HUNGRY OR FAMISHED? LAUGHABLE OR
AID? GO OR DEPART? THINK OR POND
SMELL OR AROMA? HELP OR AID? GO O
PECULIAR? AWFUL OR TERRIBLE? GOO
AVAIL? GIVE OR OFFER? ODD OR PECULIA
ST? TALKATIVE OR GARRULOUS? FUCK O
AUTIFUL? TRUTHFUL OR HONEST? TALKA
COMMENCE? ASK OR ENQUIRE? FUN O
ER OR RESPOND? BEGIN OR COMMENCE?
OR DUKE? LOVING OR AMOROUS? HUNGR
UE OR LANGUAGE? EARL OR DUKE? LOVI
LOOKING GLASS OR MIRROR? SMELL OR
GHABLE OR HILARIOUS? LOOKING GLASS
K OR PONDER? WORK OR TRAVAIL? GIV
GO OR DEPART? THINK OR PONDER? WO
RRIBLE? GOOD LOOKING OR BEAUTIFUL
IAR? AWFUL OR TERRIBLE? GOOD LOOK
LOUS? FUCK OR COPULATE? ANSWER O
ATIVE OR GARRULOUS? FUCK OR COPU
UIRE? FUN OR AMUSEMENT? TONGUE O
E? ASK OR ENQUIRE? FUN OR AMUSEME
OUS? HUNGRY OR FAMISHED? LAUGHAB
VING OR AMOROUS? HUNGRY OR FAMISH
SMELL OR AROMA? HELP OR AID? GO O
OR MIRROR? SMELL OR AROMA? HELP
AIL? GIVE OR OFFER? ODD OR PECULIAR
WORK OR TRAVAIL? GIVE OR OFFER? O
TIFUL? TRUTHFUL OR HONEST? TALKAT
D LOOKING OR BEAUTIFUL? TRUTHFUL O
OR RESPOND? BEGIN OR COMMENCE?
OR COPULATE? ANSWER OR RESPOND? B
OR LANGUAGE? EARL OR DUKE? LOVING
AMUSEMENT? TONGUE OR LANGUAGE? E
HABLE OR HILARIOUS? LOOKING GLASS
OR FAMISHED? LAUGHABLE OR HILARIO
O OR DEPART? THINK OR PONDER? WOR
MA? HELP OR AID? GO OR DEPART? THIN
AR? AWFUL OR TERRIBLE? GOOD LOOKI
R? ODD OR PECULIAR? AWFUL OR TERRI
TIVE OR GARRULOUS? FUCK OR COPULA
OR HONEST? TALKATIVE OR GARRULOU
ASK OR ENQUIRE? FUN OR AMUSEMEN
? BEGIN OR COMMENCE? ASK OR ENQUI
NG OR AMOROUS? HUNGRY OR FAMISHE
GE? EARL OR DUKE? LOVING OR AMORO

ENDPAPERS
The endpapers are published with a mosaic of word options which continue the pattern of synonyms for which 'Loving or Amorous' is the first example. These are just a handful of the thousands that exist in English. In every case, the Old English/Saxon derived word comes first, and the French/Latin derived alternative comes second.

AMOROUS OR LOVING?

The Highly Peculiar Tale of English and the English

by
RUPERT GAVIN

UNICORN

DEDICATION

This book is dedicated to my sources of constant pride

ANDRA & BELLA

Neither of whom believed it would ever be completed,
and will be grateful for no longer needing to ask:
'And so, how's it going?'

AMOROUS OR LOVING?

The Highly Peculiar Tale of English and the English

How did a marginal dialect spoken once by only 200,000 people, facing existential threat, become the language spoken by 1,600,000,000 people across the world today?

⇒ ◆ ⇐

How did a naturally reserved and very private nation of people become creatively among the most expressive in the world?

⇒ ◆ ⇐

How did English accumulate a vocabulary so varied and rich? Such that we can endlessly choose to be 'mad' (from Old English) or 'berserk' (from Norse), 'hungry' (from Old English) or 'famished' (from Latin/French), 'amorous' (from Latin/French) or 'loving' (from Old English) with all the subtle distinctions between each of these many choices.

Published in 2025 by
Unicorn, an imprint of Unicorn Publishing Group
Charleston Studio
Meadow Business Centre
Lewes BN8 5RW
www.unicornpublishing.org

Text copyright © 2025 Rupert Gavin

All rights reserved. No part of the contents of this book may be reproduced, stored in or introduced into a retrieval system, or transmitted, in any form or by any means (electronic, mechanical, photocopying, recording or otherwise), without the prior written permission of the copyright holder and the above publisher of this book.

Every effort has been made to trace copyright holders and to obtain their permission for the use of copyrighted material. The publisher apologises for any errors or omissions and would be grateful to be notified of any corrections that should be incorporated in future reprints or editions of this book.

ISBN 978 1 917458 08 5
10 9 8 7 6 5 4 3 2 1

Design by newtonworks.uk
Jacket front design by Steph Pyne
Printed in Malta by Gutenberg Press

CONTENTS

INTRODUCTION AND ACKNOWLEDGEMENTS   vii

CHAPTER ONE
'AMONG THESE DARK SATANIC MILLS'   1

CHAPTER TWO
THE LAND OF THE TATTOOED PEOPLE   11

CHAPTER THREE
WHEN GIANTS WALKED THIS LAND   19

CHAPTER FOUR
REX ANGLORUM   33

CHAPTER FIVE
THE FORGOTTEN TRIBES   38

CHAPTER SIX
NORSE CODE   42

CHAPTER SEVEN
THE UNIQUELY ENGLISH CULTURAL REVOLUTION   47

CHAPTER EIGHT
LIVING WITH THE NEW NORMAN   57

CHAPTER NINE
THE PLACE AT THE OVERFLOWING RIVER   66

CHAPTER TEN
LE LANGAGE NOUVEAU EST ARRIVÉE   79

CHAPTER ELEVEN
CHAUCER – 'THE FATHER OF ENGLISH POETRY'   93

CHAPTER TWELVE
THE WORD IS GOD   104

CHAPTER THIRTEEN
FINAL BUILDING BLOCKS – REFORMATION AND BREAK WITH EUROPE 117

CHAPTER FOURTEEN
THE THUNDER RUN 126

CHAPTER FIFTEEN
AN EXTRAORDINARY CONJUNCTION IN TIME AND SPACE 142

CHAPTER SIXTEEN
'GRAND, ECHOING, ELOQUENT WORDS' 150

CHAPTER SEVENTEEN
AND THE LIGHTS WENT OUT 158

CHAPTER EIGHTEEN
RESTORATION – LIFE RENEWED 164

CHAPTER NINETEEN
WHEN ALL IS SAID AND DONNE 171

CHAPTER TWENTY
THE GREAT AMERICAN EXPERIMENT 185

CHAPTER TWENTY-ONE
GREAT EXPECTATIONS 195

CHAPTER TWENTY-TWO
WHERE WE ARE TODAY 206

CHAPTER TWENTY-THREE
DRAWING TO CONCLUSIONS 216

SOURCES, ATTRIBUTIONS, REFERENCES, AND TRANSLATIONS USED 226

BIBLIOGRAPHY 237

INDEX 242

INTRODUCTION AND ACKNOWLEDGEMENTS

This book presents my opinions about the unique development of the English language, English culture and the long interaction between the two. Having been brought up as English, albeit from long Scottish descent on both sides of my family, I have throughout felt it permissible to describe this as 'our' history, 'our' language, and the people as 'us'.

This book does not aim to be a dry academic study, but seeks to engage readers of all levels of expertise, and constitutes a new perspective on our cultural history that is designed to spark interest broadly. I have entitled the work 'Amorous or Loving? : The Highly Peculiar Tale of English and the English'. This reflects the approach. My primary sources have been many decades of personal experience in the field of the arts, storytelling, theatre, history and heritage – and from treading the streets of the world promoting what this country has to offer. The canvas of my story stretches across several thousand years and countless different but interrelated topics. I have drawn heavily on a range of texts and works by other authors, in specific areas of this narrative, to support my opinions, to give examples and provide quotation. I have not wanted to footnote endlessly the text for fear of making it seem less accessible. I have mentioned sources within the flow, when they have been particularly important to the argument. In addition, chapter by chapter, in the appendices I specify other sources I have leant on for quotations, for translations, for examples used and specific thinking. I have also included a bibliography, ordered by subject matter, as further reference for an interested reader. I am most grateful to all the writers in their respective fields much more knowledgeable than I, who have added immeasurably to this work.

As to acknowledgements, I would like to thank the following, without whom I would never have written this book, and certainly not in this final published form.

Caroline Michel insisted that I write it, having heard me countless times speak on the subject matter, in private and public, and had the mad/brilliant* notion that it would make for an absorbing and useful book. She has also painstakingly acted as my literary agent, ably assisted by Kieron Fairweather and the rest of the PFD team. (*Delete as applicable)

The ever-patient Tim Binding acted as editor in an imaginative, and often insistent fashion, which was invaluable.

Joe Ashworth had the crucial and arduous task of being my fact checker, and conducted it with great diligence. Any facts that are still contentious or incorrect are down solely to me.

Helen Clifford, the ebullient archivist of the Grocers' Company, acted as my picture researcher, and my constant reference point on City history, of which she is expert.

Lucy Worsley, Michael Wood, Arthur Smith, Daisy Goodwin, Decca Aitkenhead, Sabina Berman, Nicholas Kenyon have all kindly read it, at various stages of its development, and given me extraordinary help and advice on so many points of interpretation, scholarship and style, from which I have learnt immeasurably.

Arthur Smith generously drew together, in his inimitable style, his comparison of swearing in French and in English, especially for this book.

Jez Butterworth has kindly permitted me to quote extensively from his seminal play, 'Jerusalem' which has provided a starting and end point to the work.

Faber and Faber Ltd have graciously granted permission for a poem and quote by T.S. Eliot to be used from 'The Poems and Plays of T.S. Eliot' which provide fitting finale to the narrative.

The whole team of Historic Royal Palaces, and of the Grocers' Company, have both been extremely helpful and supportive throughout this endeavour, touching as it does closely on the histories of both organisations.

The wonderfully able publicity team of Fiona McMorrough and Emma Mitchell at FMcM have been absolutely essential to the enterprise, and I thank them for their implicit faith in this somewhat quirky take on our cultural and linguistic history.

And finally, Ian Strathcarron, Lucy Duckworth and the publishing team at Unicorn Books have kindly and unflappably overseen the birthing of this book, bringing it to a wider world.

If, for whatever reason, this book provides you with any helpful insight or moments of inspiration, then the credit is theirs. If it leaves you cold, unedified, or even annoyed, then the fault is entirely mine.

RUPERT GAVIN

London, January 2025

CHAPTER ONE

'AMONG THESE DARK SATANIC MILLS'

'You got nowhere else to go? Come on over. The door's open. You don't like it? Stay away. What the fuck do you think an English forest is for?'

— Rooster Byron in Jez Butterworth's play 'Jerusalem'

The idea for this book struck me, suddenly, one evening in 2011. I was sitting in the Apollo Theatre on Shaftesbury Avenue. I was watching for probably the fifteenth time a performance of the play 'Jerusalem', written by Jez Butterworth, starring Mark Rylance, directed by Ian Rickson, lead produced by Sonia Friedman. Having worked all my life in the theatre, I was lucky enough to be a long-standing co-producer of this particular and extraordinary piece of drama, and had the privilege of working with four of the most exceptional theatrical creators of our generation. It was an intoxicating time.

Eighteen years earlier, I had been the producer of one of Jez Butterworth's earliest plays, and had worked with him regularly ever since. 'Huge' was a two-hander comedy, one hour long, acted by Ben Miller and Simon Godley. It told the tale of an aspiring comedy double act that had absolutely everything going for them, other than for one important missing ingredient, they were not actually funny. It ended memorably with Simon in a giant chicken suit, about to perform in a fast-food TV ad, and Ben raging at him for copping out, just as their long-awaited comedy breakthrough beckoned. Potentially. We first produced 'Huge' in a hundred-seater room at the Edinburgh Fringe Festival in 1993, and then transferred it to the King's Head Theatre in London. We got enthusiastic reviews, sell out performances, and Jez decided he wanted to keep writing. On Edinburgh High Street on the final night of our Fringe Festival run, I handed Jez 200 pounds in cash. He eyed the Scottish notes suspiciously. I explained that although they looked odd, they were indeed legal tender down South. Not satisfied, he asked me why I was giving him notes of any description. I said he had written and directed the piece, which meant that we were all 'on a share', that I had not yet done a final tally, and so this was a quick estimated advance of his cut to cover some expenses. 'Oh!' he said, 'I didn't realise you got paid for doing this.'

Whereas 'Huge' was in fact very small, 'Jerusalem' by contrast is a highly complex, large production. Its running time is over three hours with two intervals. It has a cast of sixteen, plus a flock of chickens, all of whom are live, rather than actors in suits. The 'Jerusalem' set was a recreation of a Wiltshire clearing, overshadowed by giant ancient trees, with a decrepit hippy-style caravan at its centre. It was located outside the fictional town of Flintock, modelled on real life Pewsey. The action takes place, in the manner of Greek tragedy, on a single day – in this case St George's Day and the day of the Flintock Fair. The tale is told of a charismatic, drug and drink fuelled pied piper of the woods, Rooster Byron, who leads the youth astray and vies to the death with all forms of authority, discipline or constraint. The language is part Wiltshire vernacular, part foul swearing, peppered with specific and local allusions that a London, let alone a Broadway audience, sometimes struggle to understand fully. The role of Rooster Byron is so demanding and pivotal to the piece that it could only be uniquely delivered by the acting genius of Mark Rylance. As a result, Mark had no understudy. If ill, no performance could be given.

This is not just any tale that is being told. It is one that reaches back into our forgotten Saxon and Celtic past. It conjures images of pagan gods, and pre-historic lore. It tells stories – ancient and new. It pictures enemies in every form of restrictive authority, describing them as 'the puritans', with as much venom as the rebels of Cornwall and Devon expressed, when they rose up against the new Protestants and their nanny proscriptions back in the late 1540s. In their case, they were mown down in their thousands by the state's brutal enforcers, and we have to anticipate that the same fate awaits Rooster Byron.

Every night this complex show was delivered like clockwork. Not a performance missed. The lights would dim and in front of the giant St George flag of the stage cloth, the innocent figure of the May Queen, Phaedra Cox, would sing unaccompanied of how 'those feet in ancient time (did) walk upon England's mountains green.' The cloth would rise and the revels begin.

The sheer financial challenge of putting such a beast of a work on in the West End, with no Hollywood star to lighten the load, was surmounted, the imagination of audiences was captured, and it became profitable during the course of its initial West End run. In the closing weeks, young camped out in the street all night, putting aside their social media and digital apps, hoping for the chance of a last-minute ticket to see something so time-honoured and primordial as the live telling of this complex tale. Each night the passions of the audience were fired and transported. At every performance I went to, as

Rooster Byron made his final impassioned speech, the hairs sat up on the back of my neck, tingling. Closed in on by petty authority from all sides, horribly beaten up, deserted by all his young acolytes, in the middle of the wood, Rooster finally took up his giant drum. With massive resonant thumps of his palms, he pounded out his defiance. He summoned the ancestral gods of our pre-Christian past to his aid, for the preservation of hot-blooded, sentient humanity. He spoke as follows:

> 'I Rooster John Byron, hereby place a curse
> Upon the Kennet and Avon council,
> May they wander the land for ever,
> Never sleep twice in the same bed,
> Never drink water from the same well,
> And never cross the same river twice in a year...'

Upon the repeated, desperate, insistent beating of his drum, the trees of the forest began to rustle and were bent by a powerful swirling wind. The dull thud of footsteps grew louder. 'Thud, thud, THUD.' The theatre shook. The giants have answered the ancient call. As the curtain started to fall, we knew that the denizens of our past have risen up. They have come at the very last to protect Rooster Johnny Byron. Once more against all odds, they pluck him from the crushing grasp of Puritan authority, preventing his obliteration. Their spirits will live on in England, embodied in the magic of Byron blood.

As I sat there mesmerised each night, I was gripped by the straight line connection between the sung poetry of 'Beowulf' and the epic speeches of Rooster Byron, by way of the stirring verses of William Blake. I marvelled at how a nation perceived to be emotionally reserved and usually tight-lipped, could be both those things and yet also present a complex work immaculately, with consummate skill, repeatedly reaching deep and directly into the heart of every member of the audience, with a display of such unbridled, atavistic passions.

Since that night I have wrestled with this puzzle, and this book is a quest to answer these two underlying questions. How did a cluster of marginal dialects spoken by just a few hundreds of thousands of people in the 870s, who themselves were under an existential pressure from their Viking enemies, every bit as crushing as that felt by Rooster Byron, survive and end up today as the world's most ubiquitous language, spoken by around 1,600 million people? Was this chance? Was this historical accident? Was this solely the result of the imposition of imperial and military might? Did the characteristics of this language help determine this outcome? And to what extent has the resulting language, the language of 'Jerusalem', shaped temperament and culture?

The second question is more complex. How did the nature of the people who now speak English as their mother tongue, although renowned for their reserve, for their cold nature and for their formality (all of which fits very logically with our primarily Scandinavian and Germanic origins in the middle of the first millennium) become so highly creative, so imaginative, so theatrically and so musically expressive? Yet lose none of their appreciation for discipline and organisation?

This emotional dichotomy seems to run through our language as much as through our national personality. I first used the title of this book in a talk in the White Tower at the Tower of London, while I was Chairman of Historic Royal Palaces. No building embodies more vividly the conflict between its French-speaking Norman creators and the English-speaking Anglo-Saxon capital that they sought to subjugate. Through the richness of our vocabulary we are constant participants in that conflict today. We might, of a relaxed evening at home with our spouse, seek to establish the level of affection that was to be the order of the night. To do so, we might 'ask', using the colloquial Old English word, or we could choose to be marginally more formal and thus 'enquire', using the French/Latin term. He/she then could either 'answer' (Old English) or 'respond' (French/Latin). Both words similar but noticeably different in implication. Then together, they might 'start' or 'begin' (Old English, both), or instead they could 'commence' (French/Latin). And in the end, we might be 'loving', using the Old English term, or we might be 'amorous' using the French/Latin. The underlying emotion is the same, but I think we all appreciate the world of difference between the two. It shows that throughout our lives, we have a richness of linguistic options; each option connotes a different feeling and frame of mind, between the more formal and the more personal, between the more restrained and the more demonstrative, dependent on the context. Our behaviour correspondingly see-saws between the 'theatrical' and the 'reserved' continuously.

o o o

I offer three fairly recent examples of this dichotomy of Englishness.

The first was the grand spectacle that opened the London Olympic Games in 2012. It was called 'The Isles of Wonder', the vision of two great directors, Danny Boyle and Stephen Daldry, and an inspired writer, Frank Cottrell-Boyce. All English. They marshalled artists, designers, choreographers and performers to mount a spectacle that beamed out to the whole world. It was four hours long and watched by apparently 900 million viewers around the globe.

The resulting spectacle projected the imagination, wit and visual splendour of this country, in a way that few nations, I believe, can equal. In a matter of moments, the show morphed from the epic portrayal of the satanic mills, seen sprouting from the ground accompanied by the beat of costumed drummers, to the comedy antics of Mr Bean, trying to get a note on a keyboard right, to the wondrous cheek of watching what appeared to be the Queen and James Bond sky-dive from a helicopter circling overhead. And all of it delivered seamlessly, on time and in perfect synchronisation.

It took years to devise, and to rehearse, in total secret. It involved thousands of actors, and 7,500 volunteers, many of whom played performing parts in the arena – all meticulously drilled. It required 70 sheep, 12 horses, 3 cows, 2 goats, 10 chickens, 10 ducks, 9 geese and 3 sheepdogs.

The organisation had to withstand the lead actor for the event, he of 'Jerusalem', Mark Rylance, being forced to pull out, due to a tragic family bereavement, to be replaced at short notice by Kenneth Branagh. On the final morning before the opening, GCHQ received credible intelligence that a cyber-attack would be mounted with the aim of taking control of the whole lighting system at the stadium. Senior government officials had to meet to assess contingency plans.

In the end, the 'Isles of Wonder' was delivered immaculately. It surprised and delighted a whole nation. Judging by hundreds of comments I received subsequently, it impressed many around the world, most markedly for surpassing the passionless precursor of Beijing, with something equally eye-catching but with infinitely more feeling. The most recent opening of the Paris Olympics in 2024, despite the huge budget, the massive preparations and the near closure of the centre of the city for months in advance, showed how hard it is to deliver spectacle with engaging narrative, with a convincing display of national culture, with touches of humour and true 'coup de théâtre'. London, in my view, outscored Paris on every level, and not just because of the rain at the latter.

A sovereign seemed to descend from the sky, and Kenneth Branagh spoke the fanfare of Caliban's speech from William Shakespeare's 'The Tempest':

> *'Be not afeard. The isle is full of noises,*
> *Sounds, and sweet airs, that give delight, and hurt not.*
> *Sometimes a thousand twangling instruments*

*Will hum about mine ears, and sometimes voices,
That, if I then had wak'd after long sleep,
Will make me sleep again; and then, in dreaming,
The clouds methought would open and show riches
Ready to drop upon me, that, when I wak'd
I cried to dream again.'*

Our language and our spectacle interwoven. All very specifically British.

o o o

The second example took place two years later in the moat at the Tower of London. During the course of five months, a field of ceramic poppies was planted to commemorate the hundredth anniversary of the start of the Great War. The artistic vision meant that these poppies appeared to pour from one giant 'weeping window' in the Tower's massive defensive wall, and to flow in an ever-increasing lake of red around the full circumference of the Tower. It was entitled 'Blood Swept Lands and Seas of Red'. It echoed both the history of bloodshed for which the Tower is notorious and the massive human sacrifice of that war. The right words were pivotal to the endeavour, both in the title and also in the solemn words declaimed each evening at the setting of the sun. A total of 888,246 ceramic poppies were planted in a detailed daily process – one poppy for every British and Commonwealth fatality in the four-year conflict. Each evening, the names of the fallen would be read. This was a spectacle that captured the imagination of the country. But more than that, it was a prodigious feat of organisation, involving the recruitment and training of around 30,000 volunteers. These were necessary to be able to plant each poppy day by day, to manage the crowds, and then uplift the poppies, pack them and dispatch them to around half a million donors all over the world. Each of the ceramic poppies had to be lovingly manufactured in five different production studios. Such was the short timescale for the whole project that these capabilities had to be set up only months ahead of the November finale. At the start, nobody had known what demand, if any, would be created for making the donations to buy this number of poppies. But the response was so overwhelming that there was a worrying moment, when a quarter of a million more poppies had been 'sold' than actually had been created. The logistics kicked in like clockwork.

None of the public were aware of the challenges behind the scenes, and nor did they need to know. About 5 million people in person came and viewed the awe-inspiring display. Extraordinary overhead pictures of the

Tower surrounded by what seemed like a sea of blood, played out on TV screens and on newspaper front covers, all around the world.

Ultimately the proof of the emotional power of the endeavour was brought home by the letters and messages from the recipients of the poppies. They were so many and so varied. Some with memories and connections to losses that their family had suffered in the Great War. Others from people unconnected to the war itself, but who had themselves suffered loss and found solace in the spectacle. One letter I remember especially. It was from a father and mother who had lost a much-loved daughter in her teenage years. They had kept her bedroom exactly as it was the day she died. They donated to the appeal, and upon receipt of the poppy, they placed it in the centre of the pillow on her bed. To this day, I expect it still sits there. They wrote wanting to express their feeling of huge gratitude; their letter, penned in the most moving and beautiful phrases, expressed how, although unconnected to the Great War, the glass poppy served as a lasting tribute to their daughter, which in some small way kept her spirit alive to them. Spectacle, symbols, words, solemnity, all combining to capture an acute emotion.

I was lucky to be involved personally in the latter stages of the poppies. I was able to see at first-hand how theatrical spectacle, when organised peerlessly, can produce unique emotional responses. I was then delighted to be able to continue the tradition of the poppies, with 'Beyond the Deepening Shadow' in 2018 (the anniversary of the end of the war), and subsequently the Superbloom in honour of the Queen's Platinum Jubilee. The former involved the choreographed lighting of ten thousand giant candles each night around the Tower, and was inspired by the poetry of one of our greatest female war poets, Mary Borden. *'They do not know that in this shadowed place, it is your light they see upon my face.'* The Superbloom was a lasting transformation of the moat into a colourful meadow of wildflowers that circled the Tower. The earth was rescaled into a rolling sea, and 20 million seeds from twenty-nine different plant species were sown by hand, to create a new bio-diverse environment for pollination in the heart of the city. The moat became an ever-changing tapestry of wave upon wave of colour and a place for quiet reflection for thousands of visitors, soothed by Erland Cooper's special musical composition which had been inspired by Peter Maxwell Davies' poetic 'Farewell to Stromness'.

○ ○ ○

The third example is the more recent mourning for and the funeral of Her Majesty Queen Elizabeth II. At a moment's notice, and like the workings of a giant metronomic clock, a continuous eleven days of pageant and ceremony unfolded from its start in Balmoral to its finale in Windsor. Although the panoply of events had been endlessly planned for, the potential configurations of precisely when and where the Queen would pass away, could never be fully predicted. The opportunity to pause after the announcement of death, so as to prepare, was non-existent. The commemoration of her life had to commence immediately and be on a scale so as to capture the imagination of the world. Tens of thousands of soldiers, sailors, airmen, police, officials, dignitaries had to be drilled, dressed, marshalled and bound together into a unified whole. Each day had its peculiar set of ceremonies, its different cast of characters, all executed flawlessly.

But this was not solely an exercise in organisational zeal, it was also a giant piece of highly charged theatre, designed to deliver a massive emotional punch. From the sombre, tearful march with the monarch's coffin up the medieval streets of Edinburgh, to the final goodbye at Windsor by her pony and her favourite corgis, from the catafalque vigil to the symbolic snapping in two of the Lord Chamberlain's staff of office over the tomb, the ceremonial displays worked at a level that was exceptionally deep. 250,000 people queued, many for 10 hours or more, in order to file past the coffin. Even though the time spent in Westminster Hall was no more than a few minutes, not one mourner seemed to question the value of the time spent in order to be there. The ancient stone walls were imbued with a thousand years of history, the visual richness was surrounded by an eerie silence, interrupted only by the echoing sound of the 'clack, clack, clack' of the commander of the watch signalling with his sword, the periodic changing of the guard. This created a unique piece of theatre that touched everyone to the core. As a result 'The Queue' became a phenomenon in its own right. It was a democratic pilgrimage that wound its way along the historic banks of the Thames, from its start in Southwark. Very tellingly, this gathering point was very close to the spot that six hundred years earlier, Chaucer's fictional, and no less universal, pilgrims met at the Tabard Inn to begin their journey in 'The Canterbury Tales'. One pilgrimage went east, and one went west.

The funeral itself was watched by not just a million people lining the London streets, not just by around 30 million people in the UK on television, not just by about 500 foreign heads of state and dignitaries in attendance, but by estimated billions around the world. Most of them had no direct connection with the Queen, or her realms. It was the most spectacular royal funeral that the world had ever seen. This scale of global attention is attributable to the extraordinary virtues of the Queen herself, undoubtedly, but also to a recognition that this country may well be the only one in the world that can mount at no notice, a rolling ceremony of scale and precision, without flaw or slip up, that can powerfully convey a universal emotion. A sense of awe, of reverence, and a belief that our future is best shaped by a deep respect for our past.

In the end it also all came down to the right use of words, at every step of the way, right up to the moving, poignant message from the royal family, quoting 'Hamlet', of course: 'Flights of angels sing thee to thy rest.' So often we take this ability for granted.

The Edinburgh Festival, for example, is the biggest arts gathering in the world. On the Fringe alone currently, 2.6 million tickets are sold to around 3,700 different shows, presented by performing companies in some 250 different venues. There are no invitations; anyone can come, who can find some space and register themselves. They come from all over the world. Meantime, Glastonbury is a gathering in a landscape of open fields of 200,000 people, inspired by music and by the latest in the long tradition of the English lyric. Recently, around 2,000 different acts have performed in a single festival, on up to 60 different stages, spread across fields requiring an 8 mile perimeter wall. Meantime, Hay Literary Festival brings 125,000 people together over a week and a half to exult in the power of words and thoughts. In Notting Hill, the Carnival attracts some 2 million visitors over 3 days, to its celebration of song, dance, community and spectacle, and to participate in what was founded in 1966 and is now said to be the largest street festival in Europe.

It is not just that these things speak to the passion of the cultural soul of the nation, and our endless engagement in the power of our language, but they require superhuman acts of organisation. In Edinburgh, a whole city is reshaped to create hundreds of workable performing spaces. In Glastonbury, a new city in itself is built and then dismantled one week later, in the open countryside. At Hay, and in Notting Hill, comparable feats are achieved. There is a natural tendency to take this for granted. But from my experience of the organisation of Jubilees, many festivals, umpteen spectacles and countless theatre shows, there is nothing innately natural in the skills required to make these things happen seamlessly, in a way that is harmonious with the creative imagination.

Failures happen too. With ambition comes inevitable risk-taking, and dreams dashed are a necessary consequence. One has only to remember the blighted Mound at Marble Arch in 2021, or the very anonymous 'Unboxed' or 'Festival of Brexit' in 2022, to understand the thin line between triumph and disaster. But endlessly trying is the key ingredient.

How did we get to here? From what does this marriage of strictly conflicting abilities, derive? Where did this all begin? Time and time again in our narrative, I will focus on events, conflicts, people and places in our history that are relatively unknown, and may be new to you (or at least new in the context that I describe). I have not done this purposefully. It is how the story unfolds. It does however indicate that to find our answers, we are walking along relatively untrammelled paths. That is part of the joy.

CHAPTER TWO

THE LAND OF THE TATTOOED PEOPLE

'I attribute my whole success in life, to a rigid observance of the fundamental rule, never have yourself tattooed with any woman's name not even her initials.'

– P.G. Wodehouse

Where it began, properly began, was on the edges of the great and ancient Selwood Forest. This is a giant wood that once stretched all the way from Chippenham in Wiltshire down to Gillingham in Dorset, forming a natural boundary between East and West Wessex. It began only thirty miles from where Rooster Byron subsequently ended up, defying the encroaching authorities, in these same ancient forests. Where this tale starts, so it concludes.

It was at Ecgbert's stone at the edge of these woods in May 878, that the Wessex king Alfred, seven years into his reign, called the muster of the West Saxon men-at-arms from Wiltshire, Dorset, and parts of Somerset and Hampshire. Alfred had come to the throne, succeeding three of his elder brothers, all now dead, to lead the existential struggle against a Viking warrior horde fixated on spreading their domination. After a series of defeats, the odd inconclusive victory, cruel examples of Viking treachery, and a period of hiding in the Somerset marshlands, Alfred emerged to make the final throw of the die. The muster point he chose was significant. The Wessex kings were proud of their descent and thus their legitimacy from the great King Ecgbert, Alfred's grandfather. Ecgbert had defeated the Mercian forces at Ellendun in 825, and then again in 829, earning him the moniker of 'Bretwalda' ('wide-ruler'), which heralded a period of pre-eminence for the West Saxons in Southern England. Alfred is said to have called his forces to gather at the location of Ecgbert's Stone. He was joined there by forces from across the south and south-west. With this assembled body of fighting men, he moved north-east to a point thought to be Iley Oak; here he was probably joined by more forces, possibly by some Mercian warriors. Subsequent coins show the twinned heads of Alfred and the Mercian overlord Ceolwulf in equal prominence, emphasising an alliance between the two.

The Viking battle horde had previously come south. After a plundering perambulation through Wareham, across to Exeter, they had journeyed north to capture the Wessex royal base at Chippenham, a key crossing point on the River Avon. To take over such a significant town was designed, we can assume, to make a symbolic statement of strength. The Vikings wintered here for several months. At the time of the approach of Alfred's army, the Vikings had left Chippenham moving east to an area originally known as Ethandun, where today the village of Edington is located. Close by is sited the ancient Bratton Fort, which sits perched on the Wiltshire Downs staring out at the plains to the north and overlooking the modern-day village. This may have been an attractive defensive point for the Vikings.

Alfred tracked them, and it is here that battle was engaged. A bloody conflict that defined the course of English history. Specific details of the sequence of the battle are hazy. The contemporary historian Asser only makes reference to the King 'fighting fiercely with a compact shield-wall'. Recent opinion indicates that the Vikings did not hole themselves up in the fort, but felt confident upon sighting Arthur's army, to descend to the plain and confront them there. It must have been a bloody and intense engagement. Neither side would have given up the struggle easily, but the outcome was decisive. By the end of the day, the Anglo-Saxon army was victorious; the Vikings turned, and ran defeated the sixteen miles back to their fortification, Chippenham, with Alfred's vengeful warriors in pursuit, cutting down and killing many in the rout. Asser then says that after fourteen days, the Viking host was worn down by fear, cold and hunger, and they surrendered.

A month after the battle, Guthrum, with a group of his senior officers, came to Aller, east of Athelney, where he agreed to be baptised a Christian. He was given the name Athelstan, the same as Alfred's eldest brother. Subsequently a significant agreement, the Treaty of Wedmore, was signed between Alfred and Guthrum, which reflected the new status quo after the Battle of Edington. The Vikings were to be confined to the east and the north of the country, which came to be known as Danelaw, while the Anglo-Saxons were left free to rule the South, the West and much of the middle of the country. An early copy of the original document is held in the Corpus Christi collection in Cambridge. It states:

> *'This is the peace which King Alfred and King Guthrum and the councillors of all the English people, and all the people who are in East Anglia, have all agreed and confirmed with oaths. First*

concerning our boundaries: up the Thames, and then up the Lea, and along the Lea to its source, then in a straight line to Bedford, then up the Ouse to Watling Street.'

This was the basis of a new nation loosely uniting Wessex, Kent and Mercia. The speakers of Old English were to survive. But it was not just the language but also English culture that had been deeply under threat of extinction. In the two previous centuries, England had transformed itself into one of the finest centres for learning, writing and artistic activity in Europe. This had come to a grinding halt as the Viking raids targeted monasteries, abbeys and places of learning. For much of the 9th century, not a single original work in literature in Latin was completed. Manuscript copying slowed to a trickle. According to Alfred himself writing to the Bishop of Worcester:

'...it has very often come into my mind what wise men there formerly were throughout England, both church and layfolk... and how men came from overseas in search of wisdom and instruction, which we now have to get from thence... So far has it fallen in England that few there are on this side of Humber who understand the English of their service or can translate a letter from Latin...there are so few of them that I cannot remember one south of Thames when I first began to reign.'

Edington reversed that process of decline. It started to unify the Anglo-Saxon nations, and rebuilt the culture as a vibrant English speaking one. The treaty is one of the earliest documents to make reference to 'Angelcyn' as one nation. It is appropriate to describe Edington as one of the most important, defining battles in the long history of England. It is surprising that it is so little known to many, how rarely Edington is visited and how infrequently it is studied outside of scholarly circles.

Conflicts between the Vikings and the Anglo-Saxons continued for many decades to come, but the core territory was never conceded again to the Viking invader.

I would encourage anyone interested in the English to make pilgrimage to Edington. It sits today, as a small attractive village, a few miles outside the town of Devizes, positioned on the north-facing slope of the Wiltshire Downs, with magnificent views across the plains towards Malmesbury. Edington's 14th century priory, and priory house, constructed in the local honey-coloured stone, are both still standing, substantially intact. They reflect the location's importance in medieval post-Norman times. In every way, it is a beautiful, sleepy West Country village, with decorous old rose covered cottages, identical to a thousand other villages in the area.

You would have no sense that this was a defining, possibly even the defining, location in the history of the English. There is no real indication of the great battle, nor commemoration of its significance. A directional sign up to Bratton Fort is all, and a brief memorial stone, erected in 2000, to the Battle of Ethandun. It is certainly the most important battle that most people do not know.

o o o

While the events at Edington proved to be the turning point for the formation of Englishness, this should be understood in the context of the much longer emergence of the peoples of these islands as peculiar and different.

The name for these islands which we now call British was first recorded around 200 BC in a work by the Greek historian Polybius. His text was based on the notes of the writer and explorer Pytheas, who claims to have circumnavigated the islands looking for trading opportunities and cultural exchange. He called the islands 'Pretannike', or the 'Pretanic Islands', and this eventually became 'Britannia' to the Romans, long before any concept of England (or even Engelond) emerged. That took place 1,000 years later. The name 'Pretannike' is believed to be derived from the Celtic expression for 'tattooed people', and this fits with other descriptions of the early British penchant for daubing themselves in woad. Pytheas was clearly struck by the cultural and artistic difference of the native folk from what he considered to be normal life.

The alternative term that the Greeks used for these islands was 'Albion', which is fancifully thought to have derived from the chalky south coast cliffs that greeted their sailors. While Albion has had some currency over the years, it is Britain that has achieved official status. So the 'tattooed people' are what we remain, rather than the 'white cliff folk'.

I am not sure how much cultural exchange Pytheas expected to achieve between the sophisticated Greeks and these strangely daubed people, but not a huge amount occurred, at least at first. The British inclination to get their skin impermeably drawn upon, often from head to toe, has continued over the centuries. Being a maritime nation has helped; sea-faring folk, used to working on the open decks barely covered, kept the British tradition of tattoos flourishing, and gave them a rugged, manly image. Tattoos have entered so deeply into British culture, that P.G. Wodehouse, felt obliged to lay down the law in relation to them, as quoted as the heading to this chapter.

His is a rule that neither David Beckham nor Tyson Fury have ever been particularly bothered to follow.

Three centuries after Polybius was writing, Ptolemy, the famous geographer of the ancient world, identified according to some accounts, thirty-three separate groups or tribes spread across the land mass of the Pretanic Isles – with no perceptible unifier or dominant body. Within this, England was to emerge as a concept and its territorial identity, along with its language, from the shadow of Britain a thousand years after Britain had been so named.

A few other critical points need to be made about the Land of the Tattooed people. Apart from it being a set of islands, with a well-defined territorial boundary, they were the largest such land mass off the coast of Europe. They also sit in a particular meteorological position, lying in the direct line of the Gulf Stream. They enjoy (or to some, endure) a perfect mild maritime climate, which means plenty of rain, and relatively few frosts. While parts of the islands are mountainous, much is rolling planes, with good woodland, relatively fertile soil, and highly productive land for food and resources. This is especially so in the south, the south-east, in the Midlands and the south-west.

Our history, and thus our language, and consequently our culture, has been shaped overwhelmingly by our geography, our weather and our soil. These three things lie at the heart of our story.

The rich supply of food and the mineral wealth has meant the ability for the country to support not only a labouring class, but also a clergy, an artisan community, an academic and intellectual class, and of course an aristocracy. Our cultural, artistic and philosophical development has followed as a result. Scholarship, craftsmanship and patronage have been essential ingredients.

The richness of our land has also meant that our island has been attractive to invaders, either as replacements for their homelands, or as profitable additions to their own. The lure of a plentiful choice of oysters to the Romans supposedly. Because of the continuing wealth of the land, our surrounding waters and the productivity of our soil, our invaders were not simply plundering parties on hit and runs; they were not marauders, stripping bear the spoils and leaving. All of them, even the Vikings, may have started out as plunderers but turned into settlers and stayers, determined to exploit the richness of the land long term.

Over the course of a thousand years, England was subjected to four major waves of invaders. First the Romans who arrived on a long-term basis in the year 43, and stayed for the best part of 400 years, but leaving a considerable and enduring legacy. Then the Anglo-Saxons came in their various phases, and settled permanently. Then the Vikings, followed by the Normans. All attracted by the relative wealth of these islands.

o o o

All these invasions were important to our history, but the arrival of the various branches of Germanic tribes, which we now call the Anglo-Saxons, was especially significant. The first sign of their presence on English shores was the arrival of raiding parties around 350. They were attracted by the rich pickings of late Roman Britain. The collapse of the Empire offered opportunity for invaders to encroach on the more fertile outposts of Roman rule. The Franks invaded Gaul; Huns and Goths headed for Italy and Rome itself. The primary, near contemporary record of the Anglo-Saxon arrivals, was written by the British 6th century monk, Gildas, who in his 'De Excidio et Conquestu Britanniae' gave his coruscating verdict on the poor judgement and loose morals that allowed Britain to be conquered by a bunch of Saxons. Gildas painted in primary colours; he would have been well equipped as a modern tabloid headline writer, and his florid descriptions have shaped subsequent accounts. If Gildas is to be believed, the British king Vortigern, getting no help from Rome, invited a mercenary force to help the Britons defend themselves against Pictish raiders from the North. Three boats of warriors landed at Ebbsfleet in Kent, led by the Saxon warriors, Hengest and Hortsa. This is almost certainly fanciful.

The earliest arrivers were to be followed by others of their tribes, initially in small parties. Saxons first settled successfully in Kent, but paused in their expansion during the balance of the 5th century. Then later in the 6th century, more incoming Saxons began to push westwards and southwards, while groups of Angles spread across the middle of the country and northwards. By the time of Bede's writings in 700, Anglo-Saxon kingdoms covered most of what we now call England.

There is much debate as to the speed at which the Anglo-Saxons took charge of the heart of the islands. Traditionally the Anglo-Saxons were believed to have dominated quickly, sweeping aside the indigenous Britons and establishing themselves speedily as a new ruling class. This is based primarily on Gildas' writings, and then expanded upon by Bede, who, particularly proud of the Angles, chose to give an emphatic verdict in favour of rapid Anglo-Saxon hegemony. Gildas writes:

> '...the ferocious Saxons (name not to be spoken!), hated by man and God, should be let into the island like wolves into the fold,

to beat back the peoples of the north. Nothing more destructive, nothing more bitter has befallen the land...a number of the wretched survivors were caught in the mountains and butchered wholesale. Others, their spirits broken by hunger, went to surrender to the enemy; they were fated to be slaves forever, if indeed they were not killed straight away...'

He continues in similar vein at length. This account is further supported by the proliferation of Anglo-Saxon artefacts among the remains of the wealthier families, suggesting a rapid replacement of the ruling class. As a result, it had been believed that Old English was free of influence from the indigenous Celtic languages of the British, and that Anglo-Saxon language and culture took root on a relatively blank canvas.

More recent evidence contradicts this. Integration seems to have taken place between the Anglo-Saxons and the Britons. Romano-British life continued intact for several centuries after the Romans themselves had left and the whole process of change was much more organic.

Recent DNA studies of burial sites support the conclusion that there was strong Anglo-Saxon genetic presence, but also countless signs of intermarriage with indigenous Romano-Britons. A 200-year process of intermingling and absorption seems to have taken place. If Anglo-Saxon styled objects were increasingly found in high status burials, and affluent settlements, then this could be explained as a conscious act of fashion or appreciation by Britons, rather than a sign of the Anglo-Saxons achieving rapid political dominance.

There is strong evidence now for the process of dominance by the Anglo-Saxons being more gradual.

This is not to suggest that this elongated process was entirely harmonious and consensual. There were clear moments of brutal ferocity inflicted by Anglo-Saxons on the Romano-Britons. For example at Pevensey in 491, it has been suggested by some accounts that the indigenous locals retreated inside the castle for protection from an attacking group of Anglo-Saxons; they were surrounded, captured and slaughtered, one and all. The fierce antipathy this form of brutality created in the Celtic minds, lives on to this day. The favourite Scottish insult to anyone living south of the border is to call them 'A f****** sassenach', which in translation simply means 'Saxon'. A persistent part of the progress of the English, their language and their culture is an immensely violent streak. This is still with us today, never far beneath the more cultivated and restrained surface. There is a history of aggression, and exploitation, that we will see repeatedly, and provides an important counterbalance to the achievements. In my working life, I have always been surprised by how more violent behaviour is in everyday Britain by comparison to our main European counterparts.

The Battle of Edington was pivotal in the survival of Englishness, in all its contradictions. The architect of that victory, King Alfred, is the first towering individual in our narrative. In him, we have the template for what was to become the epitome of the English champion – a warrior, scholar and visionary.

CHAPTER THREE

WHEN GIANTS WALKED THIS LAND

*'Therefore it seems well to me, if ye think so,
for us also to translate the books most needful for all
men to know into the speech which all men know, and,
as we are well able if we have peace, to make all the youth
in England of free men rich enough to devote themselves
to it, to learn while they are unfit for other occupation
till they are well able to read English writing...'*

– King Alfred, writing to the Bishop of Worcester

King Alfred's exceptional record and reputation dimmed under the weight of the Norman and Plantagenet rewriting of our story. What you might call '1066-and-all-that-itus', which has affected much of our historical perspective. He has always exercised a degree of control over the English imagination, but for periods of time, he was overshadowed by Edward the Confessor as our national, monarchical icon, and often confused with the identity of King Arthur. But Alfred's reputation was considered afresh during the reign of Henry VI, who campaigned for Alfred's sanctification. However ineffectual Henry was as a king, he took regal inspiration from Alfred's commitment to scholarship, faith and education, as witnessed by Henry's most notable legacies in Eton College and King's College, Cambridge. Three hundred years later, in Hanoverian times, Alfred, now dubbed 'The Great', attracted new attention. The German-speaking monarchy enjoyed promoting their English credentials, and patriotic tunes like 'Rule Britannia' were written and first performed. George III, or Farmer George as he came to be known, was particularly fascinated by Alfred. Equally the political circles were keen to emphasise to their new rulers, the tradition for consensual and constitutional monarchy, of which they felt Alfred represented a good model. In the Victorian era, the Alfred reputation grew further. His story chimed with the romantic sentiment of the 19th century; the Pre-Raphaelites and the Arts and Crafts movement's love of our supposedly more innocent past reflected this reappraisal. The rebirth of monarchy, under Prince Albert's influence, as a much more rounded, subject-oriented, artistic and literary institution, created a greater appreciation of our earliest polymathic, scholar King. The statue of King Alfred that stands proudly in Wantage, his place of birth, was unveiled in 1877. The statue of Alfred majestically holding his sword aloft, and warrior shield at his side, prominently displayed in Winchester, was commissioned in 1899, the penultimate year of Queen Victoria's reign.

It was Alfred the Great who referred to all his people as 'Angelcynn', which was a term first previously recorded in a Mercian charter in the 850s, and found in Worcester, differentiating those of Germanic origin from others. It was he that determined that the language they all spoke would be 'Englisc' (or 'Anglisc', or more rightly 'Aenglisc', but for simplicity I shall use the former). It was an expression of faith that a single language would create a single and unifying identity. This was a unique and critical decision, by a man who understood that the power of the word could exceed that of the sword. He had remarkable vision, and that vision has been rewarded by around 1,600 million people now speaking the derivation of his language. It is made doubly interesting by his determination to refer to the language as 'Englisc', especially when Wessexonian or Saxon might have been more accurate. But for various powerful and important reasons, 'Englisc' is what it was called. It was a decision fashioned to unite.

To understand Alfred, fully, we have to look at the three key figures that came before him that influenced him the most. One being Augustine, the other being Bede, and the third, and least well known, the Saxon king, Ine. They represent an interesting mix of attributes: one religious, one literary/philosophical and one political. Without Augustine, Bede and Ine, one cannot appreciate the extraordinary bedrocks of philosophy, religious organisation, legal construct and scholarship that Anglo-Saxon society developed in Alfred's days and thereafter.

○ ○ ○

Augustine was a Roman monk, clearly of good scholarship, and known to the Pope, Gregory, for his organisational ability. Augustine was chosen to lead a mission to Kent to re-establish the Christian faith in England. The country had been subsumed by a Saxon version of paganism in the years after the Romans left. Augustine landed in 597, at the invitation of the Kentish king, Aethelbert. That invitation was most likely prompted by his Christian Frankish wife, Bertha.

One wonders how Augustine must have felt arriving on the shores of this strange island for the first time, equipped with his cross, his images of Christ and other paraphernalia, all alien to the inhabitants. Knowing that he had a decreed task of converting the population, conversing in a language that may have been unfamiliar to either him or them, he must have sensed the scale of the challenge on his hands. Accounts indicate that Aethelbert was suspicious of the arriving mission and insisted on meeting them in the open air, fearing the power that their sorcery might exert in an enclosed space.

Whatever was said, and whatever was done is unclear, but the result is not disputed. Augustine established a foothold for Christianity, that others after him, like St Aidan, and St Cuthbert expanded upon. Canterbury was founded by Augustine as the location for the archbishopric, and Aethelbert was persuaded to fund the formation of a school and library. It was not just a faith that had arrived, but a whole approach to knowledge and learning. What Christianity brought to England was a culture based on books, on study and writing. This was a transformation of the Anglo-Saxon way of life. The speed with which they embraced this different world was impressive. In under a hundred years, all of the various separate kingdoms, large and small, had converted. It was as though the Anglo-Saxon mind was ready for this new faith and its more scholastic approach to life.

Canterbury was the primary archbishopric and was to develop into one of the most prominent centres for scholarship and philosophy in Europe. With support from the Northumbrian kings, York was established as the second archbishopric. Dioceses were established in both archbishoprics. Each provided the basis for scholarship and learning – most notably in the diocese of Lindisfarne in the North, whose monastery produced the extraordinary, illustrated manuscripts known as the Lindisfarne Gospels.

The foundations of a Christian, text-based, learning-oriented society was formed in England as a result. Augustine ensured it was well organised and well administered. Two critical building blocks for the future were thus put into place: the importance of the written word, and the primacy of good organisation. This provided a template for Alfred and the way he wished to preside as a model Christian monarch.

The enduring power of Augustine in our national psyche is exemplified by the still-surviving book of gospels that he brought with him from Rome. It is kept in the library of Corpus Christi, Cambridge; for the enthronement of each new Archbishop, it is moved to Canterbury, where it plays a central part of the rich theatrical ceremony around the swearing of oaths.

o o o

As exceptional as Augustine was, Bede was a colossus of the era, fully equal to Augustine. Bede was born probably in Sunderland, in around 672, some 80 years after Augustine landed. At a young age, he became a Benedictine monk in the local monastery of St Peter. Although preceded by great scholars, monks and writers such as Gildas, Theodore of Tarsus, Adrian of Canterbury and Aldhelm, it was Bede who was most acclaimed for his scholarship, and achieved a reputation stretching across Europe. Bede has an exalted standing among the first historians of Christian Europe. He is the only Englishman who was called a 'Doctor of the Church', and was without doubt, the only Englishman featured in Dante's 'Paradiso'.

What made Bede different was his prodigious output. Dozens of his works still survive, and many more no doubt were lost over time. He dealt in ecclesiastical and philosophical theory but was also a practical adviser to kings and senior churchmen. He was a master of dating, and we have him to thank (or blame) for the system whereby we define the years by the elapse since the imputed date of the birth of Christ – the AD system.

Above all he was a historian, and his masterwork was his 'History of the Church in England': 'Historia Ecclesiastica Gentis Anglorum'. He told the story of the formation of England from the first arrival of Caesar's legions, through the Anglo-Saxon invasion and up until his present day. Whereas his learned predecessors and contemporaries wrote in an opaque style, Bede's mastery of a fluent, lucid Latin was second to none. He was thorough in his history, but most importantly highly readable.

At the heart of his writing, especially the Ecclesiastica, he had a certain agenda. He wrote as a compassionate Christian, believing in fundamental Christian values, but more notably, he was an 'Anglicist'. His history was designed to present the totality of the Anglo-Saxon tribes as fundamentally interlinked, and England as a definable whole, united by kin, by blood and by religious belief. In that regard he was the first 'Anglicist', and had far-reaching impact on Alfred and his successors. It most probably determined Alfred's decision to call the language 'Englisc', as a tribute to Bede's unifying principle.

Bede was a capable translator; he authored compositions not just in Latin, but also in the vernacular, especially poems. He was known by a contemporary as 'learned in our song'. All of these set examples for Alfred.

It is remarkable how many writers, thinkers and scholastic churchmen were active during the period after Augustine's arrival; monasteries as seats of learning were established in sizeable number across the whole of the British Isles. The fact that we can still name and read much of their output is extraordinary, without even contemplating all that must have been lost.

During the course of the 7th century, there had been few signs to indicate the burgeoning to come of accomplishment in both scholarship and writing by the English. But by a century later, monasteries as seats of learning had been established all over England, becoming centres of Christian culture. This was to have an extraordinary impact on the whole of Western Europe. The rich agrarian economy of the country was able to support such monasteries, and these men of learning. Our separate island-bound status promoted a certain freedom of thought and divergence from orthodoxy. But it still took the emergence of remarkably gifted individuals like Augustine and Bede, to bring the potential to life.

There was a third important inspiration to Alfred.

o o o

Ine, was a direct contemporary of Bede, and reigned as King of Wessex from c. 689 until 726. Like Alfred he survived on the Wessex throne for an impressive length of time. During his reign, Ine's influence spread across all of the West Saxon territories, occasionally into Sussex, and even to London. The impact of his reign was significant. His kingdom was divided into areas we now know and recognise as Hampshire, Wiltshire, Devon, Dorset and Somerset. West Saxon coinage was issued, reflecting the fast growth in trade during this period, and the influx of gold and silver from Northern Europe. The important trading port of Hamwic (later called Southampton) with its excellent maritime access was established – the start of a strong potential rival to London. Ine espoused the principles of Christian kingship throughout his reign and built the first network of nunneries across Wessex. Most significantly, he had recorded in writing a comprehensive set of Anglo-Saxon legal codes, covering a wide range of topics from theft to marriage, to manslaughter, and ecclesiastical crimes. These codes were coordinated with the adjoining kingdom of Kent, to give the sense for the first time of a common Saxon set of legal principles. What made King Ine's code remarkable was the language they used was the vernacular – either from the outset, or else has been argued, subsequently by translation. His code of laws potentially represents one of the oldest surviving texts in any dialect of Old English and pre-dates by several centuries, any substantive attempts in Europe to put legal codes into the common tongue. The lawbook that Alfred himself commissioned, appended a record of the laws of King Ine. Alfred was happy to incorporate lock, stock and barrel, Ine's previous doctrines relating to property, theft, trial and so much more. Ine was also one of the earliest to refer to the groupings of Germanic people he ruled over, as 'Englisc', as a whole. Once again, a guide to Alfred.

A mark of the uniqueness of Ine, is the manner of the end of his reign. No Shakespearian exit. No diseased death, no treacherous poisoning or bloody defeat on the battlefield. Instead in 726, he abdicated, handing the throne to younger men. In retirement he left these shores to travel, accompanied probably by his wife, ending up in Rome, the place on earth supposedly closest to heaven, and where, by all accounts they were thoroughly happy. How modern a sovereign Ine now seems to us. And how little known to the majority of us.

o o o

There was of course a fourth inspiration to Alfred, of a very different kind. More ominous giants had arrived in the form of the Viking raiders, which provided the threat of a barbaric murderous enemy. This did much to help unify the disparate and often fractious groupings of the Anglo-Saxon peoples.

The newly flourishing world of learning, authorship and law making was suddenly thrown into chaos by the vicious attacks of this brutal foe from across the North Sea. The word 'Viking' literally meant raider. The 'Anglo-Saxon Chronicles' recorded the first such arrival, in a phlegmatic style, for 787, that can be identified as quintessentially English:

> 'This year king Bertric took to wife Eadburga, king Offa's daughter; and in his days first came three ships of Northmen, out of Hearethaland (Denmark). And then the reeve* rode to the place, and would have driven them to the king's town, because he knew not who they were, and they there slew him. These were the first ships of Danishmen which sought the land of the English nation.'

(* steward of the shire)

The subsequent attack on the Island of Lindisfarne in 793 was preceded by far more apocalyptic warnings in the 'Chronicles':

> 'This year dire forewarnings came over the land of the Northumbrians, and miserably terrified the people; these were excessive whirlwinds, and lightnings; and fiery dragons were seen flying in the air. A great famine soon followed these tokens...'

The sacking of Lindisfarne that ensued, with all its brutality and destruction of fine works, sent a wave of revulsion across Europe. The Vikings were not only willing to prey upon the weak and the helpless, but also to strike at the heart of Christian learning and knowledge. Widespread opprobrium meant nothing to them. Their terrifying intent was made plainer in the following year, by the sacking also on the east coast, of the Monkwearmouth-Jarrow Abbey and Iona Abbey on the west coast, for four successive times. First in 795, but again in 802, again in 806 and 825. The 806 raids involved the wholescale massacre of 68 monks in what came to be called Martyrs' Bay. It must have been clear that not just the material wealth of the country was under attack, but the life, religion and culture as well. Men and women of peace and learning were being regularly butchered. It was the stuff of collective nightmares, which would haunt many for centuries to come.

Of late, there has been a fashion to emphasise the trading and culturally more acceptable side of the Viking raiders once they became settlers, but there is no doubting their brutality and their contempt for the Christian religious way of life in their early visitations. The Vikings had an aptitude for cutting up their victims. An ancient, and possibly apocryphal, Viking ritual practised on defeated enemies was called the 'blood eagle'. This entailed hacking through the ribs and yanking the lungs out of the chest, so they could be draped over the back like bloodied wings.

After many decades of repeated brutal sea-born raiding, the pattern changed. The Viking strategy turned into something far more permanent. The raiders came to recognise that greater wealth could be created by possession of the land, rather than a policy of plunder. In 865, seventy-two years after the Lindisfarne massacre, the 'Great Heathen Army' arrived on these shores. The Vikings followed a policy of moving from fortified point to fortified point, subjugating people as they went, and using their bases as more permanent footholds to conduct raids deeper and deeper into the centre of the country. With the north, with the eastern half of Mercia, and all of East Anglia terrorised and vassalised, the 'Great Heathen Army' turned its attention to the rich and fertile lands of the West Saxons. Under the leadership of Guthrum, they set up bases across this part of the country, even as far south as Wareham in Dorset.

This was the existential threat that Alfred faced in 871, when he became King. If no substantial parts of England remained under Anglo-Saxon control, Old Norse could have easily become our dominant language form. We would be conversing happily today with the inhabitants of Iceland, whose language is the closest survivor of Old Norse.

This was the challenge that Alfred had to confront, and during the early years of his reign, his prospects did not bode well. The folklore is well known. As befits any defining moment in history, mythology is legion and becomes an essential part of our national storytelling. It is riddled with tales of flight across the marshes of Athelney, of disguise and of burnt cakes. These were desperate days; the Vikings both outwitted, and outmuscled him. Half victories were followed by bigger defeats. Wessex was under threat and could have succumbed. This book could have easily ended around here.

But as we heard earlier, the triumph at Edington altered all that, and the story continues.

o o o

After Edington, Alfred remained King for a further twenty-one years, much of the enduring value of the achievements of his reign can be attributed to his longevity as monarch, providing as it did, stability in a very tumultuous period. His long survival on the throne was unusual for the violent life of that period. His three elder brothers, all Kings of Wessex before him, held the throne for only around fifteen years combined, so only a half of Alfred's sole tenure. Alfred was the youngest brother, and therefore as he grew up, not necessarily believing that the throne would ever be his. The odds were against, which must have affected both his upbringing and his outlook. He was trained as much as a thinker, writer and man of faith, as he was as a warrior. Often in our narrative, you will find that the most influential figures were either outsiders to our core society, or else succeeded to prominence against the odds.

Alfred was to be our first scholar King, a unifier, dedicated to his nation and his people, and the shaper of our legal, linguistic, administrative and educational system. He busied himself applying the religious principles of Augustine, the scholastic and unifying principles of Bede, and the legal principles of Ine. His long survival on the throne made it possible for these reforms to take hold. Alfred was able to play the Viking threat to his advantage. A real and present danger can make change achievable that would otherwise be met with resistance.

The structure of England prior to the Viking invasions has been described as the 'heptarchy' – a division into seven kingdoms. It might suggest inaccurately a very ordered division of rule, rather than the layered hierarchy with smaller kingdoms subsumed within larger. A document known as the 'Tribal Hidage' from around the 8th century gives a glimpse of the complexities. Thirty-five different groups are listed, specifying their relative scale in terms of their number of hides, which was the measure of land needed to support one family. The Mercians and the East Angles are noted as having 30,000 hides each. Kent 15,000. The South Saxons and the East Saxons 7,000 each. The West Saxons had a much larger 100,000, but this probably included other subsidiary groups. Certain hidages were as low as 300, for example the

Gillingas, from whose name is derived Ealing. So you get a picture that is very fragmented, with very differing scales of power and influence.

One of the first defining characteristics of Alfred's reign was one of collaboration and integration. The pressure of the Viking invasions made survival impossible while such a cellular structure of rule persisted. Alfred married into the Mercian royal family, and his daughter married the Mercian Lord. This formed the basis of a central alliance of the two major tribal groupings that were still largely out of Viking control. The Battle of Edington and subsequent campaigns were won by his realisation that the defeat of the Vikings could only be achieved by drawing together Saxon forces under a single command. Strength came from unity, and the recognition of Alfred as initially Rex Saxonum, and then subsequently Rex Anglo Saxonum was a visible expression of that unity.

The second defining characteristic of his reign was one of scholarship. Previous kings had been judged solely by their military prowess. They would usually be illiterate; reading was a capability readily delegated by Kings to their churchmen or scribes to take care of. Mightiness with the sword and bravery on the battlefield were requirements of sovereignty. By contrast, Alfred, while still an accomplished warrior, made literacy and learning paramount goals in their own right. He introduced the great religious and philosophical texts of the time to his court and his people.

Alfred existed in a world shaped by the legacy of Bede, St Augustine, Aldhelm, St Cuthbert and all the monastic thinkers and writers. Why did Alfred become the first in the long line of Wessex and Saxons kings to take this very scholarly approach as central to his reign? Asser tells us of him travelling at an early age to Rome with his father, to meet with Pope Leo IV, and the trip providing him with an early exposure to the world of letters and theology. There is also the story of him winning in a contest, as the prize, a book of Saxon poetry. Alfred set about learning poems by heart; he gained a lifelong affection for the literary artistic form. Many of his contemporaries could have had similar experiences but without the same consequences. My own belief is that he was helpfully shaped by being the fourth and youngest son of his father, Aethelwulf.

It is because of Alfred's passion for the written word that we have unparalleled records of these times. Asser started his detailed history of Alfred's life and reign, and it survives to this day. Prompted by the example of Bede's own Ecclesiastical History, the 'Anglo-Saxon Chronicles' began to be written. These chronicles recorded the narrative of the Anglo-Saxon era until after the Norman conquest. The final edition of the 'Chronicles' petered out in Peterborough Abbey, in 1154, when a Norman-sounding abbot was installed and such Anglo-Saxon 'propaganda' ceased. The chronicles are a unique contemporary record of the era; they are unmatched in any other European country. Undoubtedly, they betray an editorial slant; among many other things, they were designed to validate the Anglo-Saxon succession and legitimacy. But they still represent a remarkable framework to help understand these times, and a loud advertisement for how this new nation intended to be based on the written word.

By contrast in Danelaw, in the northeastern half of the country, no charters survive from the pre-Scandinavian era. Written texts did not have the same importance in Viking culture; they were not kept, if indeed they were written in the first place.

The third defining characteristic of Alfred's reign was the impulse to determine language, especially the written vernacular language. To make the great texts accessible, both to the reader and also the illiterate listener, Alfred knew that they needed to be translated from Latin, Greek or Hebrew into something more broadly intelligible. What Ine seems to have decided for our legal codes, Alfred decided for our religious, scholastic and poetic works.

This emphasis on the vernacular was relatively unique. Other invaders of the old Roman Empire, such as the Lombards, the Visigoths and Franks, were to drop their vernacular in preference to variants of Latin as their official language. By contrast, many of the great Anglo-Saxon texts of the age, such as the 'Chronicles', were written not in Latin or Greek, but in Old English. This was unusual.

There were several choices of language available to Alfred. He could have elected to popularise Latin. He had various local dialects to choose from – the most notable being the Kentish, the Mercian and the Northumbrian. Or other Germanic tongues. However his decision was to pick a vernacular form and not surprisingly his own dialect, West Saxon (now known as 'Early West Saxon', subsequently dubbed 'Alfredian English'), to form the basis of the original unifying language.

The next key decision was to refer to this new 'national' tongue as English. In a literal sense the language technically is not English (i.e. 'of the Angles') but West Saxon. The reason for the choice of name, or for the misnomer, probably was reverence to Bede. By calling it English, Alfred was acknowledging Bede and his ideas of a united nation of Angles and Saxons. He was also acknowledging the inspiration of the King and lawmaker Ine, who had previously used the generic term 'the Englisc' to distinguish those inhabitants of Germanic descent from the original British (or 'foreigners'). It is notable that foreign commentators at the time referred to the dominant occupants of the country as the 'Saxons', which reinforces the view that 'Englisc' must have been an internally driven choice.

There is another possible inspiration, which would neatly underscore the English eternal love of a good pun. Pope Gregory the Great, the initiator of St Augustine's mission in Kent, supposedly noticed some fair-haired slaves from these isles, up for sale in the market in Rome. He asked who they were. 'Angles' was the answer given. 'Not Angles, but Angels', was his alleged retort. By this reply, the Pope gave acknowledgement to the 'Land of the Angles' that Christian Anglo-Saxon kings will have been happy to bask in. Whatever the truth be of this story, Pope Gregory demonstrated an affinity for a pun. In one letter, he described the missionaries that he sent to Britain, as being for the 'gens Anglorum in mundo angulo posita' – namely the 'people of the English nation placed in the corner of the world'.

o o o

Whatever the influence, English (or 'Englisc') is what Alfred ensured our language would be known as (even if strictly speaking, it wasn't), and thus the name of a tongue that around 1,600 million people speak today may technically be considered a misnomer. The country itself was then referred to in Latin as 'Terra Anglorum', and in English as 'Aenglaland' or in due course, 'England'.

The administrative and legal structure evolved impressively throughout Alfred's reign; it provided the basis which subsequent kings, such as Athelstan and Edgar, were to build upon. Alfred was responsible for instituting the system of burhs across the country. Their primary purpose was to create a defensive network of towns that could repel marauding invaders. Many of these burhs still exist today, and their names reflect their origins – such as Shaftesbury and Malmesbury. But more than a defensive network, this prompted an urbanisation of the population, and the creation of a formal administrative structure.

He continued with the division of the country into hundreds as the smallest land unit and shires as the larger land body, many of whose boundaries remained unchanged until as recently as 1974.

The code of laws was potentially intelligible to the common man, and the judicial process accessible to all free men. But what Ine had done originally, Alfred extended across a larger territorial footprint. Unlike other European countries at the time, the vernacular was the basis for the legal system. For example, of the fifty-eight written wills that survive from around this period, fifty-four of them were written in English. Latin culture never became as ingrained in England as elsewhere in Europe.

These underlying principles of a well-run, fair society were laid down in Anglo-Saxon times. This structure was bequeathed to the Normans, who being a pragmatic people, recognised that it was much more advanced than anything that they had to offer. It has provided an important basis for English life thereafter.

Alfred's style of kingship was peculiarly Anglo-Saxon; it did not have firm principles of succession. Kings were chosen on the basis of affirmation of the people (or at least, of the ruling class). As a result, Anglo-Saxons put emphasis on government by Assembly, by participation of the people in the legal processes, and by constant, visible progress through the nation. It was kingship constantly on tour. This helped provide the legitimacy for sovereignty, as much as primogeniture did. A visionary such as Alfred understood that the availability of authoritative texts in the vernacular was an important means by which he could create unity, and underpin his authority. At this distance of time, there is no firm basis upon which to question the veracity of works such as the 'Anglo-Saxon Chronicles', or Asser's record of Alfred's own life. However it is easy to detect what we now call 'propaganda' and 'spin'. If Alfred was one of the earliest users of such arts in English, then he certainly was not the last.

o o o

One of Alfred's most significant steps was the re-establishment of London as a strongly defended city within its massive old Roman walls. Had that decision not been taken, our narrative would be very different. After the departure of the Romans, the arriving Anglo-Saxons, fuelled by a superstition towards their antecedents, gave London a wide berth. The original Roman London gradually became a deserted ghost town, inhabited by a dwindling number of Romano-British.

Despite its post-Roman decay, Alfred understood the strategic value of London, the advantage of its walls and its critical river crossing. Alfred's defence against further Viking attacks was the system of fortified burhs. London represented an ideal base for an excellent and very strategic burh. In the treaty that Alfred concluded with Guthrum, the boundary between their lands followed the course of the Thames estuary, but then turned north in what is now docklands, and followed the course of the River Lea. London was therefore located at a pivotal border point, only a few miles from Viking territory. As an ironic footnote, this critical fulcrum of the borderline is now known as City Island, and is where the English National Ballet has sited its new headquarters. As Chairman of this world-leading dance company, I am often based there. I regularly point out to amazed dancers, musicians and visitors, the historic significance of this 'island' to the formation of our identity and the re-establishment of London, and the appropriateness of siting an 'English National' institution there. I am not surprised by the baffled reactions I usually get.

This assessment of London's critical defensive role was borne out by subsequent events. Sweyn, the father of the Danish ruler Cnut, was to fail in his attempt to besiege London in 1013, and Cnut himself, in exerting a period of rule over England, was to attempt the same in 1016. Cnut's army cut a massive ditch around Southwark so as to bring his ships to the west of London Bridge, and surround the city. The Anglo-Saxon defenders, led by the fearsome Ulfcetel of East Anglia, managed to hold out for long enough for King Edmund to arrive with a relief force that defeated Cnut's army. The walls of London over the coming centuries were to do their job repeatedly.

Alfred, in 886, not only moved the City of London back to its position of strategic strength, close to the original Roman bridge but reaffirmed London as being Mercian. This reflected its location on the north bank of the Thames. The great river had been seen as a boundary between the Wessex and the Mercian kingdoms. Ever since the claims that Ine had for London failed to achieve support, the Mercians had ruled over this key city. Alfred could have changed that, but once again his decision proved critical to the evolution of our language. His confirmation of London as Mercian, ensured that his Old English, based on West Saxon, gradually evolved to Mercian-based Middle English. This was to be the language of Chaucer and Wycliffe, that we can recognise comfortably today.

o o o

Alfred died on 26 October in 899. He was buried in his capital city, and one of his core seats of learning, Winchester. He was aged about fifty. The cause of his death is unclear, but Asser recorded the detail of his lifelong illness, and the description of these symptoms would suggest that he might have suffered from Crohn's disease. As a consequence of his remarkable twenty-eight years on the throne, Alfred left the basis of a single Anglo-Saxon nation. He had enabled a cultural ethos to emerge, a national language to be determined. The future great city of the country had been set on an unswerving path; the importance of learning and scholarship had been established; the founding principles of our state based on legitimacy among educated people was established. None of this would have come to pass except for the apocalyptic presence of the conquering Vikings. There is no galvanising impetus greater than that of a common enemy. But the remarkable character of the man who led this disparate group of Saxons and Mercians to victory, was an essential part of the response. 'Cometh the hour, cometh the man' is an overused quotation, but is certainly applicable to Alfred. But for his determination and vision, England might have continued as a series of fragmented kingships festering under Viking sovereignty and England might not have built the foundations of a nation for whom creativity and learning emerged as its crucial hallmarks. In his obituary in the 'Anglo-Saxon Chronicles' he is recorded as 'king over the whole English nation except for that part which was under the dominion of the Danes; and he held the kingdom one year and a half less than thirty years.' An important tribute, but an equally important exception clause, which would take some of his successors to rectify.

The final words in this chapter are best left to Alfred himself. In his introduction to his translation to Boethuis, he wrote, 'Study wisdom then, and when you have learned it, condemn it not, for I tell you that by its means you may without fail attain to power, yea even though not desiring it.' These are unusual guiding thoughts for a king at this time, and importantly more Anglo-Saxon kings, who believed in this principle, were to follow.

CHAPTER FOUR

REX ANGLORUM

'I will not cease from mental fight,
Nor shall my sword sleep in my hand;
Till we have built Jerusalem,
In England's green and pleasant land'

– William Blake

On Alfred's death, his son Edward the Elder became King. He ruled for a total of 25 years, from 899 until his death in 924 – another reign of exceptional length. He continued the process of expanding the scope of the Anglo-Saxon territorial base, especially after another resounding victory against the Vikings at Tettenhall in 910. During his reign, he ejected the Vikings from their areas of East Anglia and reconquered the Mercian territories that had succumbed to the Great Heathen Army. Towns like Derby, Leicester, Lincoln, Nottingham and Stamford were all returned to Mercian rule.

Edward seems not have had Alfred's scholarly focus. Relatively few original manuscripts or writings survive from this period. The medieval chronicler William of Malmesbury passed verdict as follows: 'much inferior to his father in the cultivation of letters' but 'incomparably more glorious in the power of his rule.'

This emphasis changed again on Edward's death, with the succession of his son, Athelstan, a king in the mould of his grandfather, and one even less known or appreciated today. His succession to the throne however was every bit as unexpected.

Edward's eldest son, Athelstan, had lost out in favour to the sons of Edward's second wife. The eldest of these, Aelfweard was considered the heir apparent. Athelstan was sent away from the Wessex court when young. He was brought up in Mercia by his aunt Aethelflaed, at their court, which in those days was centred on Tamworth. He was educated as a scholar prince, probably the first to do so from birth, and was given the highest level of tuition and learning of the day. As with Alfred, he probably had the advantage of believing that his favoured brothers would be king, not him. The focus of his upbringing was therefore different.

A series of incidents in 924, changed all this rapidly. Edward went north to Chester probably to suppress a rebellion. On his return, he stayed at a royal settlement in Farndon on Dee; he fell ill and died on 17 July. Aelfweard, the eldest son by the second wife, was promptly chosen as the new Wessex king. Athelstan was selected by the Mercians as successor to their Crown; they clearly now saw him as 'one of them'. But before proper coronations could occur, and before the issue of division of the kingdom could be confronted, Aelfweard unexpectedly died in Oxford. Athelstan was left to succeed to both thrones – Saxon and Mercian.

There was initially much resistance to Athelstan from among the leading Saxons. Their fears of his Mercian bias were reinforced, when he opted against their political centre, Winchester, for his coronation. Athelstan instead chose Kingston-on-Thames. The location signified his intent to unite Saxons and Mercians. Kingston lay on the traditional dividing line between the two dominions. It also was the historic and symbolic location of a significant Anglo-Saxon conference convened by Ecgbert, Athelstan's great-great-grandfather. But none of that appeased the Bishop of Winchester, who refused to attend.

The ceremony took place on 4 September, and was conducted by Archbishop Athelm. It included the full regalia of crown, sceptre, sword, finger ring, and in homage to King David, and echoing Frankish regal custom, he was bestowed with the ritual of the anointing oil. The symbology of the regalia and the holy anointing all survive to the present day. Athelstan's coronation was the first to use a crown, rather than the traditional Saxon battle helmet. It represented both the imperial ambition of the new King to rule across a growing union of separate dominions, and the transition of kingship from a purely martial role.

Athelstan's coronation signalled the formation of a substantial and united essentially English-speaking nation. It was the elevation to the throne of the man who was to become the first King of the English (Rex Anglorum), as acknowledged at the time on his own coinage.

The coronation coincidentally took place within a couple of miles of the site that was to become Hampton Court Palace. It was on the route that William the Conqueror probably marched his army as he progressed upstream to find a crossing from which to approach London for the first time. It was only twelve miles from Runnymede where the Magna Carta would be signed. As sometimes happens, we find so many determining moments of our history occurring in close proximity over the ages.

Athelstan lived up to the example of his grandfather, both as battlefield commander, and as scholar and cultural champion. By the end of his reign, he had established his claim to be known in future as one of the truly great monarchs of England.

His army overran the Vikings' northern stronghold in York; he extended the boundary of the English state to roughly the line of Hadrian's Wall. Despite subsequent ebbs and flows, this geography has served as the continuing footprint of England, and the launch pad for the English language. Athelstan's unification of the country was in stark contrast to the disintegration taking place in continental Europe. The large state structures, such as Charlemagne's empire, had started to fragment from the Treaty of Verdun in 843, and continued to separate thereafter. They would not come back together again in a set of steady unified nation states for many centuries to come.

More than solely a battle hero, Athelstan was determined to reign as a scholastic, wise ruler. Apart from his support for literature and scholarship, Athelstan did much to shape and codify the Anglo-Saxon laws. The most significant steps were made at the Assembly in Grateley. Now a sleepy small Hampshire village south of the A303, it lies not far from Stonehenge. Much of the decision-making process and system of leadership in Anglo-Saxon society depended on a series of Assemblies. At these, the powerful lords and thanes gathered with the aim of reaching consensus on key issues, and of resolving major disputes. The Grateley Assembly devoted much attention to the codifying of the laws; these were recorded in Latin but also, notably, in vernacular English.

Athelstan not only helped form this new nation, but also fought to keep it together. In 937, the external forces ranged against him became united. Olaf Guthfrithson, Viking King of Dublin, Constantine, King of Scotland, and Owen, King of Strathclyde put aside their differences and formed an alliance against Athelstan. Their combined forces arrived in the North, to challenge the Anglo-Saxons. Athelstan was at first slow to respond to the threat and the omens were not good. The ravens were a Norse and Anglo-Saxon symbol of warfare; a group of ravens is known as 'An Unkindness of Ravens'. They were said to fly in formation after marching armies, aware that any significant body of armed men usually led to a battle, and presaged a good supply of carrion. In the epic poem, 'The Battle of Maldon', recording the bloody conflict of 991 on the Essex coast, the anonymous author makes much of how 'ravens circled over the battle'. This symbology was taken up by Shakespeare centuries later. Famously Lady Macbeth expressed her impatience for the arrival and then murder of the King; 'The raven himself is hoarse that croaks the fatal entrance of Duncan under my battlements. Come, you spirit that tend on mortal thoughts, unsex me here...' This serves also as an early example of

Shakespeare's ability to bend the English vocabulary to his needs, inventing the expression 'unsex me', to capture Lady Macbeth's muscular pursuit of her ambition.

As Athelstan journeyed north with his army, he was followed by several unkindnesses of ravens. These would have perturbed his soldiers. They expected much meat to feed on, and they were not disappointed. Athelstan engaged the enemy at a place called Brunanburh and a battle of the most violent nature ensued. In terms of combined body count, it is considered one of the bloodiest fought on British soil. The ravens were not left hungry. Through the carnage of the conflict, through the grim bloodiness of the fight, Athelstan emerged the victor of the day. The combined enemy forces were either killed or turned onto their heels. While the precise location of the battle is still in dispute (the Wirral and near Doncaster are both the strongest contenders), its significance is not. The union of the English nation was cemented by the victorious blood of his warriors, and Athelstan, earned on the battlefield his legitimacy as King of the nation as a whole.

His reputation and status were not confined to these islands. His influence as a model of modern kingship stretched across Europe. His two sisters became the wives of two of the most important European kings of the period – King of the East Franks, and the King of the West Franks – and many of the offspring of these marriages came to Athelstan's court to be tutored on the sophisticated art of modern monarchy.

Late Anglo-Saxon England was emerging as an influential nation state internationally. It was an entity with a functioning central authority, uniformly organised institutions, a national language, a national church, defined frontiers and a sense of national identity. While the entire 500-year Anglo-Saxon hegemony was important, we have to recognise that the combined 70-year rule of Alfred, Edward and Athelstan was the defining period for our national character and was to become the template for subsequent monarchs centuries later.

o o o

Athelstan passed away in Gloucester on 27 October 939, as Rex Anglorum. Despite having been originally passed over, he was to die the epitome of a sophisticated ruler. Unmarried and childless, he was succeeded by Edmund, his half-brother, in the majority of his kingdom. Northumbria however chose as their King, a Viking, Olaf from Dublin. It took Edmund until 944 to reassert control over York and Northumbria, and the boundaries of England to be once more reestablished.

The subsequent decades were to highlight the strength but also the weakness of Anglo-Saxon succession. This was to remain a feature of English and indeed British subsequent history, and reflects the underlying nature of the people.

There is a belief in the Anglo-Saxon system of the significance of legitimacy. Succession did not observe the absolute primacy of bloodline and primogeniture. It had to be based also on worthiness, on consent or on exertion of authority. For example, two of the most successful, long serving Mercian kings happened to follow one another, but were not related. Aethelbald reigned 41 years from 716 to 757, and Offa succeeded him, after overcoming the other equally unrelated main contender, Beonred. Offa then reigned a further 39 years from 757 until 796, during which he instigated his eponymous Dyke. This system could lead to a more byzantine and often disruptive process of succession which could create vulnerabilities at times of change. While, on the one hand, the Danish kingship of the powerful figure of Cnut could be accepted, and the country prospered as part of his much wider empire. On the other hand, when Edward the Confessor died childless in 1066, many contenders came to the fore for consideration. Initially King Harold was chosen, who had absolutely no bloodline connection to the previous kings. This prompted the challenge of William of Normandy, the first cousin once removed of Edward the Confessor, who claimed legitimacy and was to emerge victorious, but only after considerable violence.

With the Normans, this process of succession largely disappeared. As in many aspects of the state, the Normans took the country to a top-down centralised autocracy and lineage was more precisely observed as the source of legitimacy. But equally, as with so many aspects of Norman rule, with the passage of time, the underlying Anglo-Saxon principles re-emerged, appropriately modified, but essentially intact. We will come to the Normans in greater depth soon.

CHAPTER FIVE

THE FORGOTTEN TRIBES

'Shoo-Be-Doo-Be-Doo-Da-Day'
— Stevie Wonder

In the meantime, we shall turn to the Anglo-Saxon precursors, the Celtic Britons. The long-standing thesis was that their influence on English culture and language was minimal. The supposed blitzkrieg nature of the Germanic invasion was thought to have wiped out or uprooted the native inhabitants rapidly, with no intermingling and no chance of infusion. More recent analysis challenges this theory. The DNA records in particular, point to a more extended period of intermarriage and assimilation. In fact, the more you look for the remnants of the various Celtic tribes among the English, the more you see.

The Britons were certainly the source of one of the longest surviving Anglo-Saxon jokes in the English language. The arriving Anglo-Saxons dubbed the indigenous Briton a 'wealh', which in their tongue meant 'foreigner'. In the plural, 'wealas' or 'foreigners'. This must have been strongly ironic; there was only one set of foreigners around, namely the freshly landed Saxons, Frisians and Angles. The Britons were definitely not foreigners, but 'wealas' was what these people came to be called. Over time, as the Anglo-Saxons increasingly encroached, many of those Britons that did not wish to stay to be assimilated, were pushed further and further to the West and the North, closer and closer to the Irish Sea. The west side of the island came to be known by the Anglo-Saxons, as the land of the 'wealas', the land of the foreigners, or Wales, as we know it now. And the people became known as the Welsh. A bunch of foreigners. In their own land.

The Welsh themselves rightly came over time to choose a more propitious name for their land: Cymru. The land of fellowship.

There are other examples of this ironic nomenclature. The derivation of 'wealas' can be found in places in Hertfordshire. St Albans (or Verulamium to the Romans) was a location of particular religious significance to the early Christian Britons, based on the martyrdom of St Alban. By the time the Saxons arrived, an important shrine had been established and an enclave of

Britons probably held out in this area longer than elsewhere. This stubborn adherence to the location of their faith is celebrated in the name of several nearby towns and villages. For example, King's Walden, situated between Luton and Stevenage today. 'Walden' in Saxon means 'The Dene of the Wealas', or 'The Vale of the Foreigners'.

This word form for foreigner has lived on in other German languages as well. One of the German names for Italy and for French-speaking Switzerland is 'Welschland'. And the Walloon territory on the frontier with Germany was dubbed 'Wallachia'. The difference for the 'Welsh' was that the Saxons were in their own home territory referring to *them* as the foreigners.

The Britons got their own back in various ways. The word 'Avon' is used in English as a river name. The word is derived from the Celtic for rivers generically. When we now describe a stretch of water as the River Avon, we are in fact saying simply River River. Similarly 'Ouse' is the Celtic word for water, and therefore the Ouse River means, unedifyingly, the river with water in it. Ironic naming apart, there are other telling impacts of the Britons hidden away in English. Words to describe the features of landscape are regularly derived from Celtic, emphasising the lyrical values of the language, and our underlying Celtic feelings for the wilder aspects of our countryside. Words such as 'tor', 'glen' and 'crag' are all generally held to be Celtic. Place names such as 'Penrith' and 'Torpenhow' are Celtic. There are various Old English words, no longer with us today, that were derived from Celtic, and that were used in their day, such as 'Bannuc' meaning a loaf or a cake, and 'Broc' meaning a badger.

One of the more surprising is the extremely modern sounding word 'slogan'. This originally was the Celtic word for a war cry, combining 'sluagh' meaning an army, and 'gairm' meaning a cry. 'Sluagh-gairm' over the years evolved to 'slogan', as an expression to be proclaimed loudly. Which justifies its inherently shouty nature in the hands of modern advertising professionals, and marching protesters.

But Celtic influences run deeper than simply the words, and the ironies. They have in fact informed some of the grammatical structures of modern-day English, in ways that billions of speakers of it, are totally unaware. Here I have been especially guided by Professor John McWhorter, who summarised these in his book 'Our Magnificent Bastard Tongue'.

There are a number of sentence configurations in English that are not shared with any other German languages. There are two particular examples, both oddities in English grammar, which he calls, 'meaningless do's' and 'verb-noun presents'.

The 'meaningless do' refers to the common tendency of English to put repeatedly the word 'do' into sentences where it seems to add no real value, and in any other language is not present. Some grammatical texts refer to this as the auxiliary 'do'. At its simplest, we will ask our partner: 'do you love me?'. We use a 'do', where no other language would. In French simply 'Tu m'aimes?'. Or our greeting 'How do you do?' has an extra 'do' that no other language has. French simply says 'Comment allez-vous?', Germans say 'Wie geht's?' and Italians say 'Come va?'. The moment you become aware of the phenomenon, you start to spot meaningless 'do's all over the place. 'Does anyone know what I am talking about?' 'What do I do if someone catches me?' 'Do you want to come round to my place tonight?' etc.

No European language has this bizarre configuration. The Germanic group of languages, English's closest cousins, have no hints of 'meaningless do's' among them. There is only one other language apart from English, that does, which is Celtic. It is fair to assume that the latter bequeathed it to the former.

Why did English acquire this Celtic trait? I would suggest that it comes from the oral nature of these two languages. The 'meaningless do' can provide emphasis when spoken. It also provides rhythm to our phrases, and to both the Celtic and the English, poetic qualities are important. It is no chance that the 'meaningless do' pops up frequently in songs. Titles such as 'Do You Know the Way to San Jose?', 'I Do Like to be Beside the Seaside', 'Love Me Do,' 'Do You Want to Know a Secret?'. Having myself spent twenty years as a marginally accomplished song lyricist, I can attest to the usefulness of the additional 'do's' to bring rhythm and singability. In the words of the title of the Stevie Wonder song: 'Shoo-Be-Doo-Be-Doo-Da-Day'.

A similar story applies, according to McWhorter, to the verb-noun present. In English we explain our actions invariably with a participle ending to our verbs. When someone tries to interrupt us, we reply 'I am talking'. The French would simply say 'Je parle'. By contrast in English we would never reply simply 'I talk'. Or we say, 'I was hunting' rather than the German form which would be 'I was on the hunt' or very simply 'I hunted'. It is unique versus other related European languages, with the exception of Celtic. It adds a certain fluency, and rhythm in the same way that the 'meaningless do' does. 'We are living in a material world' is a much better lyrical rhythm than 'we live in a material world'. Thank you, Madonna.

Why does any of this matter? It matters because it gives better evidence to the process of evolution of the English language. It has not been solely about the conquerors imposing upon the conquered in a one-way traffic. There is evidence of transfusion in both directions, especially when it makes language richer and more poetic.

Because of our Celtic roots, we have a language that is more evocative, and that is more rhythmic. The application of layer upon layer, with that which works, enduring, and that which does not, eroding, has produced the beauty of what we have today. And we are able to appreciate the various influences, as they signify the elements of character that we have inherited.

To me at least, the 'meaningless do', is surprisingly meaningful.

CHAPTER SIX

NORSE CODE

Unlike the Celts, the Vikings have not been so easily airbrushed out of our history, but still their contribution is seen as more marginal and more ephemeral than the Anglo-Saxons, or the Normans or even the Romans. This would be a mistake. So what precisely did the Vikings do for us, you might ask. The most apparent surviving legacy of the Vikings tends to be considered to be in York (or Jorvik) as the Viking capital city. A southern centric view of our history can easily downplay their influence. But as soon as one starts digging, their impact can be seen to be pivotal on our cultural development, and certainly on our language. We are the beneficiaries of Norse code.

You can start small. The '–by' suffixes of many northern towns (Grimsby, Derby, etc.) are based on the Norse word for farm or place of habitation. All the town names ending with '–thorpe' use the Norse word for a village (Scunthorpe, Althorp, etc). Family names which end with –son use a characteristic Norse derivation, which can be found frequently today among northern families (Robinson, Michelson, Harrison, etc). These reflect our Viking roots. The Johnson family, of Boris fame, perhaps incorrectly ignore the strength of their Viking roots. Their very blond hair may be more Viking than as previously contested, Turkish.

And then, there are a good number of current words which have clear Norse parentage – often in activities that conform with Viking-assumed behaviour. The word 'slaughter' is derived from the Norse 'slatra' meaning to butcher meat. The fabulously evocative English word, 'berserk' is thought to have probably derived from 'berserkr', the Norse name for the bearskin covering that a Viking warrior wore into battle. It has been speculated that he dosed himself up on a magic mushroom drug called Amanita Muscaria, stripped naked, pulled on a bearskin and hurled himself into the frenzied fray. Their behaviour was wild, violent and unpredictable, and gave us the adjective 'berserk', derived from the only thing that they were wearing.

The Norse also gave us more manly words for our cuisine, such as 'steak', derived from the Norse word 'steik', meaning to roast on a spit. And 'rotinn' which gives the English word 'rotten' for decaying food. Perhaps not unsurprisingly, Norse gave us words for some of our fouler aspects of weather. 'Fog' is derived from the Norse 'fok', and a 'gust', derived from the Norse 'gustr'. Some of the more daunting aspects of our terrain, such as 'mire', derived from the Norse 'myr', meaning a bog. So if you happen to be stuck in a bog as the gusts bring in a thick fog, you have the Vikings to blame for much of what has been said.

There are some interesting combinations and juxtapositions that the Vikings contributed to. When someone says that 'you don't know your arse from your elbow', they are giving you an intriguing cocktail of origins. 'Arse' is derived from the Norse word 'ars', meaning the rear end. Whereas 'elbow' is Old English, most directly deriving from the Anglo-Saxon 'elboga'. Is it coincidence that Norse gives us the darker of the two, the arse, while Old English gives us the brighter, the elbow?

The most interesting amalgam of influences can be seen in the names of the days of the week. Thursday is inspired by the Norse God 'Thor'. It is unlike the Latin-derived Jeudi, Jovedi or Jeuves in French, Italian or Spanish respectively. At the other end of the scale, Saturday is Latin, and is derived from the Roman God of agriculture, 'Saturn'. The rest of the days come from Old English/Germanic influences. Monday is the day of the Moon ('Mona' in Old English). Tuesday, Wednesday, Friday are derived from the gods 'Tiw', 'Woden' and 'Frig'. Sunday from the Old English, 'Sunnandaeg', literally the day of the sun. This summary reflects the little influence that Latin had, by comparison to the more Germanic, Saxon and Norse roots, on the linguistically important names for the days of the week.

But these influences on our specific words, miss the bigger picture. The Vikings did a lasting service to our English, by way of our grammar and word constructions.

There was an enormous simplification which took place during the transition from Old English to Middle English. There were many changes. But there were three that are particularly striking. And Viking influence seems to lie behind all of them.

The first was the removal of the gender definition of nouns. English is almost unique among European languages in reserving gender solely to the specific sex of a human or animal. Hence 'she' or 'he'. We do not require a gender to be assigned to inanimate objects or concepts. In French, for example, we describe sticks of bread as being either 'un pain' (masculine), or 'une baguette' (feminine), for no obvious gender-based reason. A glass can be 'un verre' or 'une tasse' – why different gender? It makes the language harder to master. Old English had three genders like most languages. By the time that it had morphed into Middle English, it had lost all case genders, making it easier to speak.

The second is the simplification of the sentence structure into subject, verb, object.

And third, Old English also like its European counterparts leant heavily on suffixes to define its verbs. On the journey to Middle English and then on to modern English, these suffixes have largely gone. Today, we decline the verb 'love' as follows, depending on the strength of the pronoun to make the meaning clear: 'I love, you love, he loves, we love, you (plural) love, they love.' No change in ending other than the single 's' on 'he loves'. Old English was much more complex 'ic luf-ie, þu luf-ast, he luf-aþ, we luf-iaþ'. French today, like all other European languages, still retains the bundle of suffixes that English dispensed with: 'J'aime, tu aimes, il aime, nous aimons, vous aimez, ils aiment.' As in this example, 'you' singular in most languages is differentiated from 'you' plural or 'you' formal, in a way that English doesn't bother with.

These are but three examples of how Middle English managed to simplify Old English. How did this happen? The evidence points to the impact of the ebb and flow across the border between Danelaw and England. This interaction over the decades forced the simplification of our colloquial speech. The Vikings, while they were raiders, were also settlers and inveterate traders. Their mercantile instinct took them far and wide, to all points of Europe to find good markets. The border between England and Danelaw was long, imprecise and prone to change. Today we worry about the trading flows across the Northern Irish border and the cultural and religious impact of restricting it. The activity across the Danelaw border was even more complex and certainly covered a much larger body of land.

The languages spoken on either side of this trading border were related. They shared a common derivation, but by this stage they were distinct. Some of the core verbs remained the same, and yet the suffixes had grown apart. There is the example of the verb 'to judge' (or 'deem') which McWhorter quotes. In Old English this conjugated 'I judge, you judge…' as 'deme, demest, demeþ, demaþ, demaþ, demaþ', while in Old Norse it conjugated as 'dœmi, dœmir, dœmir, dœmum, dœmiþ, dœma'. The difference lay in the suffixes between the two languages. This was the same with many other verbs. Over time, Viking traders and their Anglo-Saxon counterparts, eager to understand one another, must have dumped the complex different endings and focused on the main part of the verb only, which both parties could recognise, and the defining pronouns, in order to communicate and connect.

English has emerged relatively uniquely with these simplifications in the spoken form. This has made it a language not only easier to learn, but also easier to adapt. It is not a language that is bound inherently to rules and constraints. That adaptability has been part of its global success.

Lying within our third person plurals, there is further indication of this impact of Norse on English. As we explore later, the overwhelming majority of our most frequently used words are from Old English. The contribution of Norse to our top hundred includes a very important three. 'They', 'Them' and 'Their'. As suffixes disappeared from our verbs, more emphasis was placed on the pronouns to define meaning. In Old English, the third personal plural was 'hie', and sounded very similar to the third person singular 'he'. Not a problem when the suffix was doing the hard work, but a major problem once the suffix was simplified. Similarly for the third person adjective in Old English 'hiera' (their) was very close to the word for 'her' which was 'hiera'. And the same applied to the pronoun, 'hem'. To ensure that clarity survived the suffix simplification, these three words adopted the Norse terms: 'they', 'their', 'them', all of which were well differentiated from 'he/she', 'his/hers', 'him/her'. This provides further evidence of the productive interaction between English and Norse.

There are important challenges to this theory which need to be answered. Firstly, if Viking influence generated these simplifications, why did written Old English not adapt to these ways while the Vikings were still here and before the Normans invaded? Middle English in written form did not emerge until much later (around 1200 to 1400); the timing of the change of the spoken form we obviously have no record of. The answer lies in a belief that the written versions of a language maintain their traditional form much longer. They take longer to catch up with the colloquial spoken form. During the period from 1100 to 1300, in the Norman era, most documents were composed in Latin and French. Written English went largely underground for this period. Secondly, how certain can one be that it was the Viking/English interaction that was critical? In answer, English began to rise in written form again after 1300. Notably it was the texts and legal documents found in the North, where the boundary lay, that adopted the simplified Middle English earlier than in the South. An indicator of this southward spread can be seen in the 'Chronicles'. After a period of hiatus, the writing of the 'Chronicles' was resumed for a final burst in 1153. For this ultimate phase, it used a language much closer to Middle English, and distinct from the Old English of the prior text. These final chapters were authored in the Abbey at Peterborough, not far from the Danelaw line.

However dismissive we may choose to be of Viking impact on our islands, we cannot ignore their role in simplifying our language. Once again, the English had to prove flexible to the intrusion of an invading power. And also importantly, London had historically been a part of Mercia. The major seats of commerce and scholarship, London, Oxford and Cambridge, thus sat within traditionally Mercian lands, and together became a triangular powerhouse for this new flexible form of English. Alfred's original decision to restore London to Mercia had profound consequences on the future shape of our dominant language and its global potential.

As a final footnote to this chapter, we need to acknowledge that any image of the Vikings as a brutal, artless horde, misses much of the full story. The Vikings revelled in poetry every bit as much as the Anglo-Saxons. No better example of this exists than in the 'Havamal' ('The words of Odin the High One'); the manuscript still survives in the Codex Regius in Reykjavik.

> *'Fire he needs*
> *Who with frozen knees*
> *Has come from the cold without;*
> *Food and clothes*
> *Must the farer have.*
> *The man from the mountains come.'*

CHAPTER SEVEN

THE UNIQUELY ENGLISH CULTURAL REVOLUTION

> *Hear! We have heard the stories of the might*
> *Of kings of the Spear-Danes in days gone by,*
> *And how the princes practiced valiant deeds*
>
> – The opening lines of the translation of
> the epic poem 'Beowulf'

The period between the Roman departure and the Norman arrival, during which England was predominantly Anglo-Saxon, is nearly 700 years long. It tends to be dealt with in our history, as an amorphous single span of time with much of it described as being 'dark'. The same period of time after Hastings takes you from the Normans to the Hanoverians. This seems a massive and highly varied expanse of history: the subject of so many different periods (not to mention television dramas).

The problem with calling those early years 'dark', is that the more we learn through modern research techniques, the less 'dark' they become. 'Dark' implies that it is not only unknown, but also colourless, murky, obscure. But in these centuries, England established itself as the most extraordinary hothouse of learning, art and writing in the whole of contemporary Europe. Much of the roots of our English culture were defined in a period that would be better now described as the 'Light Ages'.

It helps to break this period into four phases. The first was the Anglo-Saxon arrival, and the establishment of their dominance over the heartlands of England. This took until about 600.

The culture up until this point was broadly an oral one. That changed with the arrival of Augustine and Christianity in 593. Christianity was embraced by the Anglo-Saxons with remarkable speed. It was in 680, that one of the very last outposts of paganism in England, the Isle of Wight, converted.

With Christianity came an emphasis on writing, on learning, on scripture and on philosophy. Seats of learning were established around the country and scripture-writing offices were set up at most major churches. There were 200 years of cultural transformation, against a backdrop of the improved inter-kingdom relations that Christianity helped promote, and economic prosperity that relative peace brought. This was the second phase.

It was brutally interrupted by the third phase: the bloody arrival of the Vikings in 787 at their most marauding. This phase lasted a hundred years until the end of Alfred's reign in 899.

The fourth phase was one of increasing unity among the English, growing stability, and a return to the cultural priorities of before the atrocities of Lindisfarne. Even when the wars with the Vikings continued to rage, and even when Cnut incorporated England into a larger Danish Empire, the essence of vibrant English culture prevailed.

These 700 years were not uniform, but taking these periods together as a whole, key important themes emerge.

о о о

Language lay at the heart of the creative explosion of the age. Individual dialects continued to thrive, but they were common-rooted, and importantly a single unifying language was emerging, 'Englisc'.

Even before the Latin alphabet was adopted, the Anglo-Saxon had a runic equivalent called Futhorc – a system of some thirty-one runes. Each was formed by a set of strong, simple lines, as they were designed not to be written down on paper by a pen, but scored by a blade into stone, bone or wood. Our word 'writing' still reflects this early methodology, as it derives from the Old English word 'writan' which means to carve.

Learning and scholarship were essential companions to language and writing. By the 8th century, England had become the home of Christian ethos and scholarship, which influenced the whole development of letters and learning, as it had done in Western Europe. Significant seats of scholarship emerged, primarily centred on the newly formed sacred institutions – the monasteries, the cathedrals, the abbeys and churches. Canterbury, Winchester and Malmesbury in the South, and Lindisfarne, Iona, Monkwearmouth and Jarrow in the North. These became the magnets for scholars, writers, religious thinkers, calligraphers and artists. Scholarship as we have seen was championed by kings, and England gradually overtook the reputation for learning that Ireland had established in earlier centuries through its own monasteries. It then went on to equal or even exceed the achievement of any European state of the first millennium. Aldhelm, Bede and Alcuin became the staples of the European school curriculum for many decades to come. Alcuin joined the entourage of Charlemagne in 781 as both teacher and adviser.

Alfred, as we have described, was a noted sponsor of learning, and the accessibility of it. Books and texts were translated into his West Saxon dialect. Alfred himself executed or supervised several of the translations – not a usual preoccupation of kings of that era. Alfred is said to have translated Boethuis' 'De Consolatione Philosophiae', Augustine's 'Soliloquies' and the first fifty psalms. These psalms describe the deeds and demeanour of King David, whom Alfred took as a role model for kingly behaviour. Like Alfred, David had become king, despite being the youngest son of his father. The anointment of David at his coronation directly influenced the form of the English and now British crowning ceremony.

New works were written in the vernacular during Alfred's reign. The most significant was the 'Anglo-Saxon Chronicles'. Alfred also promoted many existing works penned in English; he was, for example, a great admirer of the English verse of Aldhelm written some 200 years earlier, such as the beautiful poem 'Carmen de Virginitate'. Tellingly, the Alfred Jewel, despite its elegant design, is believed to have been the pointer end to a reading stick. It bears the charming inscription 'Alfred ordered me to be made'. In a letter, Alfred encourages his bishops to utilise a device for pointing to words when reading the translation, attributed to him, of Pope Gregory the Great's 'Pastoral Care'. The Jewel may have been such a device provided by Alfred.

His grandson, Athelstan championed literature and held in even higher esteem the scholar Aldhelm. When Athelstan died, he was buried, not in the historic graves of the Saxon kings in Winchester, but in Malmesbury, alongside the tomb of Aldhelm. A simple but powerful symbol of the importance of learning, wisdom and philosophy to the kings of this new age.

It is possible that Athelstan commissioned an early translation of the Gospels from Hebrew to English, with the help of a group of Jewish scholars he engaged for the purpose. The historian Michael Wood deduces this from references to a lost text by William of Malmesbury which described the translation process. It would be consistent with Athelstan's dedication to making learning available to broader audiences. It would predate Wycliffe's translations into Middle English by nearly 500 years, as well as being earlier than any other major Bibles known to be produced in the vernacular in Western Europe.

Literature and performance flourished. There was a profusion in religious texts but also a proliferation in creative composition; this occurred in both Latin and the vernacular.

The extraordinary epic poem 'Beowulf' consists of 3,182 alliterative lines of Old English, and although hard to date, it may have been composed somewhere around the period 600 to 700. It is well acknowledged as a defining piece of literature of the age, that reflected the hopes, dreams and fears of the Anglo-Saxons. Like so many literary creations of this period, it was written to be performed, or declaimed or even sung. Few would actually be expected to read the poem. These were performance pieces. 'Beowulf' is just the tip of a wonderful iceberg. It is packed full of heroic deeds and rich imagery, such as the following description of the odious lake into which Beowulf must enter to slay the mother of his tormentor Grendel:

> 'Steams like black clouds, and the groves of trees
> Growing out over their lake are all covered
> With frozen spray, and wind down snakelike
> Roots that reach as far as the water
> And help keep it dark. At night that lake
> Burns like a torch. No one knows its bottom
> No wisdom reaches such depths.'

The other significant alliterative poem of the period was the 'Dream of the Rood'. A shorter piece, it is among the earliest surviving examples of creative writing in Old English. In this poem the Dreamer confronts the Tree (the Rood) upon which Christ has been crucified, and the Rood's story is told in alliterative verse. It develops the imaginative use of epithets, referring for example, to the Cross as the 'wondrous tree'. It uses an elegiac tone that expounds upon the transitory nature of life, upon sorrow, upon the sinfulness of man and the ultimate consolation that will come in heaven:

> 'Listen! I will speak of the best of dreams,
> The sweetest vision that crossed my sleep
> In the middle of the night when speech-bearers
> Lay in silent rest.'

Add to this, all the poems included in the Exeter Book. These pieces had evocative titles such as 'The Wanderer', and 'Widsith' (known as 'The Traveller's Song'), and 'The Seafarer', which gives you a flavour of the tone of the poetry. 'The Seafarer' was a precursor of 'The Rhyme of the Ancient Mariner', as you can tell from this translated quotation:

> 'I can sing this truth-song about myself –
> Of harrowing times and hard travelling,
> Of days of terrible toil. Often I endured
> Bitter heartache on my ship of sorrow,
> In my hall of care, on the heaving waves.

The narrow night-watch often held me,
Anxious and troubled at the ship's prow,
As we sailed, tossing close to the sea-cliffs.
My feet were pinched by cold, bound by frost
Hunger and longing tortured and tore
My sea-weary mind.'

Towards the end of the 10th century and into the early 11th century, great prose writers emerged like Wulfstan, and Aelfric, the resident of Cerne Abbey monastery and author of homilies. The epic poem, the 'Battle of Maldon' recorded the Anglo-Saxon warlord, Byrhtnoth, battling to the death the raiding Viking army. The fact that Byrhtnoth lost but was still memorialised (and indeed his statue stands in Maldon today) speaks to the complex psychology of Anglo-Saxon authors. They were there to mourn as much as celebrate.

'Byrhtnoth and his men, ready and waiting: he ordered them
To make the 'battle fence' formation with their shields and
   hold it
Firmly against their enemies. Then it was near to fighting, glory
   in battle.
The time had come when fated men must fall.
A clamour was raised, ravens circled, eagles ready for carrion;
On earth there was noise.'

Much of the original work from this period has been inevitably lost but we still are able to enjoy poetic compilations such as the Junius manuscript, the Vercelli Book, the Metres of Boethius, as well as the Exeter Book, and standalone works such as 'Beowulf' and the 'Dream of the Rood'. These alone capture the imaginative mind of this time

It is worth contrasting this surge in creative output with progress in the rest of Europe. For example, the French equivalent to 'Beowulf', 'The Song of Roland', was not committed to manuscript until the early 12th century, and ironically the transcription was done in England. The first significant historical work written in French was Geoffrey Gaimar's 'L'Estoire de Engleis' (or 'History of the English') in 1140 and was modelled directly on the 'Anglo-Saxon Chronicles'.

This creative industry was not solely of the written word, but also excelled in art and illustration. The sheer intricate, consummate beauty of the decorated pages in the 'Lindisfarne Gospels', in the 'Book of Kells', or the

'Gospel Book of Judith of Flanders' evidence a visual skill at the time, every bit as strong as the literary.

And sometimes, the written and the visual dramatically combined. The Ruthwell Cross is a majestic example. This is a towering piece of sculpture made and displayed at Ruthwell in south-west Scotland. It was probably created sometime after the Synod of Whitby in 664. Standing some five metres high, it presents scenes from the life of Christ. It is decorated in carved vine leaves inserted with birds and animals, and inscribed with eighteen lines from 'The Dream of the Rood'. As it quotes:

> 'Christ was on the cross
> Yet eager ones came, believers from afar,
> To be with the Lord. I beheld it all
> I was seized with sorrow, humbling myself
> To men's hands, bowing down with bold courage.'

Pevsner speaking about this cross and its nearby and equally spectacular relation at Bewcastle, declared that in his opinion 'the crosses of Bewcastle and Ruthwell...are the greatest achievement of their date in the whole of Europe'.

Craft and design contributed to the creative tapestry of the period. There is a wealth of the most wonderful and beautiful objects still surviving. This especially applied to the period when Byzantine and Merovingian gold became available, which enabled the greater delicacy of detailed filigree work which this gold permits. All the surviving objects from Sutton Hoo, such as the intricately crafted gold belt buckle and the ceremonial war helmet, are breath-taking. So too the beautiful gold sea horse from the Staffordshire hoard, the Fuller Brooch, and the Alfred Jewel. These objects all indicate a considerable strength not just in craftsmanship, but also in design.

Music also played a full part in the cultural landscape of the Anglo-Saxons. We have mentioned the sung nature of the original renditions of 'Beowulf'. The advent of Christian worship only accelerated the importance of singing and music. Aethelwold is thought to have installed an organ in Winchester Cathedral in the 10th century to assist in the singing. 'The Book of St Benedict' proscribed that Benedictine adherents should sing the entire psalter at least once a week. The 'Life of St Dunstan' relates how Dunstan helped a noble woman named Aethelwynn with her embroidery. He brought 'with him as usual his harp, which we call in our father's tongue *hearpa*, intending to give pleasure with it, at intervals in the work'. The reference to 'as usual' is telling, as it indicates an expectation that our early saints would always have access to music making. Even in death, music was meant to be present, as evidenced by the pieces of a lyre found in the burial ship at Sutton Hoo, in Suffolk.

Admire for a moment the Caligula Troper, a song book with lyrics, with musical notations, and some of the most vivid and beautiful illustrations you will find. Or the Book of Kells. An album sleeve of the 1960s would have been proud of the complete artistic impact.

Humour and jest played fundamental roles in Anglo-Saxon culture. While religious texts and scholarship were conducted with due solemnity, the secular writing and composition embraced a natural sense of irony and mischief. The beginnings of the English love of the comic can be seen emerging at this early stage, continuing what we know about the English during the Roman period, including their love of Pantomimus in the theatre.

Probably the most readily identifiable example of this is contained in the Anglo-Saxon penchant for riddle. The writers loved posing amusing brain teasers for the reader to unravel. From this our national obsession with crosswords, and phenomena like Wordle derive. The master of the riddle was Alcuin, who either wrote or transcribed reams of them. His book 'Dialogue with Pippin' is largely made out of them. Pippin was the son of Charlemagne, and Alcuin was his teacher for several years.

> *'An ox ploughs a field all day. How many footprints does he leave in the last furrow?'*
> *'Who is he that will rise higher if you take away his head?'*
> *'What is that which is, and is not?'*
> *'How can a thing be, yet not exist?'*

And on and on, they went. And in the compendium of Anglo-Saxon writing in the Exeter Book, you will find ninety-four riddles in Old English. Many are complicated, some religious, some derived their humour from saucy 'double entendres' and some were uncompromisingly obscene. Riddle 42 begins:

> *'A wondrous thing hangs alongside a man's thigh under the clothing of the lord: there is a hole in front.'*
> *'It is strong and hard; it has a good firmness.'*

You get the gist of the puzzle being posed. From an early age the English mind has been fascinated by conundra and word play, delighting in comedy, especially absurdity and a bit of suggestiveness. From what does this derive? A reaction to natural adversity? A resolution in the conflict between our natural reserve and a need to express? A release valve of escapism? The rich traditions of Jewish humour provide a possible parallel.

There was an important international dimension to English culture and learning. During this period, England not only shared, in Latin, a common tongue with Europe, but also a common religion. Scholars and teachers from both sides of the Channel could exchange views productively. It also meant that travel could be conducted in the security that Christian rules of hospitality and welcome would normally apply. This prompted a surge in travel, and the expansion of ideas across the whole of Europe.

The most frequently conducted journey was to Rome. No mean feat in that era, taking potentially several months each way. The route for example taken in 990 by Archbishop Sigeric divided down into around 80 identifiable stages. One of the most frequent travellers was Benedict Biscop, the founder of Monkwearmouth and Jarrow monasteries. In the 600s, he made the journey back and forth 6 times, across a period of 30 years.

In the early decades of Christianity, many scholars came from Rome to teach in England. In the later decades the traffic increasingly went the other way. Major Englishmen of learning, such as Alcuin, were invited to Europe, and English churchmen embarked on conversion missions to heathen areas of Northern Europe.

This was a time of international exchange of ideas, in which England was increasingly seen, not just as an equal contributor, but in many ways a leading centre for thought, writing and scholarship.

This pre-eminence in cultural and philosophical fields cannot be separated from economic stability and success. Not only was England agriculturally rich, it also benefitted from sound leadership and its increasing status as a steady single nation. For example, Pamela Nightingale highlights the strength of the English economic system at this time. She writes:

> *'The advanced monetary system of the Old English also demonstrates that it was ahead of its neighbours in financial expertise. To find a parallel with the sophisticated and complex system of varying weight standards used by the mints of Aethelfred's England, one would have to go to the Byzantine Empire from where its inspiration may have come.'*

o o o

The position of women merits consideration. This was a male society, but one in which women played a more significant role than perhaps they would for some centuries thereafter.

At times, they played a prominent role politically. Aethelflaed, Alfred's daughter and Edward the Elder's sister, is a good example. She married the

King of the Mercians, Aethelred, upon whose death in 911, she succeeded to the throne. She was known widely as the 'Queen of the Mercians'. By the accounts of the local record, the Mercian Register, she was a well-loved and effective ruler. She did much to galvanise her people's response to the Viking threat, as well as to establish a proud Mercian identity. Importantly it was she who brought up her nephew, Athelstan, and helped develop him to be the great King he would prove to be.

Women were also important benefactors and patrons. For example, Judith of Flanders, who was married to Tostig, Earl of Northumberland, was a significant supporter and donor to Durham Cathedral, following his death in the battle of Stamford Bridge. Her wonderfully decorated gospel book is testament to her taste and munificence. The text of the gospels is thought to have been produced in England, reflecting our strengths in religious text production, and the binding in Flanders or Germany. The combination is stunning.

Women were sought for their wisdom and advice. For example, Hilda the founding abbess of Whitby, was the confidante and advisor to Northumbrian kings. Her abbey was chosen as the site for the Synod of Whitby in 664 on account of her personal reputation. Church leaders from all over England attended, and reached a conclusion to the tricky problem of dating Easter. She spotted and nurtured the poetic talent of the cowherd Caedmon, and thus Whitby monastery became the setting for the first Christian verse in traditional Old English metre. Her canonised memory is preserved today in the name of the Oxford college, St Hilda's.

There were well recognised female teachers of verse and scripture such as Eadburgh, abbess of Minster-in-Thanet in the 8th century, and her younger contemporaries Leoba and Berhtgyth. All were skilled correspondents, and supporters of the missions in Germany led by Boniface. In my opinion, women were not to play a role as significant until probably the 14th century.

o o o

Anglo-Saxon England was probably the leading example of a vernacular culture in Western Europe in the second half of the first millennium – expert at storytelling in its own language, excellent at all forms of visual expression, brilliant at craft skills, with a strong musical heritage.

Geoffrey Elton in 'The English' captures this phenomenon succinctly: 'Anglo-Saxon England (provided) the leading example of a vernacular culture worthy of the name in the whole of Western Europe. French and German did not achieve a like status of literary quality and use till the 12th century, whereas Old English had reigned for hundreds of years.'

What came before is hard to be certain of due to lack of records. But the comments of Tacitus, Roman Governor of Britannia in the 1st century, give a possible clue: '...they who lately disdained the tongue of Rome now coveted its eloquence. Hence, too, a liking sprang for our style of dress, and the 'toga' became fashionable. Step by step they were led to things which dispose to vice, the lounge, the bath, the elegant banquet. All this in their ignorance, they called civilisation, when it was but part of their servitude.'

There are no easy or simple explanations as to why Anglo-Saxon culture defined something so very different, confident and imaginative. Certainly none that has been compellingly advanced that I have seen. I have to attribute it to the wealth of the land and the mineral resources which afforded a learning culture, 300 years of relative peace disturbed only by inter-tribal squabbling, the rapid embrace of Christianity and its text-based doctrines, the galvanising force of the Viking attacks, our geographic separateness, the genius of leaders like Alfred, Bede, Athelstan, Alcuin, Aldhelm and many others. But at the end of the analysis, I am forced to conclude that there was something innately creative, expressive, enquiring, humorous and narrative based in the Anglo-Saxon character, of which I believe we are still living with the inheritance.

There is no clearer sign of this Anglo-Saxon inheritance than in the word 'Easter'. This is the most holy of all Christian celebrations. But contrary to expectation, Easter is probably not derived from Latin, Greek or Hebrew, but from 'Eostre', the Anglo-Saxon goddess of the Dawn and of the Spring, honoured in pagan days at around this time of year. At every Easter time, we are proclaiming the importance of our Anglo-Saxon origins in every aspect of life.

In the closing phases of 'Beowulf', the protagonist meets his fate at the hands of the dragon, and it is noted that:

> *'He has done his worst but the wound will end him. He is hasped and hooped and hirpling with pain, limping and looped with it, like a man outlawed for wickedness, he must await the mighty judgement of God in majesty.'*

Strikingly, almost the same words could have been said of Rooster Byron in the closing scene of 'Jerusalem'. In Rooster's case, it was the Kennet and Avon Council hellbent on his destruction. In the Anglo-Saxon case, it was to be the Normans.

CHAPTER EIGHT

LIVING WITH THE NEW NORMAN

*'...and always after that it grew much worse.
May the end be good when God wills!'*

So read the entry for 1066 in the 'Anglo-Saxon Chronicles', conveying the sense of apocalypse that the Norman invasion created for the Anglo-Saxon world.

William the Conqueror (or William the Bastard as he was then known) probably could not believe his luck. His victory at Hastings had been a narrow one, and his forces relatively modest in relation to the scale of the country he was invading. But it was dramatic, and importantly for William, the popular Anglo-Saxon King Harold lay dead on the battlefield. By virtue of his success in combat, and his subsequent brutal campaign of terror, he seized control of a rich and well-organised nation, many times larger and wealthier than his homelands in Normandy. One of William's chaplains made the following observation about this new country, supporting the overall thesis about its relative attraction:

> *'In abundance of the precious metal that country by far
> surpasses the Gauls; for while by its exuberance of corn, it may
> be called the granary of Ceres, from its quantity of gold, it
> may be termed a treasury of Arabia... The English women are
> eminently skillfull with their needle and in the weaving of gold,
> the men in every kind of artificial workmanship.'*

William was helped by the lack of clarity in the process of Anglo-Saxon succession. The attempts to install Edward the Confessor's great-nephew, Edgar, as the new King, proved half-hearted. So began Norman rule. So also began a bloody tussle, lasting for several centuries, between a new breed of ruler, who derived their authority from the sword, or from God (or often from both), and their people. This tussle continued more or less unabated through to its conclusion in the Glorious Revolution and William and Mary's accession to the throne in 1689. Thereafter the constitutional monarchy and representational democracy took hold as the basis of government in England, fundamentally solving this dilemma. In this context, it should be mentioned that there were attempts in late Tudor and Stuart times to overpaint Anglo-Saxon days as essentially a period of democracy with rule by Parliament, which was suddenly replaced by the Norman's imposition of monarchical autocracy. This argument was used to justify the opposition to the high-handed behaviour of Charles I, in order to emphasise a parliamentary democratic system as our natural prior state. It was never that extreme, but the Anglo-Saxon system of rule was more consensus based than what followed it. Even William's contemporaries at the time, such as Guy, Bishop of Amiens, made note of this difference. It certainly did not help the Anglo-Saxon response to the Normans, the moment Harold had been eliminated.

The simplistic assessment of the Norman Conquest is indeed one of conquest and subjugation. The Anglo-Saxon state was overrun and England turned into the vassal of a foreign totalitarian regime. While the Normans never constituted more than a few per cent of the population, they held the primary levers of wealth and power. Norman kings would make it abundantly clear who was in charge, and that any disobedience would be punished harshly. Estates and privileges were allocated to William's invading supporters, at the expense of their Anglo-Saxon predecessors. And then taken away solely on his whim. A vast network of stone castles was built to loom over the populace, threateningly. They were filled with heavily armed soldiers willing to punish harshly any transgression.

To capture the sense of Norman brutality then read the words of the Welsh bishop, Rhigyfarch, penned in around 1094. 'Our limbs are cut off, we are lacerated, our necks condemned to death, and chains are put on our arms. The honest man's hands are branded by burning metals. A woman lacks her nose, a man his genitals...'

Or read the 'Anglo-Saxon Chronicles' entry for 1124:

> *'I neither know nor may tell of all the horrors or all the tortures that they subjected wretched men to in this land...when the wretched men had no more to give, then they ravaged and burned down all the villages...then corn was dear, and meat and cheese and butter, for there was not any in the land. Wretched men die of hunger.'*

During the initial battles and the immediate aftermath, the vast majority of the Anglo-Saxon lords were killed, or stripped of their lands. A whole upper class was eliminated. Some went into exile and some worked as mercenaries abroad. An English settlement was established as far afield as on the shores of the Sea of Marmara near Istanbul, centuries before any English package holiday-makers reached the same destination. These were desperate times; an existing ruling class was rapidly removed and replaced by the Normans.

The Normans moved quickly to take over Winchester, the symbol of not only Saxon kingship, but of learning and scholarship. They demolished houses so that a palace could be built, and Winchester was never to recover its former significance fully again. They moved across vast swathes of the country, putting much of it to the sword and the flame. What the Normans lacked for in numbers, they made up for in brutality.

'The Domesday Book' underlines the extent of the takeover by the Normans. By the time that this grand record was compiled, half the whole country was in the hands of just 190 men, and half of that was held by just 11 men. And all of these were French-speaking Normans. Genuinely the country was in the sway of a foreign and alien power.

Kings were no longer called Alfred or Athelstan, but strictly Norman French names like William, Henry, Richard and John. Edward was the only Anglo-Saxon monarch's name to make a reappearance, and that 200 years later as the Plantagenets chose to rediscover some of their Anglo-Saxon roots.

In Anglo-Saxon society over 10 per cent of the population were slaves. But to the Normans, slavery contradicted their concept of the feudal economic structure and it was gradually marginalised over time. Perhaps the average serf of Norman days might have struggled to tell the difference between slavery and serfdom. But he would have been unwise to make his observation too widely known. The status of serfdom was to continue to exist for another 500 years; it was not fully abolished until 1574 in the reign of Elizabeth I.

Some things continued as before, only to disappear later. Peterborough Abbey was the final location where the 'Anglo-Saxon Chronicles' were updated and copied. But their culmination seemed to coincide with the appointment of a decidedly Norman-sounding cleric, William de Walterville. '...and now is abbot, and has made a fine beginning. Christ grant him to end thus', some monk wrote. And the candle was blown out.

The heavy violence of the Norman invasion was noted by contemporary writers in Europe, who were taken aback by its brutality. Before 1066, the English were regarded as a 'glorious and splendid people'. Contemporary commentary indicated that the Normans found English captives to be well dressed, long haired, good-looking, and much preoccupied with the brushing of their locks. Whereas Normans were shaven with crop-headed hairstyles.

As Robert Tombs quotes, William of Malmesbury, writing in the 13th century summarised the difference. The Saxons, he said, had lived richly in 'mean and despicable' houses, while the Normans lived frugally in 'noble and splendid mansions.'

The benefit of this brutal regime was its clear sense of purpose, and its fundamental efficiency. Things got done; castles were erected; cathedrals were built. A Jewish community was brought over from Normandy to help create what we would now call the 'capital markets'. The lending of money at a return was a forbidden practice for Christians. The Tower of London functioned in part to protect this important community, and indeed was part paid for by them by way of super taxation. Under the Norman system, the Jews were the King's property, the Constable of the Tower had responsibility for them, and the higher Jewish courts were located here – as well as their place of punishment. At times of trouble, they were brought within the walls for safety; the King's property had to be protected and the lending market had to continue to function.

Importantly, when the Vikings inevitably came sniffing around for plunder again, they were quickly sent packing, never to return. The economy could start functioning without fear of further invasion. Just authority had to be obeyed and heavy royal taxes to be paid. William deployed the effective money-raising notion of staking claim to all property in England by right of conquest, and then either awarding it to his closest followers or selling it back to the original occupants.

If there is an ability to get things done in an organised, determined and invariably brusque fashion, within the modern English capability set, then I like to think that this is in part derived from the massive enema of Norman culture that was inserted into the English umbilical system in these centuries. Normans do not strike me as a people who give much truck to focus groups or committee deliberations. They belong, in my opinion, to the 'get this thing done' type. The legacy of that spirit is there for all to see in the massive number of Norman fortresses and cathedrals that survive across our landscape today. So many were commenced within the first decades of Norman rule. Hopefully enough of us today have inherited that spirit, to make quite complex and daunting tasks achievable.

The Normans were ultimately practical people, and aspects of Anglo-Saxon life were preserved where it suited. The Anglo-Saxon mentality meantime was focused on quiet survival. The same might be said for the English language. The elimination of the old English ruling class allowed a new class of merchants, traders and farmers to emerge more strongly.

Anglo-Saxon society was quietly adapting underneath the Norman super structure. And the same could be said for the English culture and language. In many ways it was the vanquished that emerged in the end as the vanquishers. The Anglo-Saxons learnt to live with the new Norman.

o o o

An important part of English survival centred on London. Once again, this city is central to the narrative of our language and our culture.

While William laid waste to much of the country in the South and then went on to pulverise the North, he never destroyed London. He had no doubt as to the importance of London to his future in England. The near contemporary record on the invasion, 'Carmen de Hastingae Proelio', presumed to be written by his supporter, Guy, Bishop of Amiens, records their perceptions as they approached. 'It is a great city overflowing with forward inhabitants and richer in treasure than the rest of the kingdom. Protected on the left side by walls, on the right side by river, it neither fears enemies nor dreads being taken by storm.' William's decisions about London were once again driven by pragmatism.

Although the precise sequence of events is somewhat hazy at points, it would seem that they came to the southern banks of the Thames, and did what others, such as Cnut had done before. They attacked Southwark, in this instance, torching it to the ground. But city dwellers were unperturbed by that. Southwark in our city's history has always been thoroughly expendable. The city gates were kept locked, and London Bridge made impenetrable. Londoners meanwhile had nominated Edgar to be their new king. With further resistance gathering around the country, William did not have much time. Bringing London under his control was critical to the success of his whole mission.

The Normans started their march along the southern banks of the Thames, heading west, seeking a safe place for the army to cross in late autumn. It is not clear when Kingston Bridge was first constructed. Some accounts indicate that a bridge was there in pre-Norman days. Some records say circa 1190. Some say not until the 13th century. My assumption is that there was no bridge in 1066. This would explain his continued march west along the southern banks of the Thames. He crossed much further upstream, by most accounts at Wallingford, one of Alfred's original burhs, whose local ruler had declared for William. As the town name implies, it was a good crossing point; the large flood plains make the autumn river flows less precarious. From there, once across, he started on his way back, to the prospect of the closed gates and the manned walls of London.

A strategic decision was made by William, based on his need for speed. Rather than mount an exhausting and lengthy siege, that if successful, would have prompted the destruction and pillage of the City, he decided to strike a comprehensive, far-reaching and enduring deal. This deal preserved the City intact, protected hugely important rights, and in return the City recognised William as legitimate sovereign. The William Charter was part of that. Traditionally it has been believed that this was signed immediately after his coronation in Westminster, at Christmas in 1066, or into 1067. The precise timing is now open to debate; it may have been signed later in the 1060s. Personally I hold closer to the traditional view. I believe it fits better the narrative of William's needs at the time and is more consistent of the special treatment he bestowed on London from the start of his reign, as evidenced by the absence of destruction or major subjugation. I believe William was mindful of the long series of sieges that Cnut had mounted in 1016, which had cost him time, and in the end, necessitated a negotiated treaty.

I consider the William Charter to be one of the most important in our history, but probably little known of by the general public. In written form, it has the length of only five lines. It is only six inches long by one a half inches wide. Importantly it is written not in French and not in Latin, but in Old English. It is thought to have been drafted with the help of Bishop William of London, who as a Norman long domiciled in England, was a go-between for William and is specifically referred to in the Charter. For many centuries the bishop's tomb in the old St Paul's Cathedral was a destination for mayoral procession, recognising his significance to the prosperity and history of the City. The original still actually exists, lying in our City archives, and represents our earliest surviving charter. The original black ink has faded slightly to grey, but remains totally legible. It says simply:

> 'William the king, friendly salutes William the bishop and Godfrey the portreeve and all the burgesses within London both French and English. And I declare here that I grant you to be all law-worthy, as you were in the days of King Edward; And I grant that every child shall be his father's heir, after his father's days; And I will not suffer any person to do you wrong; God keep you.'

These short statements indicated that for the City's acceptance, as rightful, of his claim to the English throne, William, in my opinion, was committing to four fundamental principles in return.

First, he was agreeing to acknowledge London as an independent city answerable only to the Crown. This gave it unique status. The principle of independence still exists today and has been at the heart of the City's long record of autonomy. It has contributed to its success economically and culturally.

Second, he committed to recognise the validity of the principles of inheritance for Londoners. The ability to bequeath one's wealth to offspring or other family members was not a given in medieval days. By sanctioning inheritance among Londoners, the foundations of an entrepreneurial economic culture in the city became possible. At a time when life expectancy was short and often abrupt, the security of knowing that your estate could be inherited by your successors was an essential motivation for wealth creation.

Third, and of equal importance, the new King confirmed that the laws of the City, and thus of the country would continue to be the Anglo-Saxon laws.

Fourth, the Charter acknowledged that the English should be treated equally to the French.

This meant that a brutal and tyrannical invader would not, as normally expected, be imposing his own system of laws, but would recognise that of the conquered people. As a result of these four provisions, but especially the third, important parts of the underlying structure of Anglo-Saxon life were preserved.

There is recent and interesting evidence that Dr Nicolas Karn has uncovered, not only on the issue of the dating, but also of an additional, and previously unnoticed, charter between William and London in which the City paid in effect to buy itself back from the King at some point after the invasion. To me, this sounds entirely plausible given the Normans' need for funding, their regular use of this repurchase device as mentioned earlier, and represents an additional transaction to the underlying grant of rights in the William Charter. He would have been unlikely to have given the richest part of the country, which he was pointedly not allocating to a retainer, a free pass. It may also explain why it is suggested that William may have been granted a valuable tract of city land between Cheapside and London Wall. This became the location of the London Jewish quarter, and of the Grand Synagogue, unusually far away from the protection of the Tower. The street 'Old Jewry' still stands there today and the local church is still known, somewhat oxymoronically, as St Lawrence Jewry. It is possible that this land was part of the settlement for the debt, and he used it for the housing of his property – the Jewish community.

As a reflection of its continued independence from its new rulers, it is notable that no specific French/Norman trading area was established in the City, and allegedly only one City church was dedicated to a Norman saint.

∘ ∘ ∘

The English legal and administrative system endured not just in London but across England. This was testament to its quality, and also a by-product of Norman pragmatism. 'If it is not broken, then why fix it?' The advantage of the English system, and unlike the majority of Europe, was its relative uniformity across the country. This helped the Normans govern their new and much larger lands. It was unlike the plethora of individual principalities that fragmented the continent. It had a wide degree of participation; the ancient forms of representation that had been wiped out in Europe, survived much better in England.

'The Domesday Book' itself, which was such an important instrument for the application of taxation, could not have been compiled if the structure of administration was not so strongly and uniformly in place. The Normans used this as their underlying source of information.

Not only did the legal system survive, but also the culture, and the traditions of the trading system and the mercantile classes. As a result, the language was likely to survive as well – initially as an oral tongue, with the written form increasingly Latin or French. The survival of oral English was to shape the fluency of the language, and increase its flexibility and its potency, for the time of its eventual full revival.

The next important aspect of the Norman period was that England stopped being invaded with systematic regularity. A benefit of Norman brutality was the fear created in any next potential invader. The ordinary English citizen was not being endlessly displaced, and drawn into lengthy conflict, by marauding plunderers.

The final factor of importance to the preservation of Englishness, was of course the weather. This is often forgotten. In the 12th and 13th centuries (certainly up until about 1250), the climate in England was benign. The harvests were on balance, good, and these helped to support population growth, especially in the cities. London grew from 15,000 to 20,000 at the time of the Conquest, to 30,000 to 40,000 by 1200, to 80,000 by 1300. At least a four-fold growth. There are records of vineyards being cultivated in monasteries as far north as Yorkshire. This is something only just now possible again, with our current upswing in temperatures.

To contrast to the gloomy premonitions of the 'Anglo-Saxon Chronicles' in 1066, quoted at the start of the chapter, I offer you the upbeat (and probably biased) descriptions of William Fitzstephen, a monk from Canterbury, who died about 1190, recording his impressions of London.

> 'Among the splendid cities of the world that have achieved celebrity, the city of London...is one whose renown is more widespread, whose money and merchandise go further afield, and which stands head and shoulders above the others. It is fortunate in the wholesomeness of its climate, the devotion of its Christians, the strength of its fortifications, its well-situated location, the respectability of its citizens, and the propriety of their wives...the citizens have beautiful and spacious gardens, planted with trees... To the north there are tilled fields, pastures and pleasant, level meadows with stream flowing through them, where watermill wheels turned by the current, make a pleasing sound. Not far off spreads out a vast forest, its copses dense with foliage concealing wild animals – stags, does, boars, and wild bulls.'

Contrast this with the view recorded at this time by the chronicler Richard of Devizes, reporting the advice given to a French visitor to London, by one of his countrymen:

> 'Every race of men, out of every nation, which is under heaven, resort thither in great numbers; every nation has introduced into that city its vices and bad manners...you will find more braggadocios there than in all France, while the number of flatterers is infinite. Stage players, buffoons, those that have no hair on their bodies, Garamantes, pickthanks, catamites, effeminate sodomites, lewd musical girls, druggists, lustful persons...this whole crew has filled every house. So if you do not wish to live with the shameful, you will not dwell in London.'

Although taxes and punishment were harsh, in these equable climactic conditions and stable political environment, mouths were fed, learning was paid for, and sins and desires allowed to run rampant if needed.

CHAPTER NINE

THE PLACE AT THE OVERFLOWING RIVER

> 'Strong be thy walls that about the standis;
> Wise be the people that within the dwelis;
> Fresh is thy ryver, with his lusty strandis;
> Blith be thy chirches, wele sownyngng be thy bellis;
> Riche be thy merchauntis in substaunce that excels;
> Fair be thy wives, right lovesom, white and small;
> Clere be thy virgyns, lusty under kellis:
> London, thow art the flour of Cities all.'

This is a section of the verse ('In Honour of the City of London') originally attributed to the Scottish poet, Willie Dunbar, which describes London in 1500. Dunbar came as an ambassador for King James IV to help negotiate for his sovereign the hand of Henry VII's daughter, Margaret Tudor. The context for the poem was a sumptuous banquet held by the Lord Mayor for the visiting Scottish diplomats. It finishes with a complimentary flourish:

> 'Thy famous Maire, by princely governaunce,
> With swerd of justice the rulith prudently.
> No Lord of Parys, Venyce, or Floraunce
> In dignytie or honoure goeth to hymn nye...
> London, thow art the flour of Cities all.'

The success of this mission led to the creation of the Stuart line of kings of both Scotland and England, and ultimately the union of the two crowns. Whomever actually wrote it, the poem still conveys the sense of dynamism and bustle that the city had acquired by the turn of the 16th century.

It was not always thus, and in pre-Roman times was an unnoteworthy cluster of humble dwellings on one side of the river, looking out over marshes on the other. The theories about the origins of the city's name are various. To me, the most satisfying and plausible, is that London is derived from the Celtic phrase for 'the place at the overflowing river'. This accords well with the topography of the setting, certainly in early days.

The importance of the extraordinary growth, and the unique nature of London, is central to our narrative about English culture and language. London has already played an important part in our story; King Alfred's commitment to a strong, well protected London played a crucial role in fending off the Vikings. London was then pivotal in determining William's successful claim to the English Crown. The City is so important, it merits an overview of its own.

What the Romans did for us is often debated, and not just in Monty Python films. On the softer and behavioural side of life, their legacy seems to have been less than one might have expected. For example legal scholars argue that there is little sign of Roman legal code influencing English law. They did bring us our first theatres, and started something called Pantomimus, but this was different and more about dance and mime than today's pantomime. To me, their main legacies were in infrastructure. The greatest was the quality of the road system. Superbly well-built and extremely direct, it made the country easy to traverse. The union of the Anglo-Saxon nation, and the system of burhs, would not have been possible without the benefit of this road network. But their greatest legacy was the creation of London.

The site of this new conurbation had challenges. A broad, unruly river, with islands that were often tidally submerged, and with stretches of marshlands on either side. The native Britons had no particular need to surmount those challenges, or had the wherewithal. The arrival of the Romans changed all that. A far greater priority was given to the trading routes to and from mainland Europe, distribution into and out of the rich agricultural lands of the Midlands and the South, and the logistics needed to support a conquering army spreading far and wide across the British Isles. Despite the challenges, the Romans could see the potential of the London site from the outset. It sits on the north side on a stretch with higher land, and on the south side, there was a natural causeway used by the locals to weave their way through the marshes. It provided the best points at which to construct a bridge. Only builders of the skill of the Romans could have tackled the erection of such a structure across this wide, fast-moving river. Not long after their invasion in 43, they are said to have initially installed a makeshift pontoon bridge of boats. This was then replaced by a more permanent wooden structure. Once built, it became the intersection of the route west to east along the river and out to sea, with the route north to south across land and on to Europe.

The Romans initially called this city Londinium, a Latinisation of the original Celtic term. A few centuries later, as the City became grander and grander in the Roman scheme of things, they decided to rebadge it as 'Augusta,' reflecting a more imperial status for their great creation. 4th century texts can be found using this more Latinate name. But the new name never caught on, the Celtic root won out and London stuck. As so often in this tale of our island, it is the original that often lasts longest.

The Romans saw London's primary function as a trading hub and as a key supply centre for the military. The Roman road network made sure that a radial arrangement of throughfares stretched from London to the major parts of the rest of the country, establishing its logistical importance.

With growing trade, came growing wealth, and this made London vulnerable to attack, as happened in the Boudicca uprising. A visionary decision, typical of the Romans, was to embark, in around 200, on a wall-building project of extraordinary scale for this relatively new city. They built over two miles of robust defences protecting 1.1 square miles of land, originating the reference to the City as the 'square mile'. Or 'rectangular mile' more accurately. The walls were built from Kent stone, and stood over 6 metres high, and between 2.5 to 3 metres wide; the surrounding ditch was about 2 metres deep and up to 5 metres across. There were originally 5 separate gates and many more protective towers were constructed. This was a massive endeavour. These huge walls were among the most ambitious in the whole of Northern Europe. They remained impregnable to attack and future-proofed the mercantile expansion. They delineated the boundaries of the City for many centuries to come. London was forever able to play its hand from a position of strength. Rich and impregnable was a perfect combination.

Why did the Romans build the walls so large and so strong? They were out of all proportion to the scale of London at the time and its strategic significance to the rest of the Empire. I have not found an entirely satisfactory explanation, other than the Romans innate love for construction on a monumental scale. 'We can build it, so we shall'. It did comprehensively circumnavigate the full spread of the city at that time. But was this necessary, especially when considering the manpower needed to defend it? Whomever made the decision on its scale, altered the future path and destiny of the nation and the English language.

The Roman population is believed to have peaked at about 25,000 to 30,000 inhabitants, originally concentrated in the eastern half of what we now call the City, but spreading westwards over time. The Walbrook River formed the natural central divide. The enormous basilica (and thus market) was erected on the site of Leadenhall today in the eastern half. The amphitheatre was built where the Guildhall yard is now located, and could seat up to 7,000 at a time (roughly a quarter of the whole City population at its peak); several bath houses were also located in the western half. And in the very north-west corner, by Cripplegate, a Roman fort was sited.

By the time the Romans left, London had become the administrative capital of England, and one of the great cities of the Northern Roman Empire. It was on the map as a world-class city.

London Bridge has remained a vital national asset for much of our history. It was only in 1729 that it was joined by a second river crossing in London. For almost two millennia the only way to cross the great river other than by boat was at London Bridge. What is also surprising is the location of this second bridge. Putney. By the time Fulham Bridge (as it was then known) was built, the City's population had expanded to 650,000. Westminster Bridge was the third, and was not opened until 1750. London Bridge had a strategic significance for much of our history that is hard to appreciate fully today.

The arrival of the Anglo-Saxons could have potentially produced a very different outcome for London. As a result of their natural suspicion of all things Roman, they instinctively avoided it. The old City was left to rot and could have disappeared. Initially they made their base on a stretch of the Thames, at Lundenwic, further upstream, close to what is now Covent Garden. The centre of this area is still known as Aldwych, which translates from Saxon, as 'The Old Town'. Aldwych itself used to be a thoroughfare where Drury Lane now lies, but in subsequent Victorian redesigns, the name was revived for the main connection between east and west. To this day, the area around Aldwych includes the Royal Courts of Justice, and the various Inns of Court, acting as the centre of the legal system. English law is still firmly grounded on Anglo-Saxon principles, and interestingly its physical embodiment remains in the heart of the original Anglo-Saxon London.

This settlement grew to be a substantial town with a population rising to about 7,000. Bede described it as 'an emporium for many nations.' By the late 7th century, it was a centre for the Mercian trade in slaves, as well as all goods and merchandise. From archaeological finds, it is clear that it attracted dealers and merchants from all over Northern Europe. It had no significant monuments or public buildings. Its main feature was a large market laid out on a long beach strip at the edge of the river, and accordingly called the Strand, as it is still known today. The river was especially overflowing at this point, and what we think of today as a roadway far from the water, was in fact on the tidal edge.

As witness to the centuries of the gradually narrowing of the river's width, through embankments, Tube train tunnels, sewers and other building works, you can look at the placement of the magnificent water gate at the bottom of York Place. This was built by the Duke of Buckingham as the landing pier to York House, for his ducal barges to moor. Today it stands marooned like a beautiful, beached whale at the rear of Victoria Embankment Gardens, many stone throws away from where the river runs today.

Alfred set about the remodelling of the London street plan. In 898, Alfred called a gathering attended by his son Edward, the Archbishop of Canterbury, Bishop Waerfeeth of Worcester, Earldorman Aethelred of the Mercians and his wife, and Alfred's daughter, Aethelflaed. It is worth noting the inclusion of a female attendee at such a gathering. This conference confirmed the installation of a borough and a grid plan of streets between Thames Street and Cheapside. From the end of that century, the business and residential centre of London lay within the walls. The resulting street and borough plan largely remains the same today. We Londoners live in an Anglo-Saxon capital city designed within a Roman circumference and Roman external road system. No invader has ever been allowed to run rampant. The devastations of the Great Fire, and of the Blitz, have never produced a fundamental change to the underlying topography. The City has always been rebuilt largely in accordance with the original Anglo-Saxon ground plan laid over its Roman foundations. You can still today walk the labyrinth of narrow streets and alleyways, and delight in their old very English, functional names like Bread Street, Ironmonger Lane, Fish Market Hill, Shoe Lane, Poultry, Old Jewry, Cheapside (meaning market).

The Walbrook River has always been the natural central dividing line of the City, stretching from London Wall down to the Thames. It now lies buried beneath, but is remembered in names such as St Stephen's Walbrook, the magnificent Wren church, where the Samaritans was founded. The Lord Mayor's Mansion House, the Bank of England, and the primary Livery Halls such as the Mercers', the Grocers', and the Drapers' all still cluster around this central dividing line that splits east from west.

o o o

The strength of the overall deal that William concluded with London, owes much to Alfred's earlier decision to re-establish London as a fully functioning and well protected Anglo-Saxon capital. Importantly, under the Normans, the political focus for the nation began to move away from Winchester, and gravitated back towards London. This was the beginning of the concentration of all the major national functions in the same place, which has made London so powerful. Only religion has continued to be centred elsewhere – at Canterbury. But as a result, huge emphasis is placed by the

City on the primacy and majesty of St Paul's Cathedral. The original old St Paul's that dominated the City skyline, began construction in 1087. To this day the City planning committee put extraordinary emphasis on preserving the visibility of what they pointedly call 'Our Cathedral', from a whole host of far-off vantage points – one as far as Richmond Park.

While prepared to offer the city its 'independence', William meant to keep a watchful and intimidating eye over it. He commissioned no less than three fortresses to be built. Two to the west of the City, Castle Baynard and Monfichet Tower, both of which no longer exist, and the most imposing, the Tower of London, to the east, which definitely still survives. It was placed on a strategic outcrop at the point where the old Roman wall met the river.

Many today think of the Tower as a defensive structure designed to protect London. The real intent was different. It was built principally as a visually offensive structure; the exterior walls of the White Tower were elevated to a greater height than the interior structure. The Tower was taller than any other building in England at the time, and apart from certain spires, remained so for many centuries to come, literally 'towering' over London. It served as a constant reminder of Norman presence and Norman power. It was constructed to the very latest specification. No doubt in anticipation of long periods of confinement, its design boasted one of the most advanced built-in plumbing systems of any fortress. The locations of the external waste outlets from this latrine system are not as one would naturally anticipate. They are not close to the ground, nor are they directed downhill towards the river. Instead the outlets exit the building halfway up its full height, pointing northward away from the river and very visible to the rest of London. Visit the Tower and you can still easily see them there today. If ever the Normans wanted to communicate a simple clear message, then this was it: 'We are here, we are powerful and we mean to shit on you from a high height'.

The other critical addition to commercial life that the Normans introduced was the Jewish community, who they brought from Northern France. The community spread out across all the major English cities, but the London members were the most numerous and most important. At their peak it is thought they numbered between 3,000 to possibly 5,000 in England as a whole. Within Norman society, the Jews themselves and all their possessions were the property of the King. They existed outside the Christian system, and had to make specific agreement on inheritance and tax payments. They were a ready source of capital for the King but also for very ad hoc tax demands. In return the Jews had exclusive rights of usury, and thus very profitable control over the capital and borrowing markets. In Norman London, this community inhabited two areas. The first was close to the Tower of London, which was there to protect Jews in times of trouble. The second, unusually, was the area between Cheapside and London Wall, and the site of the Grand Synagogue, for reasons that we speculated on earlier. This influx enriched the diversity of London, and not just religiously. There were to be some significant female money lenders, such as the infamous Licoricia. She was well known to Henry III; she was a leading operator in the debt and financing markets, living primarily in Winchester and Oxford, but occasionally ending up in the Tower.

o o o

The Norman emphasis on London's independence as a trading centre, had a significant impact on the emergence of the guilds. While there are mentions of these stretching back to pre-Norman days, the clearest reference comes in the Pipe Roll of 1180. Henry II deemed these bodies, nineteen in total (one more than the oft reported eighteen), to be 'adulterine'. For these bodies to correct their status from adulterine to authorised, they were ordered to pay fines. So began a crucial and symbiotic relationship between the Crown and the Companies that was driven by funding. The more obstructive Parliament became upon taxation matters, the more the Crown came to rely on feeling the collars of the Companies. Of the original nineteen named bodies, many have since disappeared, but a handful still exist as livery companies today. The Goldsmiths, the Woolmen, the Butchers and the Pepperers (the forerunners of the Grocers) all still flourish today. Personally I am a former Master and Warden of the last, and thus know its history best.

All major English cities had trade guilds, but the London livery companies were understandably the most significant, and that is reflected in their longevity.

The significant growth in wealth of the Companies in medieval times, was attributable to the increasing importance of their crafts, but also the emergence of the country's leading commercial activity, the wool trade. It dominated England's economy from the 13th to the 16th centuries. Our rich, verdant, well-watered land was suited to the rearing of sheep. English wool was widely considered the softest in Europe; the fleeces were highly sought after and commanded a premium price. At its peak, the English wool industry was producing 12 million fleeces per annum, massively exceeding the total population of England. The port cities on the eastern coast of England, with easy access to the European wool markets (or Staples as they were known) in Bruges, Antwerp and Middleburg and Calais benefitted disproportionately. Norwich became one of the wealthiest cities in the country. London with its Thames port became rich on the wool trade from the more southern counties. It is said that the old London Bridge was built upon sacks of wool – figuratively if not literally. Export taxes were paid for in London to the customs controller, and appropriate prices were achieved in an orderly fashion (or you could say, 'fixed') via the Calais staples to enable the tax paid to be earned back.

Members of many major City Companies were involved in the wool trade. This reflected the mercantile spirit of the time. In the latter half of the 14th century an estimated 25 per cent of UK wool was conducted by the Grocers, although this was little to do with their core remit of trade in spices, luxuries and foodstuffs. Almost all men of very substantial wealth at this time had wool as part of their source of income. Larger importers of foreign goods naturally looked for home-produced goods to fill their ships with on the return leg, and wool was the natural candidate. The Jeff Bezos of their time were men such as Richard Whittington (a Mercer) and Nicholas Brembre (a Grocer).

The significance of the London City Companies lies not only in their governance of their particular crafts, nor only in their exceptional wealth, but their control of the administration of the City itself. From 1215, the Companies were responsible, as they are today, for the election of their Mayors (now Lord Mayors). New apprentices wishing to get a skilled job in London had to be selected by a Master from the relevant Company, who would train them. Once the apprentice had learnt his craft, he remained a member of that Company for life. Dues had to be paid to the Company, and fines were levied in the case of malpractice or poor behaviour. Philanthropy and social welfare have always played an important role, and if he got into financial difficulty, he could be expected to be supported by his Company. I write 'he' but back in the 14th, 15th and 16th centuries, women were often admitted. The Grocers welcomed their first female member to the freedom, Isabel Osekyn, in 1351. Isabel was the wife of a warden of the Company, Roger Osekyn. When he succumbed to the Black Death, Isabel inherited his business; the Company was keen to keep her in the fold. In medieval times, women, especially widows, could play an active role in commercial circles. The higher mortality rates meant that women could frequently be in charge of major commercial entities. By the 18th and 19th centuries, as mortality improved, and the direct links to specific trades had often weakened, the City Companies became exclusively male preserves – eventually reversed in the late 20th century.

The City historian, Walter Besant in his book on London, describes how all-consuming, membership of a Company was.

> 'A boy born in the City might be educated by his father's
> Company, apprenticed by the Company, taught his trade by
> the Company, found in work by the Company, feasted once a
> year by the Company, pensioned by the Company, buried by the
> Company, and his children looked after by the Company. If he
> fell into debt and so arrived at Ludgate Hill Prison, the bounty
> of the Company followed him there. And even if he disgraced
> himself and was lodged in Newgate, the Company augmented
> the daily ration of bread with something more substantial.'

The economic reach of the Companies became increasingly global. Members of the London City Companies were responsible for establishing entities, such as the Muscovy Company, the Virginia Company, and the Levant Company. The most significant conglomerate was formed in 1599, at the end of Elizabeth's reign. A hundred senior Drapers, Grocers and their peers, gathered at Founders' Hall on Lothbury, in the presence of the Lord Mayor, the Grocer Sir Stephen Soame. Collectively that day, they pledged a total of 30,000 pounds as start-up capital to found what they called the East India Company. This was intended to be the primary trading vehicle to support English expansion in the sub-continent. That decision did much to help shape the formation of the British Empire, which in turn did much to determine how the English language would reach new parts of the world, yet also become infused and enriched by other cultures' vocabulary and idiom.

Of equal significance was the Companies' creation of the Bank of England in 1694. It commenced operations in Mercers' Hall, but within a few months it was moved to Grocers' Hall, by their first Governor, a Grocer and Huguenot, Sir John Houblon. The Bank was formed to coordinate funding for the latest round of war in France. The Bank continued to operate at Grocers' Hall for the next forty years until its growing importance meant that it needed to find premises of its own. In 1734, the Grocers moved the operation into a new building constructed in its garden with its bowling green, its flower beds and its fig and mulberry trees. This is where the Bank is today. It is the basis of the wry observation that it is the only place in the country where money does grow on trees. People are often surprised to discover that the Bank did not move into public ownership until 1946.

To understand England and English, you need to understand London; to understand London you need to understand the Companies.

○ ○ ○

The William Charter set the seeds for London's role; the Magna Carta firmly ratified its independence from the monarchy. In parallel the power of Parliament grew ever stronger. During Henry III's reign, the traditional Great Council of earls, barons and senior clerics, were first referred to as Parliament. By the end of the 13th century, it was expanded to include commoners. The parliament that the rebel baron Simon de Montfort summoned included shire knights and town burgesses. Edward I then established Parliament as a permanent counterweight to the feudal nobility. At Edward II's coronation, the following words were introduced, and have remained ever since: 'Sire, do you promise to maintain and defend the rightful laws and customs which the community of your realm shall have chosen?' The legal and tax-raising powers of Parliament were established.

This saw the formation of what I dub the 'three-legged stool', which I believe has dominated much of English history. Each leg holds power, but becomes more or less important, dependent on the circumstances of the day. The three legs are the Monarch, the Parliament and the City. The monarch's own resources were finite, and very rarely sufficient to be able to wage war, or keep a standing army or navy of any strength. For additional resources, the monarch was now required to get Parliament's approval. English history is littered with instances, when Parliament refused to fund some whim, or endeavour, or overseas adventure. If Parliament refused, then usually the City became the next port of call. At times, these funds were raised by bullying or forceful edict, but often were raised by the issue of monopolies in exchange for money. These would then further enhance the power and wealth of the Companies. During this late medieval period the largest and most reliable tax source were trade and customs duties; the Companies, with their members, generated a significant proportion of these. They came to learn the importance of acting as this third leg to the monarch's first leg. The outcomes of the barons' rebellion against King John, Henry V's campaign of Harfleur and Agincourt, many phases of the War of the Roses, the support of the parliamentary cause in the 1640s, followed by the restoration of the monarchy in 1660, are all examples of the city aligning with one or other of the legs of the stools, at differing times, to suit their mercantile objectives.

o o o

Much of London's power as the third leg depended on the concentration of the economic, political and cultural centres, all in one city. There was one critical moment in London's history, when it almost lost that concentration. This possibility seems so odd now, that it often does not gain a mention.

Edwards I and III had strong military ambitions, not just in relation to securing dominance within the British Isles, but also with French territory and the French Crown in mind. The prize was substantial, but so also was the cost. Successes were often followed by defeats, and the expense grew endlessly. They turned to a new source.

The Italian traders were becoming an increasing presence in English commercial life. In the late 13th century a Castilian-Genoese fleet defeated the Muslim navy in the west Mediterranean. Access through the Gibraltar Straits, previously dangerous, became safer. Italian traders were soon setting up shop in London, exploiting the monarch's need for cash, and open to doing deals. A concentration of these merchants based themselves in an area that came to be known as Lombard Street, in recognition of the area of Italy they came from.

Edward I came to rely on the Jews less and less. He felt undermined by the spate of coin clipping that was threatening the stability of the currency. The Jews bore the brunt of the blame. Their wealth had become increasingly invested in land, which they had received in exchange for repayment of loans, which made them vulnerable. A series of statutes had increasingly disenfranchised them, and in July 1290, the King decided to go for broke, ordering their expulsion and the confiscation of all their fixed assets. All Jews, unwilling to convert, were ordered to leave England by November that year. They were allowed to take what they could carry, but fixed possessions like land, and their outstanding loan book, had to be left for the benefit of the King. Around 1,000 Jews, rounded up in the Tower, their former site of protection, unwilling to convert, had the privilege of paying for their seat on the departing boats. Formally, the Jews were not allowed to return to England until 1656, when Cromwell passed the acts of religious tolerance.

Absconding with much of the Jewish wealth met no more than a short-term need, and the King soon turned again to the accommodating Italians to fuel his financial needs – but at a price. For all the sizeable loans and grants of funds, the Italians secured privileged trading rights in the import and export of a whole range of goods including the highly lucrative wool trade. The Italians then took matters further by securing rights over the distribution structures within England – thus utterly undercutting the hard-earned monopolies of the English companies. Jews as non-Christians could not operate in the Companies' trades, but Italians as Christians had no such restriction, and thus posed a whole new level of threat.

To make matters worse for the Londoners, the Italians decided that it suited them better to make Southampton the main mercantile centre in

England. The port there was deeper and more suitable for their type of ships. It was also better sited for access from Genoa and other Italian ports. It was not only a shorter route; it avoided the narrowest stretch of the Channel, with its extremely variable conditions, and the long haul around the Kent coast.

Southampton became sufficiently attractive as a centre of wealth, that the French raided the city, unsuccessfully, in 1338. The scale of the trade through Southampton grew exponentially. Pamela Nightingale in 'A Medieval, Mercantile Community' records the growth. In the mid-1360s, foreign traders had been exporting about 211 sacks of wool each year. By 1370 they were exporting over 500 sacks each year. By 1372, they were exporting over 1,800 sacks a year. By the mid-1370s around 40 per cent of England's exports were being conducted by foreigners. The majority of this trade was channelled through Southampton. It was not just the export of wool that was at stake. The ships that were taking the wool were bringing in a whole range of goods; the Italians now had direct access to the distribution structure in all the key trades across England. They had paid the King handsomely for export rights, for import rights and distribution rights. The King had agreed an overall treaty with Genoa in 1347, which he renewed in 1371. The economics of London, and the primacy of the London City Companies was being threatened. The English were being replaced by the Italians, and London by Southampton.

The City livery companies in due course responded. The two leading Companies, the Mercers and the Grocers set aside their traditional enmity and worked together. Many of the actions that they took during the 1370s were ruthless and would never meet modern standards of business behaviour. Through a series of bribes, intimidations, murders, the Italians were forced onto the back foot. When Richard II succeeded to the throne in 1377, the Companies were quick to ingratiate themselves with the new regime. Plus pay for it. The Italian threat was seen off, and Southampton never made it to the economic big time. The Companies learnt their lesson. There was no point being the third leg of the stool, without investing constantly in maintaining that privilege.

With its commercially dominant role reasserted, London's growth became unstoppable. From a population of 15,000 to 20,000 at the time of the Norman invasion, it had expanded to about 80,000 by 1300. By 1600, the population was around 200,000, London now rivalling Paris in scale. By 1700, it was 500,000. By 1800, it had hit a million, and double the size of Paris. By 1900, after the full impact of the industrial revolution it had reached 6.5 million, and 9 million today. Markedly the largest city in what I would call old Europe.

If the reaction by the Companies in the 1370s had been different and more timid, the shape of our nation would then have echoed many other countries, with a political and legal centre geographically separated from the commercial centre. Such as Washington DC and New York for the USA. Or Milan and Rome for Italy. Or Istanbul and Ankara for Turkey. Or Sydney and Canberra for Australia.

The story of our language and our culture without that concentration in a single place, I believe would have been different. Understanding the history of London is key to understanding the history of English and the English. Languages that have influenced the world most, all emanated from nations where the capital centre has been a single unified fulcrum – where politics, culture, commerce all converged. The best examples, in addition to English and London, are Latin (Imperial Rome in its heyday), French (Paris), Spanish (Madrid). Conversely, the lack of a single metropolitan centre may, in my opinion, help explain why the Moorish/Arab Empire of the first millennium seemed to trickle away in terms of influence, despite having all the military, academic and artistic might at its height – and a single language. The eventual outcome for Mandarin will be a fascinating story to follow.

CHAPTER TEN

LE LANGAGE NOUVEAU EST ARRIVÉE

'And somme understonde wel englysch
That can neither latyn nor frankys
Both lered and lewed, olde and gonge
All undersonden English tonge.'

So wrote the English cleric William of Nasington in the mid-14th century, proclaiming that 'educated and uneducated, old and young all understand the English tongue'. Whereas the Old English of 'Beowulf' written some 400 years earlier is impenetrable to us today. By the 1300s, the language had gone through a dramatic but quiet evolution into what came to be known as Middle English, a close precursor to our language today. As these lines of verse show. All under the radar of the Norman authorities.

The long-term impact, or lack of impact, of the Norman invasion, to me, is surprising. Under Norman rule, Latin was the serious language – used in religion, and in important documents. Norman French was the dominant language of the ruling class, and the official language of communication, for many centuries. English was the colloquial language, used by the mass of people, who understood neither French nor Latin, and was preserved in spoken form in a whole range of regional dialects. The Normans were the rulers, and their language should have prevailed. But they were limited in numbers. Rather than disappearing, English survived and thrived, adapting to the circumstances and proving once again that it is a remarkably flexible and absorptive language. It is estimated that about a third of later Middle English vocabulary could be traced back to French/Latin origins. English wasn't erased, nor was it subsumed, rather it was enriched.

England, being an agrarian economy, preserved the names for animals, such as sheep, pig or cow (all Old English), while the French have given us the eaten form ('Quel surprise!'), so mutton from 'mouton', pork from 'porc' and beef from 'boeuf'. Military words tended to be derived from French/Latin: 'soldier', 'army'. Words relating to hierarchy and order similarly so: 'govern', 'duke', etc. In both cases, this reflected areas of Norman dominance.

'Art', 'culture', 'music', 'literature' are all words of French/Latin derivation. Words that reflect humour and ribaldry were usually Old English derived, like 'laughter', 'riddle' and 'tease'. The division between the formal and proper, and the informal, fun and expressive perhaps reflects the nature of the two differing sources of identity and language.

Then there are the countless times where we have been blessed with two words, one from English, and one from French, which mean approximately the same, but in reality have subtle distinctions to them. So 'hungry' (English) is roughly the same as 'famished' (French), but actually is different. Or 'smell' (English) versus the much more sophisticated 'aroma' (French). So too 'help' (English) instead of 'aid' (French). There are many alternatives (but of course not exclusively) where the English word suggests something more fluid and informal, while the French word is slightly more official or more refined or demonstrative, reflecting the hierarchy of the cultures.

One of the most interesting, in my opinion, is the difference between being 'loving' (and thus being Old English), and being 'amorous' (or in other words Latin/French – appropriately known as the Romance languages). A similar emotion but a whole world of difference in tone and meaning. These are not just word options, but they are cultural options – between being more reserved and intimate, or being showier and more romantic. We have that choice in our language and in our behaviour. Is it lit scented candles and atmospheric music? Or is it pyjamas and cuddling under the blanket?

To help determine the choice, you have the option to 'ask' (English) or 'enquire' or 'demand' (both French) of your partner. They can then either 'answer' (English) or 'respond' or 'reply' (both French). If 'yes' (English), then together you might 'begin' or 'start' (both English) or you might 'commence' (French). And so on.

As to the topic at hand, 'language' connotes both the general use of words as well as particular dialects. It obviously derives from the French 'langage' which has comparable meanings. Our more informal word 'tongue' applies to both dialect and the part of the body, in the same way that the French 'langage' does not, but 'langue' does. 'Tongue' is from Old English, 'tunge'. Formal versus informal again. Note also that it is 'LE langage' but 'LA langue'. So we are back to the mysteries of gender-riddled languages.

This duopoly of word options spills over into expressions. English idioms regularly use multiple words for the same concept. There are expressions like 'neat and tidy', 'rough and ready', 'fit and proper'. This is especially peculiar to English. Some of these couplings notably marry a French word with an

English word. So expressions like 'law and order' mix the two – English first and French/Latin second.

To add to this process of linguistic enrichment, English suffixes are added to French words. And vice-versa. A French suffix like '-able' can enrich English to create great words like 'knowable', or 'lovable', or 'unsinkable'. An English suffix '-ful' can append to a French/Latin term, creating fabulous words like 'graceful', 'plentiful' or 'beautiful'. The quintessentially English concept of the 'gentleman' is a marriage of the French 'gentil' with the very English 'man'. All beautifully rhythmic words, emphasising that easiness on the ear can determine the success and survival of a particular word, irrespective of its varied parentage.

As a result of the French/Latin infusion, English was left not only a richer tongue, but also a more versatile, and more nuanced one. It generated a spate of word creation that served the speakers and writers of later centuries well. Time and again, the language was developing vocabulary options, and the source of those options was colouring the precise meaning of the words, and enlarging the choices. English was becoming not just a flexible and simple language, courtesy of the Vikings, but also very rich, courtesy especially of French and Latin. It was becoming ready to be an even more fertile source for the poetic and descriptive imagination. In the period to 1450, English was unique among German tongues in terms of vocabulary expansion; David Crystal estimates in 'The Stories of English' that by the end of the Old English period, the language had over 50,000 different words, and that by the end of the Middle English period that number had doubled.

This overall proliferation was not attributable to peculiar areas of special interest among the English. Famously Inuits were thought to have many words for snow, distinguishing between good sledding snow, crystalline snow, soft falling snow, etc. In Arabic there are over one hundred words for camels, including the name specifically for a camel that drinks once every two days, and for one that drinks all the time. Comparably, in English there are an extraordinary number of words that relate to arrows, bows, archers, bowyers and fletchers, reflecting the importance of the long bow in our history. But the principal explosion in word numbers is quite different, it occurred across the full range of the English vocabulary, and reflected no unique concentration.

French and Latin remained the official tongues. Norman monarchs were in France or abroad for a substantial part of their reigns, and French was their predominant tongue. The chronicler Odericus Vitalis writing in the early 12th century, indicates that William I did at some point try to learn English in his forties, but we presume without much success. English continued as the spoken vernacular of the masses, but not of their monarchs. Beneath the Norman radar, however, there continued to be some scholarship and creativity still in the Old English language.

As mentioned, the 'Anglo-Saxon Chronicles' continued to be written in English until 1154. A few decades later saw the creation of the long, humorous, wonderful poem called: 'The Owl and the Nightingale.' Its author may be Master Nicholas of Guildford, and it constitutes one of the earliest records of Middle English.

> 'The Nightingale began the match
> Off in a corner, on a fallow patch,
> Sitting high on the branch of a tree
> Where blossoms bloomed most handsomely
> Above a thick protective hedge
> Grown up in rushes and green sedge.'

We have the oldest surviving example of noted music with written lyrics, the beautiful song 'Sumer is icumen in'. It was found at Reading Abbey and dates from about 1240. It opens in the original text:

> 'Sumer is icumen in
> Lhude sing, cuccu
> Growep sed and blowep med
> And spring the wude nu
> Sing cuccu...'

Once again, this language is now reasonably intelligible to us today. The full verse can be translated as follows, and gives a good sense of the joyful pastoralism of the age.

> 'Summer has arrived,
> Loudly sing, cuckoo!
> The seed is growing and the meadow is blooming,
> And the wood is coming into leaf now,
> Sing cuckoo!
> The ewe is bleating after her lamb,
> The cow is lowing after her calf;
> The bullock is prancing, the billy-goat farting,
> Sing merrily, cuckoo!
> Cuckoo, cuckoo,

You sing well, cuckoo,
Never stop now.
Sing, cuckoo, now; sing, cuckoo;
Sing cuckoo; sing, cuckoo, now!'

The author was probably unaware that the golden age of early medieval mild weather was set to end soon.

A book of religious homilies in English, called 'The Ormulum', accompanied the year's cycle of Christian services and is significant. It was written by a monk called Orm, probably at Bourne Abbey in Lincolnshire. 18,956 lines of metrical verse, which Orm wrote with a phonetic code. He wanted to ensure that the reader correctly pronounced the English. He stated as much in his preface. He anticipated this text being delivered verbally and wanted the laity to understand. The clergy was primarily French speaking and the congregation English speaking. It was written in the East Midlands and shows what was to become Middle English at a formative stage, with a clear set of pointers as to how it was to be pronounced. This work is part of the transition.

Not everyone was a fan of this process of absorption and flexibility. The 14th century Cornish author, John of Trevisa was one of those who complained about English being corrupted by foreign influences. He wrote, as quoted by David Crystal: 'by intermingling and mixing, first with Danes and afterwards with Normans, in many people the language of the land is harmed, and some use strange inarticulate utterance, chattering, snarling and harsh teeth-gnashing.'

England had become the biggest multilingual area in Western Europe. The parallel existence of languages (along with the 'chattering, snarling and harsh teeth-gnashing') could have gone on ad infinitum. But political and military events determined otherwise. The stasis became disrupted, and the balance moved, firmly in the direction of English. And a particular form of English that we now know as Middle English.

The critical tipping point came in 1214 with the Battle of Bouvines. Once again, not a conflict well known or well-studied, especially on this side of the Channel.

o o o

King John's high-handed behaviour had alienated his barons. There were many slights and confrontations. A particular indignity was the outcome of a row that John had with his bishops, about the right to appoint the new Archbishop of Canterbury. The Pope, Innocent III was consulted and unsurprisingly decided that the selection was his own right. John in a fury and fearing the Pope would start choosing kings as well as archbishops, exiled many of the bishops and abbots. The Pope's retaliation was to excommunicate John, ban all church services and order the French to invade. This was understandably unpopular; John had to abase himself to the papal legate, swear the whole country to the possessions of the Pope, and agree to pay 1,000 marks a year in order to lease it back.

John needed a major success to turn events back in his favour. That success would be the recovery of the Normandy possessions that the French had snatched back in 1202 as a result of another complex dispute.

In 1214, he took an army across the Channel; he joined up with several allies equally aggrieved by France, including Otto, the Holy Roman Emperor. They lined up on a field in Flanders at a place called Bouvines, out-numbering the French. John and his allies were confident of delivering the final *coup de grâce* on the troublesome French. But on the day, it was their control and vigour that proved too much for the more numerous allied troops facing them. The victory was emphatic, and it left John to return home and face the music, utterly humbled.

The music in this instance was not only to surrender to the barons' demands, but to recognise that England and their Norman homelands were now irretrievably separated.

Suddenly the Anglo-Norman elite had to make a choice as to which side of the Channel they belonged. Some families, such as the de Montforts, decided to split their holdings. Simon was given the English lands, while his brother Amaury was given the French. Many of the Norman elite chose to live on in England, coming to terms with the realisation that they were no longer also French.

From Bouvines, the inevitable march of language was towards English. For the monarch and the aristocracy to converse with, motivate and engage with their populace, English would have to be spoken. The disaster of the Battle of Bouvines also meant that the barons could force King John very reluctantly to sign up to a new system of governance, subsequently and currently called the 'Magna Carta'.

o o o

Symbolically this great document was concluded at a point halfway between London and the Royal Castle of Windsor. Runnymede is also the site of an ancient Anglo-Saxon gathering point and location of previous witans. As with so much around Magna Carta and the barons' revolt, there was a harking back to the Anglo-Saxon principles of legitimate rule by oligarchic consent. Magna Carta was written not in French, not in English, but in Latin – the language of universal authority at this time. It was 3,550 words long. It was translated into French almost immediately, but did not get communicated in English, interestingly, until probably around 1300. This reflects the status of English still as essentially a colloquial language until that point.

What is well known about Magna Carta is the inclusion of the founding pillars of future constitutions. Most notably:

> 'No free man is to be arrested, or imprisoned or disseised, or outlawed, or exiled, or in any way destroyed, nor we will we go against him, nor will we send against him, save by the lawful judgement of his peers, or by the law of the land.'

Once again, London proved to be crucial to the outcome of the powerplay. When London chose to back the barons, King John was forced to concede.

They extracted their pound of flesh in many petty ways, that sit uncomfortably with the enduring principles of the freedom of a citizen's rights. Much of the Magna Carta is no more than the pork barrelling of the day, down to the detail of the control of fish weirs on the river, a preoccupation of the City lobby.

While some of London's provisions in Magna Carta were small scale and near term, others were much more far-reaching, for example:

> 'And the City of London is to have all its ancient liberties and free customs, by both land and water.'

The Mayor of London had usually been a place-person appointed by the King. As part of the various accommodations made to London at this time, the King agreed that the Mayor would be independently appointed by the City itself. To this day, the Mayor (now Lord Mayor) is elected by the assembled Liverymen of the City. The Lord Mayor's pageant was instituted as a method by which not only allegiance could be sworn to the monarch, but importantly, the new Lord Mayor could be shown to both his 'electorate', but also the mass of his non-voting 'subjects' to express their vocal affirmation. This was a fundamental display of democracy that the city felt the monarchy lacked at that time. This independence has been jealously guarded and remains a defining feature of the City's history. The Lord Mayor's pageant is held on their first day of office, to prompt that approbation, and in the gilded carriage with the Lord Mayor, rides not their spouse, but their chosen priest, to reassure the populace that the Lord Mayor is umbilically linked to the Almighty.

In hindsight, it is easy to take for granted the significance of the Magna Carta. But in the context of 1215, and a nation the size of England, the authors of the Charter would be astounded by its subsequent global influence.

The King did his best to ignore and disavow it. The Pope, now receiving his 1,000 marks a year, duly declared that the Magna Carta 'shames the English nation' and that it was 'null and void…forever'. John proclaimed himself a Crusader to try to gain himself immunity, hired foreign mercenaries and required all barons to take an anti-Charter oath. The barons countered by offering Northern England to Alexander II of Scotland, in return for his support. King Louis of France arrived with an army promising to act 'for the common good of England.' Alexander II paid homage to him as King Louis of England. How many people know that we had a king called Louis or that big chunks of England were part of Scotland for a while? This whole mess came to an end in October 1216 when King John lost his war chest in the Wash and died of dysentery. Henry III succeeded to the throne in his minority with baronial support and reigned for a total of fifty-six years. The French and Scots were duly sent packing.

What was to survive from this sorry saga was the Magna Carta. And what a survival! It is a definition of Englishness founded on strong Anglo-Saxon principles that has been a part of our national character thereafter, and part of our global identity. The William Charter, the Magna Carta, subsequently the Treaty of Paris in 1783 and others besides. These have all been building blocks to the direction our country has taken, and have shaped our character, our culture and our language.

o o o

The outcome of the Battle of Bouvines, and the separation of England from Normandy, did much to determine our chosen primary language.

The gradual ascendancy of English had already begun. One of the first records of French being rejected as the proper language of formal communication dates back to 1191. Richard I's Chancellor, William Longchamp came to address the Court of Aldermen, in the City, to resolve the substantial differences between the King and the City. There was outrage expressed by the Aldermen, that the Chancellor addressed them in French rather than English. The Court of Aldermen, although operating often in Latin and French, were also a guarantor of English continuing to be practised at upper levels of society, certainly orally.

Le Langage Nouveau Est Arrivée

By 1300, the English language was seen, even by our French-speaking rulers, as an important part of our national identity, and a basis for galvanising resistance to the French. In 1295, Edward I, despite speaking French as his first language, responded to the threat of invasion by Philip of France, by stating: 'If Philip is able to do all the evil he means to, from which God protect us, he plans to wipe out our English language entirely from the Earth.'

This came to be especially important with the start of the Hundred Years' War between England and France. This long running enmity helped define what it was to be English. It is often forgotten how uneven the fight was. We think today of France and England as roughly comparable in G7 and GDP terms. In the 14th century, the balance was very different. All the various components of France added up to a population of around 16 million, while England was much smaller at about 6 million. But what England lacked for in scale, it made up for in terms of integration and functioning effectively as a state. The French-speaking, 14th century chronicler, Froissart, described England as 'the best governed land in the world'. The Hundred Years' War helped the English to rally around their single state identity and the emergence of their common language.

French language was not static either at this time. Norman French had been losing ground to Parisian based French. Just as English became increasingly London or Mercian, French was now spoken by the nobility in a Parisian style, which became a badge of status. Norman French started to sound positively rural. Change came quickly. The Hundred Years' War had started by 1337 and nationalistic feelings against the French were stirred up mightily. Identity of language became a part of those feelings. Shortly thereafter, law courts were ordered to allow cases to be conducted in English. In 1363, the Chancellor opened Parliament by addressing those gathered in the Great Hall in English. This was a first.

In 1365, the Pope helped the progress of nationalistic feeling. Urban V suddenly remembered the pledge of tribute made by King John. He was based in Avignon, and in the pockets of the French. The English assumed any tribute would go into French coffers to fund the war against them. Edward III assembled his Parliament and considered the demand. Words were not minced and were in English. 'The kingdom of England was won by the sword, and by that sword has been defended. Let the Pope then gird his sword, and come and try to exact this tribute by force, and I for one am ready to resist him,' proclaimed one baron.

On what grounds was this tribute originally demanded? Was it not for absolving King John, and relieving the kingdom from interdict? But to bestow spiritual benefits for money is sheer simony; it is a piece of ecclesiastical swindling. Let their lords spiritual and temporal wash their hands of a transaction so disgraceful, proclaimed another, with a parliamentary fervour and bluntness we would recognise today. The papal request was refused. The flames of England's fierce independence were being stoked, and anti-papacy feelings were kindled.

On Edward III's death, Richard II came to the throne in his minority in 1377. He had many weaknesses, many of the narcissistic kind, but he was the right sort of king to stimulate the cultural environment that allowed English to gain real credibility once again. He used the English language when it suited his purposes. The most significant early threat was the Great Uprising. Because the rebels were mostly fixated on the King's uncle and regent, John of Gaunt, whom they blamed for many of their woes, and because the City hated Gaunt for undermining their highly lucrative wool trade to the advantage of the Italians, the rebels found their way into London and into the Tower, surprisingly easily. An uncontrolled rampage broke out; figures like the Archbishop of Canterbury, Simon Sudbury, sympathetic to Gaunt, were dragged out of the Tower and murdered.

As Gaunt himself was wisely in Scotland, the rebels turned their ire on his London base, the Savoy Palace on the Strand. Many of his retainers were killed and beheaded. They found his son Henry Bolingbroke, who only escaped execution, due to the intercession of one of the guards, John Fervour. But for that act of mercy, his son would not have been crowned Henry IV, and arguably Richard's presumptive heir, Edmund Mortimer, would have grown old enough to succeed to the throne. That would have meant, all other things being equal, that the current royal family would be the House of March rather than the House of Lancaster.

In the face of this violent chaos, the fourteen year-old King Richard made some critically important moves. On the first day after their entry into London, he met the rebels at Mile End. He offered them a new charter abolishing serfdom, one of their key demands. At this initial confrontation, he made the surprise decision to speak to the rebels in English. It was crucial to his ability to communicate directly to the gathered rebels, rather than through the interpretation of their leaders.

The following day was pivotal. He was accompanied and supported by the leaders of the City Companies, presumably now satisfied with the bloody nose given to Gaunt's followers. He met the rebel force at Smithfield. Once again, he conversed with their leader, Tyler Watt, and his fellow leaders in English. This led to a confrontation that the City men took advantage of.

Amorous or Loving?

1. 'Blood Swept Lands and Seas of Red'. The Poppies at the Tower of London in 2014, to commemorate the anniversary of the start of the First World War. See Chapter One. *Source : Historic Royal Palaces.*

2. Edington Village in Wiltshire. The site of the Battle of Edington in May 878, and of King Alfred's great triumph over the Vikings. See Chapter Two. *Source : Dreamstime.*

3. A detail from the Anglo-Saxon 'Mappa Mundi', the earliest available map of the British Isles. From the second quarter of the 11th Century. See Chapter Two.
Source : British Library.

4. Statue of King Alfred in Wantage Market Place, Oxfordshire, 1877. See Chapters Two and Three.
Source : Greg Balfour Evans/Alamy Stock Photo.

Amorous or Loving?

5. Frontispiece of Bede's 'Life of St Cuthbert' showing King Athelstan (924-939). It is the earliest surviving, painted portrait of a king of England. King Athelstan is shown presenting a book to St Cuthbert. See Chapter Four.
Source : Corpus Christi College, Cambridge.

Amorous or Loving?

6. The Alfred Jewel. Gold, cloisonné enamel and rock crystal. 871-899. See Chapter Seven.
Source : Ashmolean Museum, Oxford.

7. The Caligula Troper, 2nd half of the 11th Century. This manuscript contains an incomplete book of chants (called 'tropes') for religious services. See Chapter Seven.
Source : British Library.

8. The Lindisfarne Gospels, St Jermone ff 2v-3, c 700. Lindisfarne Priory on Lindisfarne, Holy Island. See Chapter Seven.
Source : British Library. Copyright The British Library Board.

9. Page from the Book of Kells. See Chapter Seven.
Source : Trinity College Library, Dublin.

10. The Ruthwell Cross is a stone Anglo-Saxon cross probably dating from the 7th-8th centuries. It is the most famous and elaborate Anglo-Saxon monumental sculpture. It is inscribed with eighteen lines from the 'Dream of the Rood', and possibly contains the oldest surviving text, predating any manuscripts containing Old English poetry. See Chapter Seven.
Source : Alamy.

11. The Kingston Brooch, 7th century, is the largest known Anglo-Saxon composite brooch.
See Chapter Seven. *Source : Liverpool World Museum.*

Amorous or Loving?

12. Gold and niello buckle from Sutton Hoo. Late Anglo-Saxon 9th century. See Chapter Seven. *Source : British Museum.*

13. Helmet from Sutton Hoo. See Chapter Seven. *Source : British Museum.*

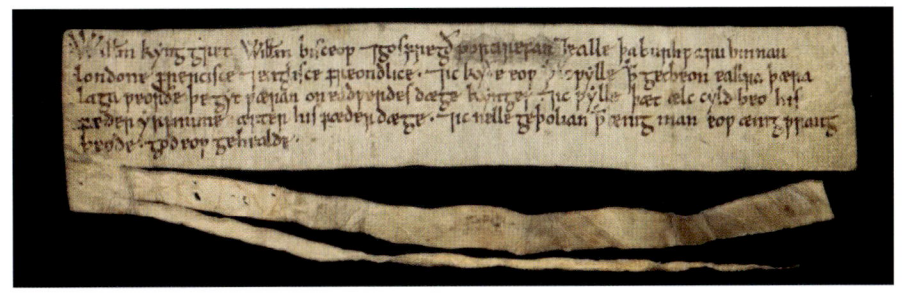

14. The William Charter : only five lines long and yet hugely significant to the future of the City. Assumed to be 1067. See Chapter Eight. *Source : London Metropolitan Archives.*

15. The landing gate at York House, designed by Inigo Jones, and built in 1626, just off the Strand. It marks the edge of the river bank in 17th century London. Following the construction of the Embankment in the mid 19th century, it now stands stranded some considerable distance from the river today. See Chapter Nine.
Source : Alamy. Credit : Eden Breitz/Alamy.

16. Map of London before the Great Fire in 1666, with crests of the leading City Livery Companies. See Chapter Nine. *Source : Alamy.*

They objected to the familiarity with which he addressed the King. William Walworth, the Lord Mayor, a Fishmonger, killed Tyler. The other leaders were then rounded up, and executed; the rebels themselves, returned home, somewhat mollified by the promises they had received in their own tongue, from their King. Use of English had been fundamental to the outcome. None of the promises were delivered in any substantial way.

When Henry IV succeeded Richard II, in 1399, he too understood the importance of language, and when he made his most significant pronouncement about the future of the realm, he expressed himself in English.

> *'In the name of the Father, Son and Holy Ghost, I, Henry of Lancaster, claim this realm of England and the crown with all its property and privileges – because I am legitimately descended from the blood of the good lord King Henry the Third.'*

The final step in achieving official status for the language was delivered by his son Henry V, with one of the more important messages in our history, written from the fields of France in English.

> *'Right trusty and well-beloved brother…right worshipful fathers in God and trust and well beloved, for as much as we know well that your desire was to hear joyful tidings of our good speed touching the conclusion of peace between the two realms…we signify unto you that…our labour has sent us a good conclusion.'*

So he wrote home in the aftermath of Agincourt. He included no apology for having the captured Frenchmen summarily killed on the battlefield. Which to the City's lasting chagrin meant that he had ruined the business model for their funding of the campaign which they had contributed to substantially. The ransoming of high value battlefield captives was an essential ingredient of the financial return. The city learnt that it was not always easy being the third leg of the power structure.

The process was completed in 1417. From the middle of that year, the King's official correspondence started to be written in English. As mentioned by G.L. Harriss, the archives of the Brewers' Company record both the moment and the rationale, stating that the King 'in his letter missive and divers affairs touching his own person…for the better understanding of his people hath…procured the common idiom to be commended by the exercise of writing'.

The same transformation was taking place in the City, as each of the Companies switched to the use of English as the language of record. As detailed by Lisa Jefferson in her analysis of City records, this did not occur uniformly or suddenly. This probably reflected the process taking place across all English institutions. The Grocers' accounts were kept in French until 1425 and then after one year of English went back to French for one year in 1427 and then used in English from the next year thereafter. The Drapers and the Goldsmiths switched in 1435, and the Merchant Taylors in 1444. The Mercers were the last of the Great Companies to detect the wind of change and continued to use French until 1459. So some forty years after the King had made the switch.

From the 1420s onwards, the status of English in the official world was reinforced by the emergence of the use of what was known as 'Chancery English'. The Chancery had responsibility for the inscribing, copying and disseminating of official notices and papers. It moved to English as its predominant language from this time. The impact of its official role was national and so it had to choose one dialect of the written English language. Based in London, it was natural for Middle English to be their preferred version, being the Mercian-based, East Midlands language, prevalent in writing in London. The scale of the Chancery activity was considerable and its influence on language was commensurate: at times the Chancery was sealing 300 documents a day and often worked Sundays and feast days to keep up with the workload.

Spelling for many centuries later was still essentially an arbitrary affair. But the influence of the Chancery, with its need to put the language into written form, started the process of standardisation, that came more fully to fruition at the end of the 17th century.

o o o

The final important building block was the crystallisation of our nation status internationally. England became acknowledged as a representative, significant nation in its own right; this had really not been so since the days of Athelstan.

After the disintegration of Charlemagne's Empire, a myriad of alignments and alliances dominated the continent of Europe. To tackle major issues affecting Christendom, a gathering of all these various sovereign entities would take place from time to time. The major conference of Henry V's reign was convened in the City of Constance. It was to last three years. The headline purpose was to find a solution to the intractable problem of the division of the papacies – three at the time. The appeal of having so many competing papacies was wearing thin. The Constance Conference had other issues to deal with as well, including the commitment of the Christian nations to weed out heretics, such as Jan Hus, the Czech writer and preacher, much inspired by our own John Wycliffe. At the conference, Hus was duly tried, found guilty, stripped of his vestments and put to death. (A powerful statue to him today movingly dominates the central square of Prague, the city where he was dean and rector.)

Of greater significance to us was the status of our representation at the Conference. Reflecting Froissart's observation quoted earlier, England sat as a single and definable entity; this was a first for this conference. England had arrived as a singular nation in the eyes of the world. The other blocks at the conference table were all amalgams of interests and different rulers. Henry V stood alone as the monarch of a single definable state with a voice of its own.

The concept of a political 'nation', in which the people participated in one single financial, legal and defensive sovereign government, ruling in the interests of the whole nation, was in a state of flux. The French would sit as an amalgam of different interests. The Italians were even more fragmented. The Germans were a bunch of states and principalities grouped under the Holy Roman Empire. Previously, for such international gatherings, the kingdom of England was regarded as part of the German grouping; their bishops and abbots sat with their German counterparts. But at the Council of Pisa, the forerunner to Constance, England started to be considered as potentially a nation in its own right. At Pisa, the Emperor (Sigismund) saw some advantage in recognising England as an independent entity. He hoped that the English would act as additional support to his German prelates, and serve as a counterweight to the French and Italians present. The French had counter-proposed that all decisions should be decided by ballot – one prelate, one vote. They received enthusiastic support for this by the Italians, who heavily outnumbered the other prelates. Inevitably the Pisa conference descended into a shouting match between the English and the French. The dispute became so fractious that at one point the English and the Germans threatened to walk out of Pisa, and not to be in attendance in Constance. Overnight the French reconsidered their position. They realised that if all the Italians participated on a one vote per person basis, then the French had little chance at Constance to get the Italians to abandon their Pope. The French returned to the negotiating table in the morning. They agreed that voting would be conducted by nations, and they agreed to recognise England as a nation in its own right. The Italians had been outflanked.

England arrived properly on the world stage on 6 February 1415; her delegation joined the Conference of Constance, sitting as a single voting bloc. The conference lasted until spring 1418. The duration was largely attributable to the need for each participating bloc to negotiate internally among themselves to reach a single coherent position. Not something that troubled England. By the end, a new single Pope was chosen, who took the name Martin. Not a name that has ever been used by a Pope since, probably for obvious reasons. The key step however had been taken for England.

o o o

The final step, by way of postscript but important to our cultural narrative, occurred in 1439. Henry VI, the son of the victor at Agincourt, formally banned public kissing. Previously it had been accepted as a ritual method of greeting between men. The official reason given for the ban was social distancing to halt the spread of the Black Death. This rings hollow; the major outbreak of the Black Death occurred a century earlier. The unpublished reason may, I believe, have been more attitudinal. Displays such as this must have seemed increasingly unEnglish. And men in England have not kissed in public since.

CHAPTER ELEVEN

CHAUCER – 'THE FATHER OF ENGLISH POETRY'

'When April with its sweet refreshing rain,
After the drought of March, hath reached again
The roots, and bathed each vein with gentle shower,
Of which virtue engendered is the flower.'

So begins the prologue of 'The Canterbury Tales' when translated from its Middle English. Its author, Geoffrey Chaucer, has been dubbed at home as the 'Father of English poetry', by Dryden, and internationally as 'the Ovid of your poetry' by the French poet Deschamps. He was the star of the literary renaissance and cemented Middle English at the heart of our cultural life.

Born in London in the 1340s, the son of a successful vintner, he spent his life holding down a series of significant day jobs, including as courtier, diplomat, administrator and lifelong retainer of John of Gaunt. Yet he still managed to pen around 43,000 lines of brilliant verse. In English.

The dialect of Middle English, which he used, had made its way south from its northern origins; it was embraced as a successful evolution and simplification from the Old English of Anglo-Saxon days. Working southwards, it became adopted within East Mercia, a region that included not just London, but the scholastic centres of Oxford and Cambridge. The use of Middle English as the basis for all the Chancery documentation produced in London was important, but as important was its use by Chaucer, and many of the other great authors of his generation.

As a tool of literature, the English language had mostly disappeared from 1100. It continued in colloquial speech. We have commented on some early flowerings, such as the poetry of Master Nicholas of Guildford and William of Nasington. The majority of writing prior to the 14th century, was in Latin or French; if in English, it tended to be translations of texts from French or Latin. It was as if the great individual creative spirit of the Anglo-Saxons had been lost. In fact it had gone underground.

During this time of invisibility, the language did not stand still. Its dominant strain moved from Wessex English to Middle English. It became a simpler and more accessible language. Arbitrary genders were eliminated; complex suffixes disappeared; the subject/verb/object order became standardised. As well as becoming simpler, it had become richer. We have commented earlier on the enormous expansion in vocabulary from about 50,000 words at the end of the Old English, with relatively few loan words, to double that by the end of the Middle English period, fuelled by many infusions especially from French/Latin.

We have records from the 13th century of a Worcester scribe glossing texts originally written in Old English. Very interestingly, in this process, he provided Middle English as well as Latin translations for Old English words. It confirms that Old English was no longer considered an active written language, and that Middle English was as important as Latin to the scholar of the day. The scribe's name is unknown but he has been dubbed 'The Tremulous Hand', on account of his consistently shaky handwriting,

A re-explosion of creativity then occurred in the second half of the 14th century, after the extended cultural winter. Middle English had been quietly fomenting its power and beauty out of sight and earshot of the Normans. The original Anglo-Saxon creative sensibilities gained confidence once again. They emerged re-equipped, with a more accessible language, supercharged with a richer range of words, opening up greater possibilities for rhyme and alliteration and with a rhythm better flexed to the poetic form.

The emergence of English as the written language for this cultural explosion may seem an obvious choice in hindsight, but it was not obvious at the time. Latin was the language of scholarship, and there were those such as Thomas More and Erasmus still arguing several centuries later that it should be the international language. The other main contender was French, which was so much more than yet another vernacular. The French court was perceived as the pinnacle of the ideals of chivalry. The University of Paris was considered the embodiment of scholarly excellence. There was a belief that French had established itself not just as the language of France, but also the 'lingua franca' of civilised Europe. The 13th century Italian writer Brunetto Latini, a teacher of Dante, wrote his major works in French, explaining: 'If anyone should ask why this book is written in Romance, according to the French language, when I myself am Italian, I should say that this is for two reasons. First, because I happen to be writing in France. And second, because that language is the most delectable and common to all people.' Chaucer himself was fluently multilingual and his choice to write in English would have been a decision, in part creative but in part political and nationalistic. What is harder to answer is: 'Why did this explosion happen then? Why in that particular half century?'

Some of the answer lies in the power of the authors of the age. Chaucer we have spoken of. But John Wycliffe was every bit as influential in the use of the English language. Chaucer was the shining star of storytelling and creative writing; Wycliffe was his peer in the religious field. Astonishingly they lived at the same time. In approximately the same period that Chaucer was writing 'Troilus and Criseyde' and then 'The Canterbury Tales', John Wycliffe was changing religious understanding among the mass of the nation, with his promotion of searing and vivid translations of the Vulgate Bible into English – Middle English of course.

To these two giants of the English language, we must add a whole group of other remarkable contemporaries including William Langland ('Piers Plowman'), John Gower ('Confessio Amantis'), The Gawain poet (writer of 'Sir Gawain and the Green Knight') and Thomas Hoccleve ('The Regiment of Princes'). Whatever they put in the mead or the wine in those days, it certainly worked. Their writings collectively transformed the progress of literature and religion in England, all within the matter of a few decades. This was a time when it could be genuinely said: 'the veins are bathed in liquor of such power, as brings about the engendering of the flower'.

There are important links between the main characters of our whole story. One of Chaucer's works was the translation of Boethuis into English of 'The Consolation of Philosophy', written in the 6th century, which was the same text that Alfred had translated 500 years earlier. Another 200 years later, Elizabeth I completed a translation of the same work. Then Chaucer's greatest piece, possibly even greater a piece of composition than the better known 'Canterbury Tales', is his long form poem 'Troilus and Criseyde'. A story that 300 years later William Shakespeare would use for 'Troilus and Cressida', written in the final year of Elizabeth I's reign. Wycliffe begat Tyndale, the great 16th century Bible translator, as much as Tyndale then begat the King James Bible. It feels we have had planted for us, firm stepping stones from Alfred to Chaucer to Shakespeare and the Elizabethan age, and from Wycliffe to Tyndale and the Stuart age.

o o o

But aside from the presence of certain inspired individuals, how can we more broadly explain the sudden creative resurgence in the second half of the 1300s, in what is known as the Ricardian period, named after the young new King? It was an explosion in writing to rival the explosion in drama in the 16th century. There are a few explanations worth examining.

The Hundred Years' War had begun, creating a suspicion of things French and a newfound pride in things English. It was a time when the upper-class

French in France diverged from our form of Anglo-French. The ham-fisted demands for tribute from the Avignon Pope, Urban III, further irritated English sensibilities.

The reign of Richard II had many weaknesses to it, but arguably Shakespeare, for dramatic effect overplayed these. Richard was indeed narcissistic, self-obsessed, and prone to satisfying the whims of favourites. He certainly knew how to create enemies. However he was a man of extraordinary faith, and a lover of the ceremonies and performance of religion. Today, we would recognise him as a 'man of theatre'. He invested heavily in churches and in particular Westminster Abbey, where he instigated the formation of one of the first full-time choirs. Musical performance was hugely important to him for worship, but also self-image. He was the first monarch to insist on introducing more ornate forms of address. 'My Lord' was no longer sufficient, and 'Your Majesty' and 'Your Royal Highness' became required as necessarily dramatic, and have successfully survived to this day. He had an innate love of culture, his sponsorship of literature and writing was undoubtedly significant. In the same way that the sponsorship of theatre by Elizabeth I and James I was a catalyst for the explosion in drama in the late Tudor and early Stuart period. Richard's reign witnessed the great growth in popularity of the Mystery Plays. These were religiously based productions mounted in major cities, by the local guild Companies (otherwise known as Mysteries) designed to tell the Bible stories in a way that the masses could understand. They formed the basis of drama in medieval England.

Richard looked more to Europe and especially the Holy Roman Empire than his predecessors. His marriage to Anne of Bohemia, the daughter of the Emperor Charles IV, provided a bedrock for the link. Sizeable trade benefits between England and the Empire were created; it also formed a model for a cultured royal court. Charles IV made much of architecture, of art, of vernacular literature and the works of humanist thinkers, and the foundation of the first Northern European university. In return, Anne's appreciation of the work of John Wycliffe meant that he gained an audience in Bohemia. Wycliffe's thinking was to influence the Prague-based philosopher, Hus, who in turn proved to be an inspiration for Luther's work and the Reformation. Anne and her husband Richard II deserve credit for their sponsorship of art, philosophy and literature, that was to go on to change the shape of the modern world. Characteristically, when Anne died, Richard made the most profound public expression of grief that he could imagine. In an utterly theatrical flourish he demolished her favourite home, Sheen Palace. It was as if the court had been nothing more than a stage set, to be swept away at the end of the performance.

Peter Ackroyd when writing on Chaucer reinforces this analysis.

'If a reign is also to be celebrated for the culture which it creates, then that of Richard must be remembered for the work of Langland, and of Gower no less than that of Chaucer himself. It was a resplendent literary period, only to be equalled by that of Elizabeth in the late sixteenth century. It was the age of a masterpiece such as 'the Wilton Diptych'. It was the first age of the mystery plays. It was the age of the great religious works of Margery Kempe, and Julian of Norwich... Richard II had a fully conceived and almost theatrical sense of his own Kingship; he believed that he ruled by divine authority and was inspired by the divine will. It was a court of ceremony and of formal ritual...'

Importantly the English language had emerged.

o o o

Chaucer and his fellow poets came from all backgrounds and from all parts of the country. This was not a cultural movement emanating from one particular quarter, one class, one seat of learning, or even one sex. Consider how unique a person Chaucer was. The first reference to his existence appears in 1357 in the accounts of the Duchess of Clarence, the wife of Lionel, the third son of Edward III. He is first to be spotted as a young valet in the household of the Duchess of Clarence. She gave him a short cloak, shoes and breeches of red and black. Thus dressed, our greatest poet takes our attention for the first time.

He made rapid progress in court circles. He was soon to be on campaign in France with Lionel, the Duchess's husband, where he was captured. It was significant that the King helped pay his ransom of no less than sixteen pounds. By 1366 he had married one of the Queen's ladies-in-waiting, Philippa de Goet, sister to Katherine Swynford, who was later John of Gaunt's third wife. By 1367, Chaucer was attending the King himself, and was referred to as 'Dilectus Valettus Noster' ('Our dearly beloved valet'). He rose to the status of envoy, and went to Italy on several occasions serving the King as diplomat. He negotiated the complex inter-dependence of the English monarchy with the various Italian paymasters which we discussed earlier. By 1374 he had been appointed the comptroller of the customs of the Port of London, and for over ten years had his office at the Customs House on the wharf just by the Tower of London. In Richard's reign, in 1389, he was appointed Clerk of the King's Works, giving him responsibility for projects in a range of royal palaces including the Tower. His principal building project was the reconstruction of the Tower wharf to enable access to larger ships. Chaucer spent several years in close association with the Tower, and subsequently had a range of other royal roles and appointments until he died in 1400. It has been suggested that some among his contemporaries considered that his role as public servant, courtier and diplomat was what he would be most remembered for.

History concludes differently. But how did he find time to write? In this, he had similarities with Shakespeare, who for much of his life had to juggle being actor, shareholder in his company, with being author of a unique body of plays. Chaucer had a full-time role at court and in public life, but still found energy to write copiously.

It is not known when Chaucer started to write, but probably on his return from his first trip to France. He seemed to be taken by the French tradition of romantic poetry, and possibly translated the epitome of that poetic style, the 'Roman de la Rose', a famous 13th century piece devoted to the exploits of love. But it was his various visits to Italy that were to transform his writing, and provide him the lasting inspirations for his work. His fluency in the Italian language allowed him to appreciate the works of Dante, of Petrarch and of Boccaccio. The latter provided him with the strongest influences; Chaucer's 'Troilus and Criseyde' borrows directly from Boccaccio's 'Il Filostrato', and 'The Canterbury Tales' from Boccaccio's 'The Decameron'. Without his extended period of time on missions to Italy, and without his knowledge of the language, Chaucer would not have achieved his transformation of English literature.

While the Italians provided him with much of the style and structure of his writing, these things alone would not have made him the acknowledged master of the art form. The critical ingredient he brought was his choice to write of the common man, as much as the Knight and the Merchant. It was his use of vernacular, not just in English, but the recognisable dialects and speech forms of those he wrote about, which gave his work the capability of engaging and amusing those from all walks of life. It was his fondness for the humour, the vulgarity, the sauciness and not just for the grand moral and philosophical. It was his skill at describing the mundane, and for conjuring the natural world in a way recognisable to every reader, which marked him out. 'The Canterbury Tales' had, as its target reader, not only members of the court, but people of all walks of life.

Chaucer himself spoke of the diversity and richness of the English language, his constant tool. In 'Troilus and Criseyde', he writes:

> 'And for ther is so gret diversite
> In Englissh and wrytyng of oure tonge

*So prey I God that non miswrite the
Ne the mysmetre for defaute of tonge;
And red wherso thow be, or ells songe,
That thow be understone, God I biseche!'*

I believe that Chaucer was acutely aware of the original core of the English language. In calling his major work 'tales' and not 'stories', he chose the Old English word, derived from 'talu', meaning a narrative, rather than the French/Latin/Greek alternative.

Chaucer's ability to move from the high-faluting, to the commonplace and then the downright bawdy in a matter of a few lines is a hallmark of his style. What may be less appreciated is how great an innovation this was. There cannot be a teenage English student today who hasn't come across sections of 'The Miller's Tale' with gleeful relief. Passages such as this in translation read:

*'Dark was the night as pitch, as black as coal,
And at the window out she put her hole,
And Absalon, so fortune framed the farce,
Put up his mouth and kissed her naked arse
Most savourously before he knew of this.
And back he started. Something was amiss:
He knew quite well a woman has no beard,
Yet something rough and hairy had appeared.
'What have I done?' he said. 'Can that be you?'
'Teehee!' she cried and clapped the window to.'*

Chaucer's writing carries the reader through time, to a different age. You can hear the sounds, you can tread the dusty paths, you can even smell the breath of the characters, as you feel the sweaty reality of their lives. Much of this speaks to the theatricality of his writing. Although he wrote in verse poetry and not drama, in some ways he can be considered England's first great playwright; so much of 'The Canterbury Tales' is inherently theatrical in its tone and its devices. The concept of the gathering of the diverse range of characters and their processional progress to Canterbury, while each narrates their own story, is essentially a dramatic device. The role of the narrator at the end of the General Prologue, is similar to a Master of Ceremonies in folk plays of the time. Both the first two tales borrow heavily from medieval theatre. 'The Knight's Tale' makes much of the spectacle of the tournament and its accompanying festival. 'The Miller's Tale' contains much reference to and inclusion of the stagecraft of Mystery Plays. 'The Canterbury Tales' lays the basis of the style of storytelling that would become quintessentially English, and demonstrates how the language could be used to project performance and three-dimensional character. The metaphor that 'All the world's a stage' is one that many of our writers have utilised, not least Shakespeare himself, and Chaucer was the first most effective exponent of in English.

His consummate range and his innate theatricality ensured his popularity in the hearts of the English audience, even in his own day. Parts of over eighty contemporary copies of 'The Canterbury Tales' still survive today, some 700 years later. Although it should be recognised that none of Chaucer's original manuscripts survive, and all copies were known to be inaccurate to varying degrees. This was the scourge of the medieval writer as Chaucer as he noted in the earlier quote from 'Troilus and Criseyde'.

His peers certainly recognised the scale of his genius. His fellow poet Gower spoke commendingly of his work. The prose writer Thomas Usk wrote of the 'noble philosophical poete in Englissh'. This recognition continued in following centuries. In 1470, the writer George Ashby in his 'Active Policy of a Prince' ranked Gower, his more famous contemporary Chaucer and Chaucer's successor John Lydgate, at the very top flight of our poets.

And to these attributes, has to be added the most English of them all – self-deprecation. Typically, Chaucer inserted himself as a character in the narrative, whom he then disparaged. As the fictional 'Chaucer' seeks to entertain the company of pilgrims with a rhyming yarn of his own, he is promptly cut off by the host of the Tabard Inn, Harry Bailey, with the following expletive:

> 'By God' quod he, 'for pleynly, at a word,
> Thy drasty rymyng is nat worth a toord'

A tradition of English pathos is observed in the 14th century as much as it is today with the buffoonish figure of Basil Fawlty, or Mr Bean fumbling the rendition of 'Chariots of Fire' at the Olympic ceremony.

As George Ashby's quote indicates, Chaucer's contemporary poets, in this period of great creative flowering, were also hugely important. Most significant was the author of 'Piers Plowman' presumed to be William Langland. This enormous piece of alliterative poetry, which preceded much of Chaucer's writing, was highly influential in its day, telling the tale of an 'Everyman', Will, and his travails and his visions, as he rails against a corrupt religious and political elite. This was the use of English, and the tongue of the ordinary people, to create a 'Fanfare for the Common Man' and a biting satire on the evils of the 14th century.

This was not literature by and for the noble classes. This was writing for a broader audience. Langland was a highly idiosyncratic churchman. Hailing from Shropshire, he moved to London where he found a poor living singing the chantry masses for the souls of the rich, and transcribing documents. All the while he devoted his creative energies to the single work of 'Piers Plowman' which he revised and improved endlessly. Based on the autobiographical aspects of the poem, he had the unconventional habit of dressing up as a beggar, and experiencing at first-hand the life of the impoverished. There was no keener critic of social injustice, and his tract served as a rallying call for the disgruntled. A noble tradition was established.

With Langland and Chaucer, the use of Middle English was reaching the full range of its power as an expressive medium, from which the nation has never really looked back. Dialect was plundered and slang put to work. The breadth of the appeal of their work was an essential ingredient.

Chaucer himself is said to have coined or be first known to have used some 2,000 new English words. Whether he specifically invented them is impossible to say, he may solely be the earliest remaining record. In either case, it is a magnificent array of words, including some with a very modern ring. His is the earliest surviving writing that makes use of the word 'twitter' in relation to birdsong – he might be amazed to see what 'twitter' was then to become. He would certainly be intrigued by Twitter's (now X's) salacious, gossipy and scandalous postings. He coined terms such as 'femininity', 'narcotic', 'erect' and 'plumage'. He also invented some delightful additions to the language, like 'newfangleness' for novelties, and 'thunderclap' for a mighty sound.

This constant splurge of word creation was not always accumulative, but inherently experimental. Words were added, but some disappeared. How often today do we describe the skies/clouds/heavens as 'the welkin'? And are you surprised? See p184 for a more recent unfortunate example. And as David Crystal notes in 'The Stories of English', both 'impede' and 'expede' were introduced at this time, but only 'impede' survives.

o o o

Two prominent women writers are a tribute to the diversity of the age. They commanded attention irrespective of their sex, and their consequential lack of a formal scholastic education. Both lived in Norfolk, at a time when that area was noted for its religious fervour, and considerable wealth from the wool trade.

Julian of Norwich was a writer inspired by visions. Aged thirty and very ill, she believed she was on her deathbed; while being administered the death rites by a priest, she experienced a series of visitations of Christ bleeding on the Cross. Upon her unexpected survival, she chose to live as a reclusive nun (or 'anchorite') in the Carrow monastery near Norwich, and used her various visions for the basis of her work, 'Revelations of Divine Love'. She wrote in English; Latin would not normally be learnt by a woman. Thus she is the earliest female writer in the vernacular that we know of. Her writings were mystical, and enthused with optimism and compassion, she advanced the principle, unusual at the time, of God both as mother as well as father. She received in her visions repeatedly the promise of reassurance, which she constantly questioned, from Christ: 'All shall be well, and all shall be well, and all manner of thing shall be well.' This open-hearted kind of religious devotion, which argued against the horror of eternal damnation, popular at the time, has gained her many adherents in recent decades, as her work has been latterly translated and become better known. T.S. Eliot refers to her writings as having been an influence on his conversion to the Anglican Church.

Margery Kempe was the daughter of a mayor of Bishop's Lynn, wife of a burgess, and gave birth to fourteen children before deciding to live a life of chastity. She journeyed to the Holy Land, Italy, Spain, Holland and Germany. She has the distinction of writing the earliest surviving autobiography in English, 'The Book of Margery Kempe'. Or at least she dictated it, being unable to read or write herself. Her work was also mystical in nature, passionate, religiously ecstatic and featured visitations from, and conversations with Christ. Julian and Margery both stand out for the visionary nature of their writing, for being two of the earliest women contributing to written religious thinking. They both proposed pathways to divine acceptance that was highly personal and divergent from the strict teachings of the Church at the time. It was a reflection of this fresh-thinking age.

Ultimately the legacy of the English poets of the 1370s, and the dominance of the East Midland dialect of Middle English became guaranteed with the advent of the printing press in England. Caxton began printing in 1476. The first known output from his new press, not surprisingly, was 'The Canterbury Tales'. To make his economics viable, Caxton needed to produce works with mass appeal, and in an English which the majority of his potential buyers could read. He went on to print many of the great works of not just Chaucer, but also Chaucer's contemporaries, and other later, great romantic works like Sir Thomas Malory's 'Le Morte d'Arthur'. In doing so, he reinforced the inevitability that the language of England would indeed be Chaucerian Middle English. While the presses were not perfect, they did much to overcome the scourge of the inaccurate copyists generating slightly varying renditions of their original texts.

Caxton's press was originally based at Westminster. While he printed about one hundred different books, he never printed either the Bible or 'Piers Plowman'. The controversy they would have caused with his ecclesiastical landlords, I believe, would probably have been too great. In 1500, and after Caxton's death, his apprentice, the magnificently named Wynkyn de Worde, who inherited the business, moved out of Westminster's clutches to a new site near Fleet Street. Geographically this sat happily in the 'No Man's Land' between the City, the Palace, the Cathedral and the Abbey. It became the early basis of the free spirit which would in due course be known as 'The Fleet Street Press'.

By way of finale, I will summarise how England appeared to the outward eye, now that it had recovered from the ravages of the Black Death and subsequent plagues, from the vicissitudes of the Hundred Years' War, and from the upheavals of the War of the Roses. Polydore Vergil was an Italian churchman from Urbino, who settled in England, becoming Archdeacon of Wells. He described the relative calm of England at the start of the new Tudor period:

> *'Delectable valleys, pleasant, undulating hills, agreeable woods, extensive meadows, lands in cultivation, and the great plenty of water springing everywhere. It is truly a beautiful thing to behold one or two thousand tame swans upon the River Thames. The riches of England are greater than those of any other country in Europe. There is no small innkeeper however poor and humble he may be, who does not serve his table with silver dishes and drinking cups'*

For all this tranquil description, unbeknown to Polydore Vergil, a turbulent religious upheaval was on the horizon which would change everything.

CHAPTER TWELVE

THE WORD IS GOD

*'In the beginning was the Word, and the Word was at God,
and God was the Word.
This was in the beginning at God.'*

So began the opening of the Gospel of St John in the translation from Latin into Middle English in what is known as the Wycliffe Bible. It was the first complete translation of the holy work into our language. The importance of the deification of the 'Word' lay at the heart of Wycliffe's philosophy, emphasising the power of language and the sanctity of the text to reach out to all classes if expressed in words they could understand. This provided the drumbeat that would eventually lead to the Reformation.

While Chaucer is well known to a modern audience, John Wycliffe, his contemporary, is less well remembered. His influence was as great. They were known to each other, both prominent figures of their age, but it is unclear if they ever met. Their ideas would have seemed to have influenced one another. What Chaucer was to English in the poetic context and in popular culture, Wycliffe was to English in the prosaic context and in religious thinking. If Wycliffe's work had lent itself better to movie treatment or musical performance, then he would probably be better recognised now. His crowning achievement was the translation of the Vulgate Bible, from its Latin into the vernacular, that his followers undertook. How much of the translation is directly attributed to him is a subject of debate, but his influence was undeniable. Today this offers little box office. At the time, it was sensational. Wycliffe wanted the scriptures to be understood, word for word, and revered by the common man. But more than this, his credo was to put total emphasis on the power of the written text itself. The unintermediated understanding of God through the scriptures, and very pointedly not through interpretation by the clergy. This was his Holy Grail. His priority was to find the right word and the right expression. What was not readily available had to be coined or invented; as a result we owe Wycliffe and his followers for some of the most potent parts of the English language. In many ways, he is arguably the most significant figure of our story so far, ranking alongside Alfred the Great.

In both instances they seemed to have had no precursors; in both instances they have defined an agenda that has lasted centuries; in both instances they have stood head and shoulders above their contemporaries. When Wycliffe was described as 'the morning star of the Reformation', such broad sweeping acclamation is deserved. Some scholars have wondered why, given the debt we owe him, that there is not a monument in every town to his memory, and in every university there is not a college named in his honour.

Wycliffe was born in about 1324, probably in a Yorkshire village called, inevitably, 'Wycliffe', a few miles from Richmond. He went to Oxford, at around the age of sixteen where he obtained a BA, before becoming a Doctor of Theology. The Oxford of that day was small, but highly influential. It consisted of six colleges, and had some seventy-five members, mostly graduates. There were about 1,500 undergraduates, predominantly Church clerics. Wycliffe was the star of Oxford, by virtue of his writing and his skill at disputation and argument. He went on to serve as Master of Balliol. Through the course of his life, he wrote about 160 different works (96 in Latin and 65 in English); it was his denunciation of the Church, of the friars, of the clerics, and his castigation of the Pope as the Anti-Christ, which formed the backbone of his thinking. Ultimately, his vitriol and the remorseless logic of his arguments, made him too contentious even for the most ardent of his high-ranking supporters. When the focus of his attack moved from the current structure of the Church, on to portraying transubstantiation as a piece of religious trickery, with no authentication by the scriptures, he became truly inflammatory.

The argument over transubstantiation, belief in it or denial of it, was to rage from this point until the 17th century. Transubstantiation is the term given to the transformation in the Eucharist service of the bread into the actual body of Christ, and the wine into the actual blood of Christ. This is achieved by the priest through the utterance of the Eucharistic Prayer. It was a key element of the power, indeed the supernatural power, of the Church. The Protestant contention by contrast was that the entire use of bread and wine was only symbolic. They pointed out that transubstantiation was only included within Christian doctrine at the 4th Council of the Lateran in 1215, and had no support from the scriptures themselves.

Wycliffe's influential supporters, men such as John of Gaunt, were happy to back his attack on the Church, the clerics and on the papacy itself; it served some of their nationalistic purposes. But they were perturbed by his repudiation of central sacraments of Christian service. Until that point, he had withstood the pursuit of papal bulls; he had rung rings around his accusers in several trials, taking advantage of royal interventions on his behalf. But ultimately a trial at Oxford, led by the establishment clerics, found against him; he was banished from the University. His ability to continue his teachings was seriously restricted, and he retreated to the parish of Lutterworth. He at least had his life.

His truly lasting legacy was to be the translation of the entire Vulgate Bible into English – Middle English. His intent was that everyone in the country should have direct comprehension of the scriptures. He wrote that 'it helpeth Christian men to study the Gospel in that tongue in which they know best Christ's sentence'. In response to this inspiration, a group of like-minded scholars and clerics set about the huge task of creating the first English version of the full Bible, despite the opposition of the church establishment. How much Wycliffe himself was personally involved in the translation, or the organisation of its distribution, or indeed the origination of the Lollard movement that promoted the overall cause, is the subject of debate. It is possible that a period of 16th century post-Reformation popularity chose to over-play his personal and direct contribution, and that his specific involvement was minimal. However what is more certain is that his credo, as espoused in his writings and teachings, created the impetus for challenging the religious status quo, and for transforming the accessibility of the scriptures to the general populace.

At this time, there were no printing presses to mass-produce the translated Bibles. Instead a production room of manuscript copiers were employed, and an army of 'Bible-men' recruited to disseminate the translated words by readings and teachings. The 'Bible-men' were usually junior clerics, referred to as 'Poor Preachers', who shared Wycliffe's enthusiasm to take the scriptures, to the people in a language they would understand. As he himself wrote: 'The highest service to which a man may obtain on earth is to preach the law of God'.

There had been earlier translations into English, but only of passages or sections. Bede began a translation in 690. Aldhelm had translated the Book of Psalms. Athelstan may have commissioned a translation from Hebrew. In the 10th century, a translation of the Gospels was completed in Lindisfarne, with the Old English interlaced between the Latin text. The Wessex Gospels were a wholly Old English translation from the latter part of the 10th century, but solely of the Gospels. Then in the 11th century, Abbot Aelfric translated much of the Old Testament into English. The Wycliffe Bible was the first translation of the entirety of the Bible, Old and New Testament, utilising a single source, the Jerome Vulgate version, applying close attention to the language, the words and the strict meaning of the text.

Having retreated to the simple parish of Lutterworth, he was to die there in 1384, aged around 60. Throughout his final years, he worked diligently, feeling his luck would sooner or later run out, and that men would surely arrive to eliminate such a thorn from the side of the established Church. Many had been martyred for much less. He is said to have written in his later years, possibly apocryphally:

> *'To live and be silent, is with me impossible – the guilt of such treason against the Lord of Heaven is more to be dreaded than many deaths. Let the blow, therefore, fall. Enough I know of the men whom I oppose, of the times on which I am thrown, and of the mysterious Providence which relates to our sinful race, to believe that the stroke may ere long descend. But my purpose is unalterable; I wait its coming.'*

The stroke did not descend. On the last Sunday of 1384, as he was preparing to dispense the Lord's Supper, he suffered further paralysis and fell. It was his third such attack in as many months. He was taken in a chair out of the side door of the Church, back to his house. He died there on 31 December of a natural death.

It took until May 1415, some 30 years later, for the Catholic Church to summon the impetus to seek to crush all memory of his existence. Having committed his disciple, Jan Hus, to the flames of damnation, they turned their attention posthumously to Wycliffe. They condemned him as heretical on 260 counts. His books were ordered to be burnt, and his bones to be dug up and ejected from consecrated ground. The actual sentence was not executed until twelve years later. In 1427, his disinterred bones were removed from the Lutterworth cemetery, publicly burnt and cast into the River Swift. He exercised a mesmerising hold over his protagonists even in the 'after-life'.

To us today, Wycliffe's rigorously argued rhetoric sounds familiar. He anticipated the principal arguments of the Reformation and the Protestant movement. But at the time, Wycliffe's views were radical. His belief was that the scriptures were the one and true expression of God's will. He thought that everyone had the right to imbibe those scriptures in a language of their understanding. The exclusive ability of the clergy to be able to translate and interpret those scriptures, he considered an afront. The Pope's authority should be confined to spiritual matters. Temporal matters were the preserve of kings and princes, which should not be interfered with by the Church. The Pope and the Church should not debase themselves with the pursuit of wealth and political power. The preaching friars who travelled the country fleecing the people with their offers of pardons in return for money were an abomination to their religion. The whole edifice of the sale of relics, the saving of souls at a price and the commercialisation of the access to God should be pulled down, and replaced with a priority of focus on the true word of God. He questioned even the power of the Pope to excommunicate anyone.

His thesis was not proposed in a ranting, revolutionary fashion but in academically argued texts based on the teachings of the Bible. His opinions were greeted with an understandable frostiness from the ecclesiastical establishment. In his public lectures, he would speak of the Pope as 'the Anti-Christ, the proud, worldly priest of Rome and the most cursed of clippers and purse-kervers'. The context in which these opinions should be judged are the conditions of daily life of the peasant in the 14th century. The historian, Trevelyan, describes the weekly church experience of the common man thus:

> 'Around him blazed on the walls frescoes of scenes from the scriptures and the lives of saints; and over the rood-loft was the Last Judgement depicted in lively colours, paradise opening to receive the just, and on the other side flaming hell with devil executioners tormenting naked souls. Fear of hell was a most potent force, pitilessly exploited by all preachers and confessors, both to enrich the Church and to call sinners to repentance.'

The driving force of mainstream life was very different from today. Life expectancy was much shorter. Wealth was created to achieve physical comfort, but also to satisfy the greatest needs of the day – a good death, sins forgiven and a place in heaven – for yourself and your immediate family. The keys to all these things lay with the Church, and could be bought with money, either through direct payment, or by funding sung chantries. Today, wealth is created mainly to achieve physical comfort, in this life, with the endless acquisition of the material trappings and the tendency for conspicuous consumption. In medieval days, the priority was very different; an arbitrary death lurked around every corner, and an individual's ability to acquire an exalted position in the after-life, was the most important distinction versus your peers. To make doubly sure of this outcome, your descendants could keep purchasing further indulgences, even after your death, to help ensure that an exalted position could be improved upon.

His central thesis attacked the very core of this system, and the comfortable self-enrichment of the Church and the clergy. No surprise that they were angry. Nor surprising that a blizzard of papal bulls dogged him. The support therefore from the lay establishment was critical to Wycliffe's survival. His

The Word is God

message played well with the politics of the day. While renouncing the authority of the Pope, he endorsed that of the King and Parliament over all non-spiritual matters. The Church's hold over English wealth had rankled for many decades. The Church owned a significant proportion of all useful land. This stranglehold on the country's riches had irritated many of the landed barons and gentry. The regular payments made to the Church, by way of tribute, tithes and indulgences were strongly suspected of being siphoned off by the papacy, to subside pet causes, including the French forces fighting the English, especially in the Avignon era. Wycliffe was targeting a common enemy, and doing it with eloquence, and with the full deployment of the teachings from the Bible.

This political backing had important consequences. First, it enabled him to continue as a free man, and to live; the Bible project could be completed, with all its impacts on the development of the language.

Second, it enabled a substantial base of followers to be formed. These followers, Lollards, were to become in due course a major movement, including people from all strata of society. The seeds of non-conformism were sown within England.

Third, patronage at the highest level, enabled Wycliffe's thinking to spread internationally. The Queen, Anne of Bohemia's espousal of his work, meant that Prague philosophers, embraced his anti-cleric, anti-papacy stance. This in turn inspired Luther and Lutheranism. Which in turn worked its way back to England as part of the Reformation.

All of the above helps explain how subsequently the Reformation was embraced so readily by sections of the English population. The Protestant spirit, and non-conformist practice, had fermented for several centuries from Wycliffe's days of influence.

After Wycliffe's death, Catholic dogma got the upper hand again in the argument. Heresy became a capital offence in 1401 for the first time – a response to the dissemination of the Wycliffe Bible. The Church's denunciation of Wycliffe posthumously was vitriolic. Archbishop Arundel said: 'This pestilential and most wretched John Wycliffe of damnable memory, a child of the old devil, and himself a child or pupil of Anti-Christ, who, while he lived, walking in the vanity of his mind…crowned his wickedness by translating the Scriptures into the mother tongue.'

But the impact of his work is evidenced by the significant number of copies of his Bible that were produced. Each was made by hand and was prohibitively expensive, costing the equivalent of an annual wage. Yet around 250 original copies still survive, either in whole or in part.

Reflecting Wycliffe's adamant fixation on the value of the 'Word', every sentence of the Bible translation was carefully composed, and it had a profound effect on the English language. The Bible became responsible for the introduction of many Latin-based words and expressions to compete with the French influx in Norman times. Maybe not in quantity, but certainly in terms of influence. Many of the words that Wycliffe or his followers or the Bible translators coined are central to everyday modern speech today, for example:

>   Excellent
>   Problem
>   Ambitious
>   Communication
>   Irrevocable
>   To treasure
>   Sex
>   To scrape
>   Wrinkle

Then there are the words that are quirky and very contemporary in feel. The most notable being 'ecstasy'. Just as the modern use of his word 'twitter' would surprise Chaucer, so Wycliffe would be intrigued by the modern use of the word 'ecstasy'. But add to this the following:

>   Female
>   Puberty
>   Liquid

Then add to these, some of the most pervasive and evocative expressions:

>   Childbearing (a combination word first used in Isaiah)
>   Graven image (in Exodus)
>   Keys of the kingdom (in St Matthew)
>   All things to all men (in Corinthians)
>   Root of all evil (in epistle to St Timothy)
>   The quick and the dead (in epistle to St Peter)
>   Ye of little faith

And they brought additional currency great expressions like 'salt of the earth', which were already in use. If you spent a day speaking without using any of these words or idioms, it would be frustrating.

Wycliffe summed up his belief in the use of language.

> *'Christ and his Apostles taught the people in the language best known to them. It is certain that the truth of the Christian faith becomes more evident the more the faith itself is known. Therefore, the doctrine should not only be in Latin but in the common tongue, and as the faith of the Church is contained in the Scriptures, the more these are known in a true sense the better.'*

○ ○ ○

Roll forward 150 years, and another remarkable pioneer of the Bible in English emerged. William Tyndale was born around 1494, into an established family living in Gloucestershire, in an area of the country notable for a continuing strength of Lollard adherence. He was born no more than fifty miles from where another significant William would grow up. Despite this proximity, Shakespeare lived in a doggedly Catholic part of the country in neighbouring Warwickshire. Different ends of the Christian religious spectrum of the day, but both were counter-establishmentary at their respective moments of birth.

There are parallels also between Tyndale and Wycliffe. Both were driven by a belief in the power of the Holy Word. Both were determined to make it accessible to men and women of all classes and backgrounds. Both were deeply opposed to the corruption of the Church, the predominance of ritual and the monopoly of divine access exercised by the clergy. To one particular priest who challenged what he was doing, Tyndale replied in a manner that Wycliffe would have probably endorsed wholeheartedly: ''ere many years, I will cause a boy that driveth a plough to know more of the scriptures than thou dost'. A man of undoubted conviction, Tyndale was not necessarily a master of 'winning friends and influencing people'.

Wycliffe was essential as the trailblazer, but Tyndale was necessary to reignite the flame. Wycliffe had been declared a heretic. His translations were outlawed. Heresy was now a capital offence, in no small part due to the popularity of his and his followers' preaching. The philosophy that he espoused was driven underground by fear. Conformity replaced nonconformity. The success of Wycliffe, and the resulting backlash, put back Bible translation over a century. Germany had around 14 separate vernacular translations from 1466 until Luther's famous German translation in 1522. England had none.

By the time of Tyndale, principles of conformity in England had definitely not changed, nor had the brutality with which they were enforced. But other things were different. Printing had emerged and enabled mass distribution. Wycliffe never had that. Nonconformity as espoused by Wycliffe had spread from England to Northern Europe. The Church was no longer dealing with a single outbreak of revolutionary thinking, but a whole series of flare-ups, all approximately consistent in their thesis. The Church had been deeply threatened by John Hus, but Martin Luther further changed the whole landscape. Tyndale was able to spend good portions of his life, in the relative protection of like-minded thinkers in Northern Europe. In England he was hounded as a heretic and would have been quickly executed if he had stayed.

Tyndale was still ignored for many centuries by historians. In part because his name was airbrushed from subsequent Bibles using his work. From Victorian times, he started to be rediscovered, and it is Wycliffe who now is more likely to be ignored. Partly because Tyndale provided the underpinnings of the King James Bible and partly because Tyndale came to a tragic and dramatic end. When the forces of darkness came for Wycliffe, he was able to retreat and survive productively in exile. When the same forces came for Tyndale, the end was swifter and more brutal. It makes for a memorable tale, that has lent itself to movie-making.

They were both Oxford men. Tyndale went to Magdalen Hall College (now known as Hertford) in about 1506. He achieved a BA in 1512, an MA in 1515, and went on to study theology. Upon completion of his education, he took a role as the chaplain and tutor for Sir John Walsh. But he hankered after the task of translating the Bible into English. Tyndale was a linguist of distinction, fluent, or to become fluent, in French, Greek, Latin, Hebrew, Italian, German and Spanish. He decided to go further than Wycliffe, by translating the New Testament not from Latin but from the original Greek, and the Old Testament from Hebrew.

Translations of the Bible were still thought to be deeply subversive. Thomas More himself was particularly against making the scriptures intelligible to the common man, and railed publicly against such an endeavour. Tyndale was refused permission to make his translation. He therefore left for Europe to start his work in earnest there. He travelled through Germany and the Low Countries, eventually arriving in Antwerp. When his groundbreaking translation of the New Testament from Greek was finished, it was printed in Europe and copies were smuggled into England. An earlier written preface explained his commitment to addressing the 'everyman' among his intended readers. He emphasised the democratic intention of the work, which served as contrast to the strong control exerted by the Church over the Latin versions:

'If they (the readers) perceive in any place that I have not attained the very sense of the tongue, or meaning of the Scripture, or have not given the right English word, that they put their hands to amend it, remembering that so it is their duty to do.'

The translations were printed in a small pocket-sized edition, making them portable for constant reference and simpler for concealment amid folds of clothing. They caused a furore. Those caught in possession were branded heretics and treated accordingly. Wolsey and More unleashed a litany of venom and condemnation against Tyndale. They bought up every copy they could find, unwittingly boosting his earnings in the process, and burning them in ostentatious piles in public places. People marvelled at the bizarre sight of government officials busily setting fire to the word of God.

Tyndale also wrote a thesis called 'The Obedience of a Christian Man'. It argued for the supremacy of the King over the Pope. Anne Boleyn specifically brought it to the King's attention, who showered it with praise. This was short-lived as his next text, 'The Practice of Prelates', argued that the proposed annulment of Henry VIII's marriage to Katherine had no firm justification in the scriptures. This was not welcome news to Henry, who wrote forcefully to Charles V, the Holy Roman Emperor, demanding that Tyndale be found, and be extradited for trial. Charles was the nephew of Henry's estranged wife Katherine, and was happy to delay any response, on grounds of insufficient evidence.

Tyndale next concentrated on his translation of the Old Testament, completing the first five books. Having taught himself Hebrew, he hit his rhythm with this second major phase of work. 'The properties of the Hebrew tongue agreeth a thousand times more with English than with Latin,' he said. Sections of these were printed and smuggled into England, while the authorities busily compiled evidence against him and his writings. In 1535, Tyndale's safe house in Antwerp was finally betrayed by an English spy. The following year he was tried for heresy and found guilty. Thomas Cromwell, no fan of the Thomas More school of thought, argued strongly for his pardon, but in vain. He was publicly stripped of his priestly vestments and tried by a civil court. He was found guilty, and executed by strangling first, and burning second. His final words were purportedly made in a loud and unfaltering voice: 'Lord, open the King of England's eyes'.

Events were moving rapidly and eyes were indeed being opened. Not in time to save Tyndale's life but certainly to create his legacy. Failing in his endeavours to persuade the Pope to annul his marriage, Henry broke from Rome, marrying Anne Boleyn in 1533. The Act of Supremacy was passed, signalling England's formal separation from Rome the following year. Thomas Cromwell replaced Wolsey, and Cranmer became Archbishop of Canterbury. As a result, three figures, Queen Anne, Cromwell and Cranmer, all with pro-Reformation zeal, were in positions of power. Despite Henry's personal continuance of the Catholic faith, Protestantism was quickly taking root. The monasteries were destroyed and Church iconography removed. Religious fervour, nationalistic pride and mercenary greed conjoined to create rapid change.

Tyndale's faithful assistant, John Rogers, moved around Europe, and completed the missing sections of the Old Testament; he remained closely consistent with the style of Tyndale's own writing and for reasons of secrecy used the pseudonym 'Thomas Matthew'. As Tyndale's name was still contentious with the King, the resulting completed work was known by the pseudonym of his assistant, the Matthew Bible, and was published in 1537. This led to the official commissioning by Thomas Cromwell of a version by Matthew Coverdale, based on these translations. Henry VIII formally endorsed what became known as the Great Bible, which was published by Richard Grafton in 1539, and churches were compelled to use it. Thus in a period of only four years, possession of Tyndale's writing had moved from being extreme heresy punishable by death, to mass distribution and prescription as the official version.

Cranmer wrote the introduction to the Great Bible, laying out the principles and purposes of the grand endeavour.

> *'Here may...men, women, young, old, learned, unlearned, rich, poor, priests, laymen, lords, ladies, officers, tenants, and mean men, virgins, wives, widows, lawyers, artificers, husbandmen, and all manners of persons of what estate or condition soever they be...learn all things what they ought to believe, what they ought to do...as well as concerning Almighty God as... themselves and all other.'*

Richard Grafton, the publisher of the Great Bible, was formally dubbed the King's Printer. He was not a member of the Stationers' Company as many printer/publishers were (indeed still are), but of the Grocers' Company, with the better affiliations that this afforded him. Being fleet of foot and well connected was essential to the role. He produced the next most important work for the Protestant movement, Cranmer's Book of Common Prayer. He also printed Lady Jane Grey's proclamation as monarch, and amazingly, he survived Lady Jane's failure to see off the Catholic Queen Mary. He slipped into retirement unscathed although financially challenged. Like many in the City, Grafton was a strong supporter of the Reformation. Protestant beliefs, lying dormant in England, and in London in particular, had been ready to be reawoken. This owes much to the bedrock that Wycliffe and his followers had laid. And that Tyndale had strongly rekindled.

Tyndale's legacy was even further assured by the King James Bible, which leant heavily on his translations. The two most influential works in the advancement of English globally, namely the King James Bible and the works of Shakespeare, were created by two Englishmen born within fifty miles of each other, yet on separate sides of the fault line between Protestant and Catholic; both outsiders in their own way in their own time.

As with Wycliffe, Tyndale's enrichment of the English language was considerable, partly driven by didactic principles. He pointedly used the word 'congregation' for 'church', 'elder' for 'priest', 'love' for 'charity' and 'overseer' for 'bishop', which accorded with his beliefs. At every juncture, he chose a term that diminished the authority of the established Church, and tended to choose words derived from Old English, in preference to Latin. Tyndale's radical zeal shone through in the very words he chose.

We owe Tyndale for the coining of some of our most expressive words:

> Beautiful
> Brokenhearted
> Scapegoat
> Uproar

Tyndale is the acknowledged originator of some of the most powerful idioms in our language. All generated from his Bible translations, and common parlance now due to their ubiquity in the English-speaking world. Idioms including:

> Coat of many colours (subsequently to inspire Lloyd Webber and Rice)
> Brother's keeper (from Genesis)
> Eye for an eye (from Matthew)
> Eat drink and be merry (Ecclesiastes)
> Blind lead the blind (St Matthew)
> Suffer fools gladly (Corinthians)
> Busybody (St Peter)
> To fall flat on one's face (Numbers)
> The skin of my teeth (Job)

As a lamb to the slaughter (Isaiah)
To put the words in his mouth (Exodus)

One could continue: 'Seek and ye shall find', 'Let there be light', 'A law unto themselves', 'Filthy lucre', 'Stranger in a strange land', 'The powers that be', 'The fat of the land', 'Flowing with milk and honey', 'The spirit is willing', 'Signs of the times'. Ad infinitum.

While his phrases were invented, they derived from the task of translating, as precisely as he could, from the Greek, Hebrew, and Latin originals. What the Bible translators did, in their own way, was to introduce yet more influences from other tongues. Both Tyndale, and Wycliffe, placed the highest store on the power of those words; we are not left with clumsy translations, but an expressive lexicon that plunders foreign sources to create powerful meaning anew.

But more than even words, Tyndale brought to his translations a powerful ability to tell tales, and to bring text alive with narrative. In this, he drew heavily on the Anglo-Saxon tradition of verse-based storytelling. His Bible engaged uniquely with the English imagination, long schooled to appreciate not just words, but also tales.

I end this chapter where I began, the translation of the opening lines of the Gospel of St John. But this time with Tyndale's rather than Wycliffe's. If you flick back and forth between the two, they are broadly identical in their readings but Tyndale added minor differences, in the rhythm and the repeated use of 'that' to provide emphasis to so important a line. What Wycliffe first wrote, Tyndale improved.

'In the beginning was that Word, so that Word was with God, and God was that Word. The same was in the beginning with God.' Amen.

CHAPTER THIRTEEN

FINAL BUILDING BLOCKS – REFORMATION AND BREAK WITH EUROPE

The Reformation provides the central gearbox in our history, shaping the direction of our culture and language thereafter. That is my opinion. You cannot appreciate who we are today, without understanding the change and the turmoil of this period.

The narrative moves fast. In 1521, Henry VIII was being lauded by the Pope for his attack on Martin Luther, and awarded the accolade of 'Defender of the Faith'. By 1534 with the Act of Supremacy, Henry had broken with Rome, thrown off the yoke of the traditional Church, started the dissolution and plundering of the monasteries, and was subsequently excommunicated. The change is precipitate. It was driven initially by the expediency of the biological clock, and the requirement for a strong male heir. Upon such prosaic matters, national destinies are determined, and the next building blocks of the English language and of the English culture started to come into place.

To emphasise the speed and completeness of the change, there is no better example than the attitude to transubstantiation, that hobgoblin of the religious thinking of the day. In 1539, at the time of the printing of the Great Bible, the Six Articles published by Henry confirmed unequivocally the validity of transubstantiation. The death penalty was threatened to any who argued against it. By 1563, twenty-four years later, Elizabeth I was decreeing in the Thirty-nine Articles: 'Transubstantiation, or the change of the substance of bread and wine in the Supper of the Lord cannot be proved by Holy Writ, but is repugnant to the plain words of the Scripture, overthroweth the nature of a sacrament and hath given occasion to many superstitions.'

The speed of change was assisted greatly by the groundwork of Wycliffe. A good proportion of the English population was ready to accept the new model of worship heralded by the Reformation; the thinking and principles, although transformational, were not new. Henry remained staunchly Catholic at heart, despite his break with Rome, but allowed a coterie of Reformation-minded people to occupy positions of power. Most significantly, he put his only son's education in the hands of Protestant teachers. In the short period of Edward's monarchy, key elements of a Reformed Church, such as the Book of Common

Prayer in English, were introduced with a strong compulsion for it to be used universally. The backlash came with Mary's succession, and the reinstatement of Catholicism. Mary had significant popular support upon succession, based on both respect for her lineage but also a hankering after old ways. This popularity was squandered by her marriage to Philip, the Spanish King, which put England's independence in some doubt (was he to be King? Or was he not?), the loss of the country's last French dominion, Calais, the absence of a male heir, and then the needlessly brutal pursuit of Protestants – most notably Cranmer. Despite his recantations, he was still sent to the stake, when a change of heart would normally have secured a pardon. Cranmer, of course, had the last word – repudiating his repudiations, dying a Protestant martyr, and ensuring a prominent place in Foxe's massively popular compendium: 'Book of Martyrs'. Mary's stubborn refusal to save him from the death penalty only emphasised the pointless vindictiveness of the regime. Elizabeth I came to the throne, and moved the pendulum back closer to where Edward had left it. But she assuaged the extreme conservatives with appropriate modifications. Not everyone was happy; an undercurrent of rebellion and sedition was forever on the agenda. The firm path away from Catholicism had been set. Catholic service in England remained illegal until 1791, and subsequent Test Acts decreed that the holding of any public office was dependent on swearing denial of transubstantiation. Remaining thus until 1828.

o o o

Symbolically, the Act of Supremacy provided the break from Rome. Since Wycliffe's day and even before, many of the English had bridled at the control placed on the country by the self-appointed hierarchy of the Church. Much of the country's assets were owned by Rome, significant annual tributes and tithes were being paid to Rome, for often dubious uses, and judgements over daily life were being determined not in Westminster but in Rome or in Avignon. A familiar English complaint?

Although the specific catalyst was the King's marriage, more broadly the break from Rome was an act of national self-determination. Rome, specifically, was seen by many as an alien power with no mandate, and thus fundamentally contrary to the Anglo-Saxon need for legitimacy of rule. It is striking that the Reformation took greatest hold in the northern parts of Europe, where the traditions of the Germanic and Nordic tribes were strongest.

The dissolution of the monasteries began in 1536 with initially all those with an annual income of 200 pounds or less being taken over by the state. The impetus grew in the balance of Henry's reign, with larger monasteries following suit. Treasures were confiscated; lands taken over and incomes redirected to the public coffers. The exchequer was enriched either directly by taking ownership or indirectly by the proceeds of sale of monastic land.

J.C. Solomon in his 'Dissolution of the Monasteries: An Economic Study', identifies that in 1509, there were 850 monastic foundations including 500 monasteries, 136 nunneries, 200 friaries, plus several thousand chantries. A long history of donations means that collectively they owned around a sixth of the total land of the country, and about a third of the arable land, Solomon estimates. Monasteries alone accounted for a significant proportion of that. By the mid-1540s, almost all of those had been dissolved, and their wealth removed.

In terms of the pattern of distribution of this huge swathe of land, it is estimated that 14 per cent of the total was sold to members of the peerage, enlarging existing estates. 2.5 per cent was distributed by the King to reward favours, or honour loyalty. The balance, and the vast majority was sold to less wealthy families and smallholders – often at affordable prices. The process of dissolution and distribution of assets benefitted less the aristocracy of the age, and more the rural gentry. It laid the foundations for future generations of a new land-owning upper class.

The Crown made use of these funds to finance Henry's army and growing navy, to wage war against Ireland, Scotland and France, to fund his lifestyle, to satisfy his desire for ostentation and to pay for the upkeep of his many palaces. It is estimated, he had over fifty palaces or substantial manors under his control, many of which he was improving or expanding at any one time. It often seems an unnecessarily large number, but given the scale of his itinerant court, and the challenge on the countryside, simply to feed them all, it is perhaps explicable that they equalled the equivalent of about one per week. A week was about the maximum that his court could be feasibly fed in an out-of-London location, before draining the surrounding land and fisheries of food. In terms of ostentation, each of the magnificent Abraham tapestries, dazzling with their gold and silver thread, and commissioned for the Great Hall at Hampton Court Palace, where they hang to this day, cost the equivalent of building a small battleship. The importance of 'showing off' was sufficiently high to determine this priority.

In crude economic terms, the dormant wealth of the monasteries and churches was unlocked and injected into the economy. Craftsmen, artists, soldiers, sailors, ship builders, stone masons benefitted from this incontinent spending. Much went abroad (the tapestries for example were made in Belgium), but much will have entered the English economy.

A new efficiency was enabled. The monasteries had not been the most rigorous exploiters of their assets. Pooling their lands with private landowners enabled larger units to be formed, better motivated to increase yields and returns. The process of enclosure of land was accelerated. Whatever the social consequences, the piecemeal division of land into separately owned sub-plots did not produce efficient farms. Most importantly it helped the deployment of the new agricultural system of 'up and down' farming, which specialised in the long-term rotation of acreage between arable and pasture, with significant improvements in productivity for both types of use.

It was not only the utilisation of what was on the land, that dissolution transformed, but also what was below. The monastic land holdings included some areas of the richest mineral resources. The monasteries were not motivated to exploit these. Now in private hands, a mining revolution took place, with substantial quantities of lead, tin, coal, iron and other resources being unlocked.

Prior to the 16th century the English economy had been dominated by agriculture, especially the production of wool. The country was a producer of raw materials, and Europe was the finisher of goods. The economic revolution of that century transformed the balance of the economy. Not only did mineral extraction become a big business, but a heavy manufacturing sector grew off the back of it. By the time of the Civil War, England dominated the lead market in Europe (important for roofing). It was also the leader in mining generally and heavy industry. None of this would have been achieved while these resources still lay in monastic ownership.

It was upon this impetus that the expansion of England's power and influence through the 17th and 18th centuries was based, and it was critical to being able to support the rapid development of cultural life in this period. Not just as the plaything of monarchy and the higher nobility, but as something with a mass audience, able to pay a reasonable price to be amused, entertained or enlightened.

o o o

One of the crucial roles that the wealth of the monasteries had provided was support to the poor, education of the young and a very rudimentary level of hospital care. The dissolution of these institutions was understandably met with protests – the most significant being the Pilgrimage of Grace in the north, where the standing of the monasteries was higher. These protests were suppressed with speed and brutality. The hole in the system of social care was thus left to be filled.

The average peasant at the bottom of the ladder, had relatively few choices. They could live the precarious life of a jobbing farm hand, starve, or head for the City to find a new skill or way of living. When the cities began to become overcrowded, the impetus grew to move abroad, to start a new life. England (and Scotland, Wales, and Ireland too) had an impoverished and dispossessed lower class willing to migrate. No other country at this time had such a surfeit. The process of dispossession begun by the destruction of the monasteries, land redistribution, and periods of religious intolerance, created a willingness to confront considerable danger to move to new lands abroad. This in turn had a significant effect on the spread of the language globally.

o o o

The growth in the scale of the English cities became exponential. By 1600, the London population had expanded to around 200,000. In a century, the number had trebled. London had gone from being one of the larger cities in Europe, to being an equal to Paris and more populous than every other contender.

The economic impact of a single market the scale of London in those days cannot be underestimated. The wealth and the power of the City Companies grew in significance. A new social support system had to emerge.

As a result of the burgeoning wealth of the cities, and the collapse of the church-driven care system, a pivotal decision was made. Rather than exploit and pocket all of their newfound income, the City Companies decided to act philanthropically to the benefit, not just of their members, but also the poor, the needy and the disadvantaged. They did not have to do this, but they chose to – albeit philanthropy tinged strongly with self-interest.

Part of the new credo was that salvation and progress in the after-life, was no longer contingent on paying penances, and hiring clergy to sign your prayers. It was more dependent on faith from God, reflected in an individual's acts in their own lifetime. Much of the City Company wealth traditionally had gone on supporting their own members, and particularly in the payment for chantries on behalf of their deceased members. The latter function became increasingly redundant. Establishing alms houses for the poor, and schools for deserving scholars seemed a more fitting use of their wealth.

In addition the expanding economy needed a supply of well taught apprentices to enter the workforce and sign up to their respective crafts. The City had developed over time a strongly Protestant spirit, and the opportunity to build and fund schools was a chance to ensure that future generations were taught thoroughly, in the disciplines of the new religion.

A very significant number of schools and institutions were founded by the Companies in the relatively short period from 1550 to 1580. Most still flourish today; most are still run by their founding Companies. Christ's Hospital, founded in 1552, had particularly emblematic significance; this was King Edward's personal pet project to establish a new generation of bright Protestants from all backgrounds. He persuaded the Companies to back it financially. Originally founded in London, it then moved to Horsham, where it still thrives. The Grocers' Company still today has the right to allocate six scholarship places to children of restricted means. At a comparable time, around the Grocers' Courtroom table sat Lawrence Sherriff, the founder of Rugby School in 1567, William Laxton, the founder of Oundle School in 1556 and the Lord Mayor, Sir John Lyons, the first cousin of the founder of Harrow (established 1572). All three schools were built at this time, and all three flourish today. Gresham's School (established 1555) was entrusted by the Mercers to the Fishmongers. Tonbridge School was founded by a Skinner in 1553. The Merchant Taylors' Company established the Merchant Taylors' School in 1561. All of these schools promoted grammar and language, primarily in Latin and in Greek, but also in English. Richard Mulcaster, the first headmaster of Merchant Taylors' School decreed that 'I do not think that any language be it whatsoever, is better able to utter all arguments either with more pith, or greater planesse, than our English tongue is... I honour the Latin, but I worship the English.' A very modern sentiment for the time.

All these institutions were well financed, made accessible to children of ability from a range of backgrounds, and are still world class today. The majority of them were not concentrated in London, as might have been expected, but located around the country. They were designed to develop a new wave of entrants to the workforce who were schooled in the new religion, and more likely to be recruits to the mercantile and professional classes than the monastic outputs of previous generations. The seeds for a future industrial revolution and the global reach of England's trading Empire were sown here.

o o o

The Act of Supremacy had resulted in Henry's and England's excommunication. English ships were often prohibited entry to European ports, by way of punishment. The need was created to seek out markets further afield. The Muscovy Company was formed to create trade with Russia as early as in Queen Mary's reign. Subsequently the Virginia Company, the Levant Company and the East India Company followed suit. These enabled the City Companies to finance the development of trade with far flung markets by way of risk-sharing special purpose vehicles. Expanding global trade soon developed into Empire, which succinctly put, meant taking sovereignty of these foreign lands, applying legal and administrative structures, expanding their abilities to generate raw materials, shipping these back to England to be turned into manufactured products, selling them to the home market, and also back to the originating country as finished goods. This circular system fed the wealth of England. The development of the slave trade was the expansion of this principle to its ethically and morally bankrupt conclusion.

The international reaction to the Reformation speeded up the rate at which England's attention turned to non-European markets. It created the need for England to be the leading maritime power and to protect its presence in the sea lanes of the world

o o o

As importantly, the shift from Catholicism led to the removal of ritual and iconography from Christian worship, and created a focus on the written and spoken word.

The most visible emblem of that lay in the creation of the cornerstone of Anglican worship – the Book of Common Prayer. Or 'The Book of the Common Prayer and Administration of the Sacraments and Other Rites and Ceremonies After the Use of the Church of England', to give it its full, jaunty title. This was the masterwork of Thomas Cranmer, the Archbishop of Canterbury. Acting as part editor and part author, he led a team that laid down every aspect of church service and worship in the new Protestant faith as fashioned for English congregations – all in one compendium. As with Wycliffe, as with Tyndale, Cranmer operated in an environment where the value of words and expressions was paramount. By good fortune, Cranmer was one of the greatest prose writers in the English language. For over 400 years, his Book of Common Prayer has been the source of annual worship in the Church of England. Its longevity is due to the beauty of its phrasing, its simplicity of expression, its use of repetition, and its rhythm of speech when declaimed.

I choose only one example, the simple beauty of the Advent Collect:

> *'Almighty God, give us grace that we may cast away the works of darkness, and put upon us the armour of light now in the time of this mortal life (in which thy Son Jesus Christ came to visit us in*

great humility), that in the last day, when he shall come again in his glorious Majesty to judge both the quick and dead, we may rise to the life immortal, through him who liveth and reigneth with thee and the Holy Ghost. Now and ever. Amen.'

The Book of Common Prayer was published in 1549, some ten years after the Great Bible. The Act of Uniformity in June of that year made it compulsory in all churches in England. Overnight religious service moved from ornate ritualistic Latin to simply spoken phrases in beautiful English. The sudden change of the Book of Common Prayer caused its ructions. The most significant was its rejection in Cornwall and Devon, where English was less prevalent. The mandatory application of the new liturgy triggered a major rebellion, and an armed body determined to march on London to insist on the return of the old service. In their eyes (or ears) they were being commanded to give up service in one language they didn't understand, to be replaced with another language which they purported equally not to understand, and with no frippery or iconography to compensate. After hearing the substance of the protest, an armed force was duly sent to wipe out the rebels. 4,000 of them were slaughtered, and use of the Book of Common Prayer was enforced.

Although a cruel tale, it does reinforce the unifying value to the language of a common book of prayer across the whole nation – all in English. Briefly during Mary's reign the Book of Prayer was outlawed while traditional Catholic service was reintroduced. But with Elizabeth's succession, the Book of Prayer was firmly re-established and republished in 1559, incorporating a few modifications designed to placate some of the objections from the conservative wing.

This chapter finishes with all four building blocks to the English language firmly in place.

Modern Middle English had now been used to create leading written works of art: 'The Canterbury Tales', 'Piers Plowman' and 'Morte d'Arthur'.

Mass printing meant that these works were accessible, accurate and the language increasingly uniform across the nation.

Modern Middle English had been used to make the most important book of all, the Bible. The Old and New Testaments were now able to live vividly in the minds of everyone in the country, through the inspired translations of William Tyndale.

Finally the Book of Common Prayer meant that the most familiar observance in the lives of everyone, namely religious service, was conducted beautifully in their own language as a result of the genius of Thomas Cranmer.

These were the building blocks. The underlying jigsaw was now complete.

But more than complete; each piece of this jigsaw had been constructed with a power and a style of expression that deployed the richness of this particular language to the full. They set the example of what English, when written, and spoken, should be. Poetic. Vivid. Direct. Rhythmic. Fluent. Painting pictures, not with brush and canvas, but through words chosen from the broadest of lexicons, built up by the infusion of influences, of sources, and of so many inventive minds, into the richest vocabulary in the world.

What also fascinates me is the character and circumstances of the originators of these works. Chaucer. Langland. Gower. Wycliffe. Tyndale. Cranmer. They make an extraordinary collective. None of them particularly well-born, or socially advantaged. All of them had in some way the characteristic of the outsider, and the maverick mind pushing at the doors of accepted opinion. Some were lauded in their day, and others had to wait. But in due course their efforts were all embraced and all contributed to the journey of our language. I personally believe that it is something to do with our innate belief in consensus, and the democratic will, which is peculiarly Anglo-Saxon in origin, which enabled such radical minds to have their impact. This belief is reinforced by the continual rejection of the concept of the English equivalent of the Académie Française, or a similar body to regulate the language. Individual expression and interpretation were felt to be higher ideals than conformism and control.

The overall shift in priorities was not without broad, long-lasting consequences. A population brought up on the ornate performance of the mass, and celebration of saints' days and feasts, now had to be satisfied simply with the power of text. This achieved a greater focus on language, vocabulary and expression. But it also brought a thirst for performance and ritual, now no longer satisfied. The trappings of religious ceremony and saints' day celebrations may have been banished, but the underlying appetite remained. We move next to consider the massive reverberations in English cultural life that were prompted by this unsatisfied need. 'The Thunder Run'.

CHAPTER FOURTEEN

THE THUNDER RUN

'For what else is the life of man but a kind of play in which men in various costumes perform until the director motions them off the stage.'
– Erasmus from 'The Praise of Folly' published in 1511

The Thunder Run is a device invented for early proscenium arch theatres and built high above the stage in the uppermost rigging. A long sloping channel constructed of wood planks traverses the width of the theatre several times; down this, giant cannonballs are rolled by a stagehand not afraid of heights. The deafening sound of their lengthy descent shakes the theatre, and creates the impression of an almighty storm. The force of the 'thunder run' is a good theatrical metaphor for the revolution in drama that occurred after the Reformation and the reverberations that we still feel today.

Drama was always present in medieval England. However, in 1210, Pope Innocent III banned all clergy from performing in theatrical settings, and thereafter the plays were performed primarily in the vernacular, by lay folk. The most popular format for these came to be known as Mystery Plays. These told the lives of the saints, of figures from the Bible and conveyed morality stories. These were mounted annually, at length, with much display, in outdoor settings. The texts were particular to individual towns; the most famous surviving ones were from York, Chester, and Wakefield. They were mounted by the civic guilds and livery companies, who were generally known as Mysteries (based on the Latin for craft, ministerium) and thus these performances became known as Mystery Plays. Almost without exception these dramas were devoted to the promulgation of religious themes, occasionally enriched with comic interludes. They played a crucial role in explaining the scriptures to a non-Latin speaking population.

With the Reformation, everything was to change. What had been the essence of drama, suddenly became unacceptable and impossible. This included the whole theatrical nature of religious service itself. The Catholic Mass, its Latin chants, its ornate costumes, its props, its smells, and its performance of the living presence of Christ during the Eucharist service, all were to disappear. The sheer magic of pieces of bread being transformed into the body of the Saviour, and the wine being transformed into his blood, was no more. Gone too were the many celebrations of Saints' days with their associated pageants and parades.

To make matters more confusing to the average Englishman of this period, there was a swinging back and forth of the proscribed religion during this period. One day, with King Edward VI, religion consisted of spartan, unadorned services seeking the truth of God's word via a Bible written in English and conducted in accordance with the Book of Common Prayer. The next, with Queen Mary, religion reverted to full regalia and holy objects, with an ornate and ritualistic Mass delivered in Latin. And then back again with Queen Elizabeth.

The role of drama during this interim period flip-flopped too. With the initial advent of the Reformation, there was a phase when drama was deployed as a useful tool to ridicule the religious beliefs of the opposing faction. Productions were toured, most notably by the playwright and preacher, John Bale, which served up outrageous propaganda for the Protestant cause, and ridiculed Catholic beliefs. His touring company of actors were known as Lord Cromwell's Players. Their most well-known work was a history of King John, which portrayed him as essentially a good King forced into evil ways by the Pope and all the apparatus of the Roman church. The production ended in a giant singsong and knees-up with the Pope and members of the Church dancing out their ritual in ludicrous fashion. The sacking of monasteries had yielded a ready supply of free costumes for the purpose.

But this was a passing phase primarily egged on by Thomas Cromwell's mission to convert the country, by fair means or foul – theatre was just one such weapon in his armoury. In the end, one of the few things that various Tudor monarchs could all agree on is that religion should not be a feature of stage performance. It was just too serious a component of statecraft. So Henry VIII introduced the Act for the Advancement of True Religion in 1543, which permitted moral plays that encouraged virtue in preference to evil. Edward introduced the Act of Uniformity in 1551 which forbad any plays from attacking the Book of Common Prayer. Mary and Elizabeth despite their religious differences both issued proclamations at the very start of their respective reigns, decreeing that religious matters were the highest affairs of state, and not to be dealt with in things as trivial as plays. The complete hand-brake turn had been executed in the matter of only a few years. We had gone from plays dealing with religion and the scripture, almost exclusively, to never being able to be mention such things. Not overtly at least.

Under the onslaught of such legislation and decrees, of grim penalties including mutilation, or grisly death, awaiting any breach, it would have been easy for theatre to have retreated into a hole of fear and dread. But that did not happen. Quite the reverse, for reasons I believe connected directly with the Reformation itself, the foundation stones were laid for the future and continuing success of theatre in England.

○ ○ ○

First, it is helpful to appreciate the plays of this period, and how they evolved rapidly from the religious purposes of the Mystery Plays to the secular requirements post the Reformation.

The first landmark in theatrical writing at this time, was, improbably, the comedy 'Ralph Roister Doister'. It was first performed around 1552, less than twenty years after the Act of Supremacy. Written by Nicholas Udall, a schoolmaster, it was meant originally for performance by his pupils. But it quickly found a mainstream audience. Udall himself was a controversial, larger than life character. Educated at Winchester and then Corpus Christi College, Oxford. He was said to have been tutored under instructions from Thomas Cromwell. He taught at a London grammar school, before progressing to teaching Latin at Eton, becoming headmaster in 1534. His Eton career came to an ignominious end, in 1541, when forced to resign for committing offences against the pupils. He was prosecuted and found guilty under the Buggery Act. The offence usually carried a capital sentence of hanging. However he used his connections to the maximum, and managed to get the hanging commuted to a one-year gaol sentence, which he served in Marshalsea prison. Upon leaving prison, he appears to have been made the Vicar of Braintree, and then of a parish in the Isle of Wight. When he tired of this, and despite his criminal record, he got himself reinstated as a teacher, this time at Westminster School. It is said that 'Ralph Roister Doister' was originally written to be performed by his pupils here. Despite his chequered tenure, the library at Eton College boasts the only original edition that is known to still exist.

The play returned to the basic format of comedy popular in Greek and Roman times. You can find clear traces of Plautus and Terence in the work; the character Ralph was closely modelled on Plautus' pompous braggart in 'Miles Gloriosus'. The play tells of a rich widow, Christian Custance, who is betrothed to a merchant called Gawyn Goodluck. Ralph is persuaded by an artful huckster, Matthew Merrygreek, to seek to woo Christian away from Gawyn. The play follows the various increasingly outlandish attempts to achieve this, all of which fail. The play finishes with the wedding of Christian to Gawyn, and a 'happy ever after life' for them.

The comedy is in English, and there is no hint of religion. Its rambunctious style is clear from its characters and the scrapes they get into. It strongly influenced many of the Elizabethan writers specialising in comedy, including Shakespeare himself. It set the new paradigm.

The second landmark play formed the template for tragedy. 'Gorboduc' by Thomas Norton and Thomas Sackville. It was first put on at the Inner Temple in 1561, less than ten years after Ralph Roister Doister made its debut. 'Gorboduc' was subsequently performed at Whitehall for Elizabeth I. Both Thomases were Cambridge educated, both became MPs, and were well connected at court. Sackville subsequently became the Earl of Dorset. The authors were establishment figures (like only a few of the protagonists in this narrative) and seemed free to deliver the highly political message that 'Gorboduc' presented. Once again, the play goes back to Greek/Roman tragic roots, and firmly avoids religious themes.

'Gorboduc' is the tale of a mythical king of Britain who divides his kingdom in two, between his sons Ferrex and Porrex. No sooner has the settlement been reached than the younger son kills the elder in the hope of getting his share. Their mother, for whom the elder was her favourite, promptly kills the younger – leaving the King heirless. In the ensuing chaos, the people of Britain rise up and kill both the father and the mother. The nobles then take charge, brutally subdue the rebels, and they then in turn, descend into civil war between each other. Lighthearted, it certainly is not.

'Gorboduc' has all the essential hallmarks of future work. Shakespeare's 'Titus Andronicus' and 'King Lear' owe much to it, as does Webster's 'Duchess of Malfi'. The other innovation of 'Gorboduc' was its pioneering use of blank verse. Blank verse allowed the power of the metre to be retained, but ensured that weighty and emotional passages were not undermined by simplistic structures of rhyme. A new and more effective way of doing tragedy had been discovered. Great writers were to follow suit.

'Gorboduc' was controversial in its subject matter. It replaced the religious message of pre-Reformation drama, with a political one. The narrative shows the national chaos when royal succession is left unclear. This was the hot topic of the day. The country worried about the consequences of a Virgin Queen. The play was a part of the pressure on her, to find a husband and to bear sons – but to no avail. In doing so, 'Gorboduc' showed that drama could comment on political issues of the day, metaphorically. Once again this was to become an important template for much Elizabethan and Jacobean drama.

o o o

The next critical innovation were the theatres. The first specially dedicated theatre built since Roman days, was a playhouse called the Red Lion Playhouse, opened in Whitechapel in 1567. It replicated the performance spaces often used at larger inns: a rectangular courtyard with a stage at one end, standing space in front, and a surrounding upper gallery for more comfortable seats. The Red Lion Playhouse was a farmhouse converted to a theatre by a member of the Grocers' Company, John Brayne. The Red Lion was the start of the end of the wholly transient life of players. It was the beginning of professionalism, and also the start of a mass audience being able to identify certain physical structures as fixed destinations for dramatic entertainment. Just as Gresham's transformative Royal Exchange, opening four years later, was the physical embodiment of mercantile activity, so the dedicated theatres were the physical embodiment of plays and playmaking.

The Red Lion Playhouse was probably not a great financial success. Its location amid farmland was not helpful. It lasted no more than about a year. But this did nothing to dissuade Brayne from embarking on his next, bolder venture. For this he teamed up with his brother-in-law, the theatre producer James Burbage. The Red Lion experience had taught Brayne that success depended on being able to generate your own content. They built the first polygonal half-covered, half-enclosed theatre in Shoreditch, on a site closer to the city gates and closer to a main traffic route, the road to and from Bishopsgate. It was a markedly better location than Whitechapel farmland. It took the considerable capital sum of 700 pounds to build and served as the template for large Elizabethan theatres. Some of the greatest plays of our history, like 'Romeo and Juliet', were most likely first performed here. Certainly an early version of 'Hamlet' (probably not Shakespeare's) was recorded as having been performed here. Brayne and Burbage called the new building the 'Theatre', trumpeting its direct lineage from the Roman 'theatrum'. The first building known in England as a Theatre was thus opened in 1576, in what is currently a very unprepossessing part of the city. It had its own company of players, which in due course attracted influential sponsorship; they were to be dubbed in due course the Lord Chamberlain's Men and were to include one William Shakespeare. He is thought to have been working in the theatres by the late 1580s; his presence was definitely acknowledged by 1592 (the year both of the 'upstart crow' jibe by his rival, but more established, playwright Robert Greene, and the year he took lodgings in St Helen's, just down the road in Bishopsgate). Every building subsequently called a theatre owes a small debt to Brayne and Burbage. The innovative marriage of building with resident producing company took hold, and is a model that we now take for granted as core to the enduring success today of institutions like the National Theatre, the RSC and many London and regional theatres. The Theatre's appeal to the performers and to the public alike can be assumed. When a serious dispute with the freeholder of the underlying land arose, in 1596, the Lord Chamberlain's Men initially decamped and continued their work at the neighbouring Curtain Theatre, first performing 'Henry V' here. Then in 1599, they went to the extraordinary lengths of secretly dismantling The Theatre building and transporting the timbers across the river (indeed potentially made possible by the river itself being frozen at the time in the great freeze of 1599/1600), to a new site in Southwark. Here they used this wood to help construct a new version of their building, calling it the Globe.

If there ever was an example of clinical well-organised efficiency, married with a commitment to the delivery of great art, then the secret transfer of The Theatre to the Globe, is a supreme candidate. This was not the project for the muddle headed, nor those of uncertain organisational abilities. Using my simplistic shorthand, the 'full Norman' was required for the underlying 'Anglo-Saxon purpose' of making great art.

The rest, as they say, is history. The Globe operated with the same company in it, the Lord Chamberlain's Men (subsequently elevated and dubbed 'the King's Men' by James I in 1603) until the closure of all theatres by Cromwell in 1642. Their success was helped by their first resident playwright being William Shakespeare, and their leading performers being great tragedians like Richard Burbage (James's son), master comic players like Will Kempe, the infamous master of the jig, and his successor, Robert Armin, and two exceptional young boys to play the lead female roles.

More dedicated theatres were built. Not just Theatre in 1576, but the theatre in Newington Butts, underneath what is now Elephant and Castle, was built at this time. The Curtain followed in 1577, just alongside Theatre. The Curtain is where Shakespeare first appears in 1597 on a cast list alongside his lifelong fellow actors and partners, John Heminges and Henry Condell, in the first performance of Ben Jonson's 'Everyman in His Humour.'

The Rose Theatre opened in Southwark in 1587. The Swan Theatre in 1595. Theatre moved south of the river to reopen as the Globe just next door to the Rose and the year after that, the Boars Head opened. The Fortune Theatre followed in 1600, the Red Bull in 1605, Whitefriars in 1606, the Cockpit (subsequently to become the Phoenix) in 1609, the Hope Playhouse in 1613 after the Rose had closed. None of these projects were acts of benevolence, or artistically driven philanthropy. They were often brought into life by the entrepreneurial spirits of middle-ranking members of the City Companies, teaming up with actor/managers with joint economic interest in the endeavours, acting in the belief that money could be made, and a market served.

I emphasise the middle-ranking nature of these entrepreneurs. City Aldermen were opposed to the consequences of public theatres, the entertainment that they plied and most importantly the behaviour of audiences. The city elders had become increasingly puritanically minded. This moral commitment had positive benefits on the development of education, but negative on theatre. With only one exception (the Blackfriars) all of the theatres referred to above, were sited outside the city walls.

Of the City Companies involved in theatre, members of the Grocers' Company were often the most prominent. John Brayne, partner of the Burbages, was a Grocer, and an active one at that. Richard Hicks who founded the playhouse at Newington Butts was as well. As too, was John Cholmley, the freeholder of the land for the Rose Theatre. Most significantly Shakespeare's closest business partners and fellow actors, John Heminges and Henry Condell, were both Grocers, and originators and editors of the First Folio. Many of the apprentices recruited into the King's Men by Heminges were Grocers, as there were no actors' apprenticeships in their own right. Heminges himself was sufficiently embedded in the Company to be elected as its Steward.

People are surprised by this close association between purveyors of spices, medicines and general produce, with pliers of drama. It is part chance but part prosaic. Early theatres had important franchises for the sale of food and drink. With theatre now a mass market, Grocers spotted the commercial opportunity. What popcorn is to modern cinema, so food and ale retailing were to Jacobean drama. Why were poor performances readily met with a hail of rotten tomatoes? How were such things ready to hand? I conjecture that this was a Grocer sideline for moving produce past its 'sell-by' date at a discount. Pure speculation, of course.

The Beaumont/Fletcher innovative classic of 1607, the 'Knight of the Burning Pestle', is renowned for being the first play known to break the dramatic convention of the fourth wall, but is also the first to make a City Company central to the narrative – namely the Grocers. Members from the audience, who are actors playing Grocers, object to what is being played, and inject themselves into proceedings onstage with the aim of improving the dramatic offering. Their young apprentice, Rafe, is made the main protagonist in the adjusted tale. At the end of the play, as he dies tragically, in his final words, Rafe pleads: 'Fly fly my soul, to Grocers' Hall'. And everyone in a Jacobean audience would have appreciated the significance of that.

o o o

The creation of established and permanent performing companies was the next critical step.

In 1572, the Statute and Act for the Punishment of Vagabonds was made into law. This act gave the towns and boroughs, including London, the powers to arrest anyone who was 'not belonging to any baron of the realm or towards any other honourable personage of greater degree'. This Act was prompted by the fear of vagrancy and of Catholic infiltration, by spies travelling under cover. It impacted badly on performers, for whom touring the country was a primary source of income, especially at times of city plagues. It prompted a change in the structure of the theatre world and had implications on the standard of work and the repertories performed. Informal groups of players restructured themselves into more established companies, with persons of standing as their named sponsors. As early as 1575, Londoners were able to appreciate the talents of players patronised by the Earls of Warwick, Leicester, Sussex, Oxford, Pembroke, Lincoln and Essex, as well as Lords Howard, Rich and Abergavenny. The artistic association, if chosen right, reflected well upon the patrons, and the players were able to protect themselves from arrest as vagabonds. Leicester's men are recorded as having asked their patron for a licence 'to certifye that we are your household Servaunts when we shall have occasion to travayle amongst our friends as we do usuallye once a yere.'

These three factors – new popular play formats that avoided the religious prohibition, new dedicated buildings to perform in and the formation of structured, sponsored companies capable of commissioning and developing new work – all of these were important springboards to the explosion of theatrical activity. But none would have been sufficient had not scripts been written and great writers been available.

o o o

Suddenly there seemed to be an abundance of them. Men like Shakespeare, Marlowe, Jonson, Kyd, Fletcher, Greene, Beaumont, Dekker, Webster, Middleton et al. What is noteworthy is that they came from amazingly diverse backgrounds. Some aristocratic but many decidedly from more working-class origins. Some metropolitan and some rural. Some had been actors; others had not. The authors of 'Gorboduc' aside, playwriting was not the preserve of the well-born. The theatrical fever gripped people from all walks of life, who felt that they had an ability with words, and could respond to the hunger for narratives told onstage. It is testament to the accessibility and the flexibility of the English language, and the new educational system that so many writers from humble backgrounds were able to be proficient. The number of new plays that each company needed each year to keep going was substantial, given the shortness of the runs. The number of scripts that an author wrote would be in the several hundred in total. A number unthinkable to playwrights today. The prodigious nature of the output kept the plays performed constantly turning over, and a broad-based popular audience regularly coming back for the latest offering.

One of the most popular plays of the Jacobean period was 'A Game of Chess' by Thomas Middleton. This was a comedy satire, making fun of the Spanish, the Catholics and King James. Each of these satirical targets guaranteed popularity; the combination of all three was unbeatable. The play ran for a record nine successive days at the Globe Theatre, and probably would have run longer, but the King intervened and had it removed. The record nature of nine successive performances gives a clear indication of the speed with which plays were rotated – many only receiving one or two performances in a single season. Traditionally the writer would only receive a share of the take on his play reaching a third performance. The pressure was on to create something so engaging to the audience that a third performance would be achieved

This rapid rotation was an extraordinary feat of organisation that would make modern repertory companies blanch.

o o o

Strong royal patronage was important to the profile of the theatrical arts. While the City elders may have distrusted the art form, the country had two monarchs in succession who were genuinely interested. Using Brett Dolman's analysis in 'Drama and Debate at the Court of King James', Elizabeth attended six court performances of plays per annum on average over a forty-five year reign. James was more frequent: nineteen per annum on average over a twenty-two year reign. A total of 421 plays were performed for him during his time on the throne, not counting masques and other miscellaneous extravaganzas. To increase the royal linkage, all of the main acting companies were brought under direct patronage of the King or his immediate family. So the 'Lord Chamberlain's Men' became the 'King's Men'. 'The Admiral's Men' became 'Prince Henry's Men'. The Queen had two companies. And Prince Charles had his own company.

Royal patronage did not mean that companies slavishly toed the line. Despite their name, the King's Men were the first to offend King James at the start of his reign, with two plays. One, performed in 1603, was 'Sejanus' by Jonson, a politically themed play about corruption in the Roman Empire, and the other was a drama about the Gowrie Conspiracy, in which Jonson performed. He was called before the Privy Council, was accused of both Poperie and treason by the powerful Earl of Northampton, and was imprisoned. Being a member of the King's Men did nothing to spare him his punishment.

This ability of the performing companies to fly in the face of royal niceties was commented on by the French Ambassador in 1604: 'Consider for pity's sake what must be the state and condition of a Prince, whom the preachers publicly from the pulpit assail, whom the comedians of the metropolis bring upon the stage, whose wife attends these representations in order to enjoy the laugh against her husband.'

As always with the English, a robust sense of humour is at work.

o o o

A profession that at the start of the 16th century had been itinerant and ephemeral, by the 17th century had become an established and well-organised way of life, capable of rotating plays on an almost daily basis, and responding to the regular plague-driven closures.

By the 1630s, there were six major permanent playhouses in London, with as many established performing companies, linked to these venues. The members of their companies numbered between twenty and thirty and remained remarkably constant. There is no better example than the premier company, the King's Men. Come the 1630s, their operations were based at the Blackfriars Theatre in winter, and at the Globe in summer. Once their resident playwright Shakespeare retired, Fletcher took over, who was then succeeded by Massinger and Davenant – all talented writers. The same was true for their onstage talent. Burbage succeeded Burbage, both legends in their day, to be followed by one of the best tragic actors Joseph Taylor, and in turn followed by Stephen Hammerton.

In 1641, an order was passed that protected plays that had not yet been published against unauthorised copying. The King's Men listed a total of sixty-one unpublished plays. When combined with all those that had been published, the total repertory is impressive, and steps were being taken to establish copyright laws. A cultural industry had emerged.

o o o

The final and probably most important factor was the audience. By 1600, there were around 200,000 people in London. A city to rival Paris in scale. By contrast, Amsterdam had a population of only 60,000 and Berlin around 10,000. The economic powerhouse that was Venice peaked in the 1570s at about 170,000, and by 1600 had already waned to about 140,000. This concentration of population in London, part prompted by the upheaval of the Reformation and the dissolution of the monasteries, provided a massive advantage to theatre.

London not only had scale, but it also had appetite for what was on offer. In Jacobean London, based on the known theatre capacities and the performance schedules, it is estimated that on average the equivalent of about a third of the entire population must have come to the theatre every month. This was truly a mass medium. As a consequence, it has shaped our cultural landscape and has affected the projection of the English language around the world. Why did this happen at this time and in this place?

We have heard about the theatre builders, we have heard about the writers, we have heard of the royal interest. But above all these was the impact of the religious change. But for the Reformation, none of this would have happened. In my opinion. This is the irony. Pre-1540 theatre had to be religious. Post-1560, theatre had to be secular. But it was religion that made it great from that date onwards.

This impact I believe was twofold. Firstly, in terms of the overall appetite for performance, in a world where religion was no longer able to satisfy that appetite. Secondly, in the way that theatre could convey stories and symbols of a religious nature, but covertly navigating the strict prohibitions – especially of anything of a Catholic nature.

Pre-Reformation, performance was delivered to people by way of the mass and all its rituals, and by the extension of the mass, through the format of overtly religious plays. All of that was taken away. Although the fundamental need must have still existed. There was a continuing requirement for community, for narrative, for explanation, for the comfort of ritual. And a need for it to be told more dramatically, than the reading of texts. The roots of modern English drama were formed from this need; it is no coincidence that they started to flourish at precisely the time that the Church and religion no longer could satisfy it.

But more than that, there is a strong theory that some of the popularity of the plays of this period was due to the subtle religious coding inserted within them. This was designed to appeal to an audience which contained secret adherents to the old religion. It would help explain the massive demand for them.

James Shapiro, in '1606', relates a tale from that year, when a Warwickshire recusant called George Badger was caught transporting a cache of Catholic trappings from one hiding place to another. A twenty-four strong jury in Stratford-on-Avon were charged with inspecting these wares so as to value them before they were handed over to the King. He imagines them staring at this trove of vestments, chalices, crosses, baubles and relics in amazed wonder. They were witnessing the costumes and props from a bygone time.

Plays and performance undoubtedly had a role in the goings-on of the wider world, greater than today. In February 1601, supporters of the Earl of Essex requested and paid handsomely for the Lord Chamberlain's Men to perform 'Richard II', on the eve of their uprising against Elizabeth. The portrayal of the story of the abdication of an unsuitable monarch, was presumably destined to rouse support for Essex's rebellion. To hammer home the significance, a further performance of the same play was requested at Whitehall, by the Queen herself, for the day before Essex's execution for treason. The perfect riposte.

The relationship between the playwrights and Catholicism is a complex one because of the serious dangers at the time, of being identified as a practitioner of the old faith. However, it is known that Jonson converted to Catholicism for a twelve-year period. Shakespeare's own relationship with the old religion is a much-debated one. His father and his daughter were both at different times identified as having made Catholic lapses. He is known to have been brought up in an area of England with strong residual Catholic leanings – not least by the Gunpowder plotters, many of whom hailed from the Warwickshire area. Shakespeare himself was too much a master of personal privacy ever to identify himself. It would have been too dangerous. A hotly contested body of work has grown up purporting to identify the secret themes within his plays, that would appeal to those in the audience hankering after the old ways. Peter Milward and Clare Asquith are two historians who have particularly espoused these analyses. Although their theories are frequently discounted by other historians who dismiss them as speculative, since we have not the slightest direct confirmation by Shakespeare himself, the comprehensive reinterpretation of his work through a Catholic lens is impressive to say the least. I list their works in the bibliography, and when you read them, you will discover a suggested network of codes. Any reference to a tempest is said to be synonymous with the cataclysmic storm of the Reformation itself. Characters that are tall and fair such as Helena in 'A Midsummer's Night Dream' are deemed to be recognisably Catholic, while those that are shorter and dark, such as Hermia are symbolically Protestant. Thus Hermia says about Helena:

'…her tall personage, her height, forsooth, she hath prevail'd with him, and are you grown so high in his esteem: because I am so dwarfish and so low? How low am I, thou painted maypole?' The maypole being the symbol of old, more traditional beliefs. Helena jabs back about Hermia: 'She was a vixen when she went to school; and though she be but little, she is fierce.'

Then when the whole narrative of 'Romeo and Juliet', with its warring sides, its errant monk and its tragic outcomes, is subjected to this analysis, a web of signals emerge to signify the true values of Catholicism. In 'Hamlet', the chaos in Elsinore becomes a huge metaphor for the desolation wrought on England by the change in religion. The arrival of the young Fortinbras at the end to bring hope and order to the people of Denmark is synonymous with the hoped-for invasion by Philip III of Spain, the son of Philip II, the former Queen Mary's husband and instigator of the Spanish Armada. In 'Comedy of Errors', the arrival in Ephesus of the merchant Aegeon of Syracuse searching for his lost wife and family, prompts his arrest and sentence to death for no reason other than being a stranger in time of conflict. This reflects the death sentences being then meted out to men solely for being adherents to their old religion in what has become a strange land. His final reprieve in the closing scene is achieved by the Abbess revealing herself to be his lost wife, and securing his pardon as a result. Some of these portrayals of supposedly happy Catholic endings overcoming the misery of an imposed alien religion are fairly straightforward, if believed. Play after play after play can be reinterpreted through this doctrinal prism.

What becomes even more complex are instances where Shakespeare is overtly writing to please a Protestant monarch, as for example, in 'Macbeth'. This was a play finished shortly after the traumatic events of the Gunpowder Plot. On the surface, 'Macbeth' communicates vividly the dire consequences of regicide and rebellion against the ruling order. This was something that King James wanted to hear after he and his family might have been brutally assassinated. However the particular analysis of this play goes deeper and can find themes implying that those characters seemingly portrayed as representing the new religion, in fact are secretly coded as the old religion, and vice-versa. In this inversion, Macbeth is no longer the Catholic tyrant set upon the unlawful destruction of the Protestant royal family, but is in fact the Protestant instigator of misrule seeking to disrupt the established order of the Catholic faith. It is in this reading, that you can find sense in the much-debated Porter scene, which is often removed as out of keeping with the rest of the play. When the audience heard the Porter identifying the King's man, Macduff, as an equivocator (a notorious Catholic trait of the day), they would understand what the coding was, and who was on whose side. If you accept that there is covert counter plot lying beneath the overt plot, then the scene starts to have relevance.

While all of this is remarkably detailed, inevitably tortuous and has of course no confirmation from the author himself, it does reflect a way in which a Catholic minded audience, hankering after the old days, might have found comforting signs of reassurance through his plays, that all will be well in the end. It would certainly help explain the popularity of the theatre at the time, and the connection Shakespeare had with his audience.

Once again, it reinforces that the Reformation was the defining event.

o o o

If you are willing to embrace this theory, it is still a precarious balance. Drama was never trusted by the Puritan factions; they closed down theatres totally in 1642. Those countries that shed Catholicism, and moved to more extreme Protestant forms, such as stronger versions of Calvinism, made sure that not only theatre was stamped out from our ecclesiastical settings, but also firmly stamped out in the secular world. Any form of theatre was too threatening, and a reminder of sin and idolatry.

Contrast this with Paris. It had dedicated theatres opening at a similar time to London. It had a number of world-class playwrights such as Racine and Molière, but never the English profusion. It had royal interest from Louis XIV. But throughout, theatre was much more the plaything of the court and the aristocracy, than the people at large. When the court moved out of Paris to Versailles, at the end of the 17th century, performance largely moved out there as well. General theatre in Paris waned. Although there were intermittent periods of revival, there seemed not to be the same fundamental need for performance as in London.

England was relatively unique in moving away from Catholic worship, but steering to a middle ground, avoiding the more dogmatic versions of reform. Protestant worship was often brutally enforced, but many a blind eye was turned, and many of even noble birth and significant influence continued to practise in secret. These were the ideal conditions for theatre to take root in the public sphere, and to flourish. In modern parlance, this was the 'Goldilocks Principle'. Demand in England was driven by a need for spectacle and ritual in a post-Catholic world. It was driven by the search for community and shared experience. It was driven by an appetite for coded messages of hope concerning the old religion. It was driven by the huge growth of London to a population of over 200,000 – a massive market for entertainment. It was driven by the increasing wealth of the city based on the growing maritime and mercantile reach of London. However it was not stamped out other than for the brief period of the Cromwellian Republic.

∘ ∘ ∘

I finish with a modest, often unnoticed statue that stands in a ruined churchyard, not far from where Shakespeare lived for many years in Silver Street. The church was St Mary Aldermanbury at the back of Guildhall; it was the parish church of both Heminges and Condell, the two lifelong actor partners of Shakespeare. The church is where many of their children were baptised, and they themselves were buried. The church was originally burnt down in the Great Fire, rebuilt by Wren, only to be flattened by the Blitz. The remains were shipped and rebuilt, oddly, in Fulton, Missouri, where it stands today. The statue is a tribute to the act of friendship that Heminges and Condell performed to their friend, and the legacy that they left. In his will, Shakespeare left them money to buy mourning rings (probably more valuable than the second-best bed he left his wife). In return, they collected up all the unpublished play scripts and what they considered to be the best versions of those that had been published. They ordered them as Tragedies, Comedies and Histories, and ensured that the world today knows all the thirty-six plays which constitute Shakespeare's First Folio, of which only eighteen had been previously printed.

Underneath a fine bust of Shakespeare, on the column is written, quite fittingly:

'To the Memory of
John Heminge
And
Henry Condell
Fellow Actors and Personal Friends of Shakespeare
They lived many years in this parish and are buried here
To their disinterested affection
The World owes all that it calls Shakespeare
They alone collected his dramatic writings
Regardless of pecuniary loss
And without the hope of any profit
Gave them to the world
They thus merited the gratitude of mankind.'

But for the First Folio, half of the Shakespeare plays we know today, may have been lost, but also other previously printed plays might have been preserved in earlier versions. Below for example is the opening of the famous soliloquy from 'Hamlet' as it appeared in the very first Quarto version, registered in 1602 and published in 1603, before it was revised in the subsequent second Quarto, which then became the basis of the authoritative First Folio version:

> *'To be or not to be; aye there's the point*
> *To die, to sleep – is that all? Ay all.*
> *No, to sleep, to drem – ay marry, there it goes.*
> *For in that dream of death, when we awake,*
> *And borne before an everlasting judge,*
> *From whence no passenger ever returned,*
> *The undiscovered country, at whose sight,*
> *The happy smile and the accursed damned.'*

Shakespeare and the plays of the First Folio were to form a cornerstone of theatrical development in England, and a basis of promotion of the English language globally.

CHAPTER FIFTEEN

AN EXTRAORDINARY CONJUNCTION IN TIME AND SPACE

'We have kept such a revel... They fled me so from argument to argument, without ever answering me directly...that if any of their disciples had answered thaime in that sort, they would have fetched him up in place of a reply, and so should the rod have plied upon the poor boyes buttocks'
– King James's reportage in a letter to a friend on the intellectual high jinks, he presided over at the Hampton Court Conference

King James gained the English Crown on the death in March 1603 of his cousin Elizabeth I. Despite the deadly tussle between the former Queen and his mother, Mary Queen of Scots, James had for several years been the heir presumptive. Of direct descent from Henry VII's daughter Margaret Tudor, and most importantly brought up in the Protestant faith, thirty-six years old, with long experience of the Scottish throne, he came with a ready-made family, a Protestant wife, Anne of Denmark, and three children including two sons. He was a noted scholar, capable on sight of turning any passage of the Bible from Latin to French, and then from French into English. He had penned several books, including one on the principles of monarchy, as well as one on witchcraft and demonology. In so many ways he was the perfect antidote to his ageing, childless and increasingly joyless predecessor. He travelled south from Edinburgh, in steady stages, and was met with enthusiastic acclaim.

Along that journey, he stopped and met with leading members of the English aristocracy; he garlanded all that he met with gifts and titles, being certain to ingratiate himself with his new court. In total during his reign, he made fifty-six new Baronies, nineteen Viscountcies, thirty-two Earldoms and three Dukedoms: a stark contrast to the more parsimonious approach of his predecessor. He wanted to be known as a peaceful and generous King – a 'Rex Pacificus'. While dispensing such favours he found it hard not to notice the grandeur of the sumptuous residences that his new aristocratic subjects equipped themselves with. The contrast between the frugal spirit of the Scottish court and the lavishness he found in England caught his attention.

He commented that he was swapping 'a stony couch for a deep feather bed'. All his previous written works were quickly put back into print, and a host of poetic tributes were rushed out for broad distribution.

He had made his way south, arriving in London by early May. His coronation took place in July, a lesser affair than planned due to an outbreak of one of the worst plagues – deaths in London alone were set to reach 30,000. The full ceremonial parade was postponed to the following year. In the autumn of 1603, to avoid London, he went to Oxford. From there he went to Wilton in the first week of December, to stay as the guest of the dowager Countess of Pembroke.

To mark his commitment to the theatrical arts, James chose to take over the patronage of the finest body of players in the country, renaming them the 'King's Men'. They were made 'Grooms of the Chamber', a formal part of the Royal Household. The first time that a group of actors had been so honoured.

The King's Men were each issued four and a half yards of red cloth for the tailoring of their royal liveries, for the coronation procession. Burbage, Shakespeare, Heminges, Condell, Armin et al, paraded the streets of London as part of the royal retinue. The number of plays increased, as did the rate of pay. Under Elizabeth's penny-pinching supervision, the rate per performance at court was ten pounds. James doubled the rate to twenty pounds. The Royal sponsorship meant that on their tours, they could perform anywhere they chose; they no longer suffered the obstructions of local authorities.

Before becoming the King's company their performances at Court averaged about three a year. In the ten years after, their known performances at court averaged about thirteen a year. This was greater than those of all other London companies combined. They had become the foremost playmaking company in England.

Due to the plague, the company spent much of 1603 performing around the regions. At the Countess's invitation they arrived in Wilton on 2 December to deliver their first performance for their new patron. Based on the Countess's letters, the play performed at Wilton was probably a comedy about a group of exiles waiting for a return to court. 'As You Like It' was written a few years prior. It was an apposite choice; its theme would have chimed with its audience, all waiting themselves to return to London, and to court.

The King's original plan had been to return to London for Christmas, but the plague did not abate, and he diverted to the rural safety of Hampton Court Palace. The new King spent his first Christmas here. The initial performance by his new company must have impressed, as the play's title had promised; he ordered them to join him at Hampton Court Palace for his further entertainment. They presented a cycle of their works during the Christmas season.

The Secretary of State, Robert Cecil, wrote to Lord Shrewsbury, with the exhausted air of the consummate civil servant: 'We are now to feast seven ambassadors: Spain, France, Poland, Florence and Savoy, besides masques and much more, during which time, I would with all my heart I were with that noble Lady of yours, by her turf fire.'

In an unbroken cycle, four plays were presented before the King and the Queen and two plays were presented before the dashing Prince Henry, James's eldest son and great hope for the future. The company were to return in February to present a seventh. For a single group to present such a body of work, written by a single author, to this new visionary King, confirmed the acting company, and Shakespeare himself, as the leading dramatic lights of the day. They had truly arrived. Hampton Court Palace is the only surviving building in which Shakespeare and his company is known to have performed a whole body of his work. Other extant locations were venues for only a single play at most.

We know the specific number of plays presented by the contemporaneous references in the accounts of a payment made of fifty-three pounds for the body of six plays over Christmas. The accountants, in their way of things, only recorded the completion of the performance and the sum paid. They thought it unimportant to record the names of the plays themselves. We know that one was 'A Midsummer's Night Dream'. A member of court, Dudley Carleton, in attendance, wrote to a friend in January, telling how on almost every night during holy week, a new play had been presented in the Great Hall, and that on 'New Year's night we had a play of Robin Goodfellow'. So we know the title of one, and the location. The Great Hall still stands, with its Abraham tapestries in place, looking broadly identical to when Shakespeare himself performed there.

The identity of the other five are uncertain, but the recently completed 'Hamlet' was quite possibly among them, as it was especially apposite to King James. The performance of plays at court, were in themselves dramas within dramas. The King and the royal family sat prominently in the centre of the Hall, upon a raised dais, visible to the rest of the audience arranged in a U-shape of seats and benches around the rest of the Hall. The selection of those sitting with the King and Queen each evening provided important clues as to the direction of royal favour. The royal party was then constantly scrutinised by the audience to monitor their reactions. What did they like?

What did they not like? When were they engaged? When were they bored? Who did they talk to? As many eyes were trained on the dais, as on the stage.

'Hamlet', which featured a play within a play within a play, lends itself to this environment and this audience. Its location of Elsinore in Denmark was familiar to the King, but even more to the Queen, whose home it had been. Hamlet believes that his father has been murdered by his uncle, with the connivance of his mother, in order to win her hand and the crown. The play's players are engaged by Hamlet to enact the whole scenario in front of the protagonists, to seek to register their reaction, and establish their guilt.

What a tale to enact in front of the new King! All in the audience knew the resonance. James's own father Henry Stewart, Lord Darnley died in similarly mysterious circumstances. He and his valet were found dead in the night lying in the orchard of Kirk O'Field in Edinburgh, after a gunpowder explosion in the building where he had been staying. No satisfactory explanation for his death was ever proven, but the strong suspicion was that the Earl of Bothwell had arranged, with Mary's consent, for him to be killed. Mary herself was attending the wedding celebrations of one of her trusted servants, while the killing occurred. Bothwell was tried but acquitted; Mary would marry him.

It would have been hard for James, as he watched this play within a play in turn playing out parts of his own family history, not to have imagined himself as Hamlet. The eyes of the audience that night must have been closely watching the King.

James must have delighted in Shakespeare's storytelling and the subtle way he provided commentary on current-day events, and massaged his ego. James was a lover of the use of words, and the power of speech in all its forms. James would not have kept coming back to plays, and to Shakespeare's plays, if he had not applauded their quality. The following Christmas alone, James had performed for him 'Othello', 'The Merry Wives of Windsor', 'Measure for Measure', 'The Comedy of Errors', 'Love's Labour's Lost' and 'Henry V'. James's patronage of and enjoyment of Shakespeare propelled him to the unassailable position of England's most revered dramatist. A role he has not since relinquished.

Long before the performance of Macbeth, and but a few days after the end of the 1603 Christmas season of plays, Hampton Court Palace bore witness to another significant event. On 14 January, James convened the Hampton Court Conference. The aim was to resolve the thorniest issue of his early reign. He had to determine the direction of religion of his new monarchy, and in particular which version of the scriptures should be used in the Anglican

Amorous or Loving?

church. Representatives of the main Protestant factions were assembled to thrash this issue to a conclusion. The other aim was for James, a serious scholar of the Bible, to be able to show off his knowledge, and his mastery of the various translations. Indeed, lengthy speeches on the most arcane points were delivered at the three-day conference in which James fully engaged.

It was a febrile time. His succession had promised the possibility of a range of outcomes. The avowed religion of his mother raised the hopes of the Catholic faction, who prayed for a return to the old faith. At the other end of the spectrum, the Puritanical wing of the evangelists had strong expectations that James would bring south aspects of the Scottish Presbyterian church to which he had been accustomed. They hoped that a purer form of Protestant worship would be introduced, which removed bishops, priestly robes and other trappings. By contrast the established Anglican Church hoped for the subtly balanced status quo, that Elizabeth had created, to be preserved.

James himself had his own priorities. He was insistent that whatever the outcome, the divine right of kings to rule must be advanced as strongly as possible. He had previously written, 'God gives not Kings the style of Gods in vain, for on his throne his sceptre do they sway and as their subjects ought them to obey, so Kings should fear and serve their God again.'

At the conference, the Puritanical faction numbered four, led by John Reynolds, President of Corpus Christi, Oxford. All of them chosen for their relative moderation. The Anglican Church faction significantly outnumbered them and was led by Richard Bancroft, the Bishop of London, soon to become Archbishop of Canterbury, and Lancelot Andrewes, the Dean of Westminster, and subsequently Bishop of Winchester. Lancelot Andrewes was a noted deliverer of massively authoritative and thundering sermons, beautifully written and much appreciated by James. The King probably spent as long, if not longer, listening to the sermons of his star preacher Lancelot Andrewes and his most able fellow practitioners, as he did attending to Shakespeare's plays. It was part of James's overall love of English and the spoken word.

Also in attendance were divinity scholars and religious men of wisdom. Even the Anglican church officials represented a wide range of views themselves. It was a cacophony of different opinions. And everyone was asked their views. The agenda for the conference had three main topics: the use of the Book of Common Prayer, excommunication in the ecclesiastical courts, and the provision of fit and able ministers for Ireland. The Bible and a possible new translation did not feature on the agenda.

James opened with an hour-long address to the conference, which was as detailed, as it was learned, and as it was interminable. James was keen to bludgeon dissenters with the strength of his argument and was quick to show his dissatisfaction with that of the Puritans, granting them little support.

All the Puritan representatives were invited to speak. Reynolds suggested that bishops should govern jointly with their brethren in a presbytery of pastors and ministers. He was assuming that this Presbyterian concept would appeal to James, but in fact it did the reverse. James had heard similar arguments expressed in Scotland, often in inflammatory terms, and had a fundamental concern that Puritans were undermining the King's role as the Supreme Head of the Church. By contrast the Anglican representatives had persuaded him that the retention of the existing Church structures and ritual would preserve his divine right to rule. This was a cunning argument to run; James himself pronounced at the conference, 'It is my aphorism, No Bishop, No King.' Argument by argument, James out-manoeuvred the Puritans. They quibbled for example at certain wordings in the Prayer Book, such as the marriage vow by the husband to his wife: 'with my body, I thee worship', on the basis that God should be the only recipient of a man's worship. James proceeded to attack the argument, finishing with the challenge to Reynolds, goading him for his celibate status: 'If you had a good wife yourself, you would think all the honour and worship you could do her were well bestowed.'

Despite his scathing private reportage of the weakness of the Puritans' arguments, James was always at heart the master diplomat. There was a danger that his dismissal of every argument of the Puritans would be counterproductive, widening the rifts between the factions, and presenting the monarch as biased. He was keen to liken himself to Solomon, in his love of peace and wisdom. Henry IV of France, on hearing this, wittily retorted that James indeed was like Solomon in being truly the 'son of David' – a sly dig at his mother's alleged infidelity with her secretary, David Rizzio, around the time of James's conception.

The conference then came to review in passing what version of the scriptures be authorised as the official text for the Anglican Church, whether it should continue to be the official Bishops' Bible or an alternative version. Despite not being on the agenda, Reynolds proposed that an alternative be considered and be officially authorised, in the hope that the Geneva Bible, which was closest to Puritan thinking with its expansive marginalia, and at the time the most popular, would win the day. Bancroft immediately objected to the proposition in strong terms. This gave James the opportunity that he needed, to disagree strongly with the Anglican faction and to present a more even hand. His knowledge of the various biblical texts was sufficiently detailed that he was able to turn to each sequentially – Tyndale's, Matthew's, Coverdale's, the Bishops', and the Geneva. He took issue with elements of each. Reynolds probably expected that while the Geneva would not be universally adopted, he hoped that it would be allowed, and would give his ministers scope to use their preferred translation.

James however took the proposition further, turning the tables on everybody in the room. He announced that a new translation would now be commissioned. He commanded that groups of scholars and translators be formed in Oxford, Cambridge and Westminster to consider different sections of the Bible, and that a joint group be formed to review and agree the finalised version. The specific decree was that 'A translation be made of the whole Bible, as consonant as can be to the original Hebrew and Greek; and this to be set out and printed, without any marginal notes, and only to be used…in time of divine service.'

Six companies of translators were then employed, applying themselves to different sections of the Bible. Around fifty learned scholars were kept busy for seven years agonising over the original texts.

Bancroft initially had been antithetical to the whole proposal, but learnt to embrace it. He spotted the opportunity to lead the process, to pack the groups with sympathetic voices, and emerge with a text close to the Bishops' Bible, without it being called such.

After an exhausting process, the commission finalised and published in 1611, what became known as the King James Bible. The frontispiece dedicates the work boldly to 'James, by the grace of God.' Describing him as 'King of Great Britain, France, and Ireland.' James was keen to establish the union of the nations and not just the crowns. James was the first to promote the concept of Great Britain. This continues a journey that has taken us from Alfred, the first king of all the Saxons, to Athelstan the first King of all the English, to James, the first self-proclaimed King of Great Britain – the great 'land of the tattooed people.'

The preface to the new Bible made the purpose clear:

> *'Among all our joys, there was no one more filled our hearts, than the blessed continuance of the preaching of God's sacred Word among us; which is that inestimable treasure, which excelleth all the riches of the earth; because the fruit thereof extendeth itself, not only to the time spent in this transitory world, but directeth and disposeth men unto that eternal happiness which is above in heaven.'*

This is a resounding reiteration of the faith in the power of the Word of the scriptures. And when in 1611, the first readers opened up their copies of the new translation, and started to read, they found a wonderful and beautiful text that was almost entirely that of William Tyndale from eighty years previous. Even down to the somewhat archaic use of the terms 'ye' and 'thou'. The proximity of the final text to Tyndale's confirms that James, Andrewes and Bancroft had a clear idea of their desired end point – even if it took seven years to wrestle to a conclusion.

It is sometimes assumed that the King James version, with its royal authorisation, became an instant success. In fact the reverse happened. It had many critics. Some of the early printings were poor, and prone to errors. A 1631 edition exhorted its readers 'thou shalt commit adultery', having left out the 'not', causing perturbation among Protestant adherents. Because the printer, Robert Baker, had paid the King handsomely for the exclusive rights, the price for each copy was high. During the first half of the 17th century, the Geneva Bible, with its full and helpful marginalia, remained the most popular – especially as far as the laity were concerned. Archbishop Laud was so concerned by the lack of acceptance for the King James version, that printing of the Geneva version was banned in England. This had little effect, as excellent versions were printed on the continent and shipped over. Laud in desperation declared that it was unpatriotic to buy the Geneva Bible, as it lined the pockets of foreign printers. But the start of the Civil War saw the Puritans back in the ascendancy, and the Geneva version once again was preferred. Cromwell mooted a further possible translation based on the Geneva version, but it never progressed. It then took a subsequent generation and the Restoration, for the King James version to achieve acceptance.

The primary purpose of this chapter is to marvel at how the destiny of Shakespeare and the destiny of Tyndale came together at the same time, at the same place. As you stand in the Great Hall today, beneath its great hammer beams, and under its massive tapestries, it is humbling to conjure what the space between those four walls has done for the projection of English around the world. James as King gets a lukewarm assessment these days; this is as a result of his various superstitions, his pursuit of witches and his reputation for indulgence and excess – 'a nursery of lust' as one contemporary writer called it. We ignore James's huge influence as a man of peace, a man of culture and a lover of words, and his importance to these two mould-breaking bodies of works. This is what Samuel Johnson in his Dictionary referred to as 'the golden age of our language.'

CHAPTER SIXTEEN

'GRAND, ECHOING, ELOQUENT WORDS'

'Jocund day stands tiptoe on the misty mountain tops.'
— William Shakespeare

In speaking of Shakespeare and Tyndale, one can embrace their similarities but also their differences; they play separate but complementary roles in the promulgation of the language.

The complete works of Shakespeare is composed of 884,421 words. The King James Bible has approximately the same number. It is a remarkable coincidence. The difference is then their range of separate words. Shakespeare uses 31,534 different words. The King James Bible uses approximately 10,000.

In relation to language, they act differently. Shakespeare was pointedly florid, varied and inventive in his word selection. The English language, enriched as it was by Latin, French, Old English, Norse provided him with a vast palate from which he painted ornate and powerful pictures with his words. Where a word did not exist, he invented it. It is estimated that Shakespeare coined around 2,000 words in total. Great words such as 'bedroom' and 'barefaced'. He was especially fond of creating combination words like 'lack-lustre', 'dewdrops', 'footfall', 'baseless', 'cold-hearted', 'hunchbacked' and 'leapfrog'. Another specialty of his was the 'un-' prefix, as in 'unmitigated', 'unreal', 'undress' and in Lady Macbeth's case, 'unsex'. It is easy to see the poetic and metrical value of many of these inventions, designed as they were to keep the rhythm of his verse.

Shakespeare's contribution to our idioms is the stuff of legends, and requires whole books to do proper service to. I repeat a few because they are a joy to write. 'Fast and loose', 'Neither rhyme nor reason', 'Be all and end all', 'Bated breath', 'The world's mine oyster', 'Mine own flesh and blood', 'Cruel to be kind', 'A foregone conclusion', 'Truth will out', 'Pomp and circumstance', 'It was Greek to me' and 'Good riddance'. How often and how blindly we pay homage to Shakespeare's inventiveness in our everyday speech. His expressions by their pithiness, have provided titles to so many books and films: 'Brave New World' (Aldous Huxley), 'Brief Candles' (Aldous Huxley again), 'The Sound and the Fury' (William Faulkner), and 'The Dogs of War' (Frederick Forsyth).

His reputation for breadth of word and phrase is well deserved, but interestingly he was not the most prodigious of his day. Through the good offices of Heminges and Condell, we have his folio of plays, and he often wins by virtue of sheer quantum. Yet, scholarly analysis of his texts indicates that he was not the broadest-ranging in his vocabulary among his contemporaries. Academics have assessed his generation of playwrights and calculated the average number of words each of them has used for every 10,000 words of text. In this Webster is the most vari-worded. For every 10,000 words of text, he uses on average 1,827 different words. Second is Dekker with 1,772. Jonson used 1,727. Shakespeare's back in seventh place with only 1,664. And perhaps that is the point. Shakespeare was inventive and expressive, yet he was a popular writer who did not overload his audience with too much profusion.

He was deeply aware of the need to speak in English, pure English, to the English. In one of his earliest histories, 'Henry VI Part 1', he ridiculed French-derived words.

Sir William Lucy
'Herald conduct me to the Dauphin's tent
To know who hath obtained the glory of the day.'

Dauphin
'On what submissive message art thou sent?'

Sir William Lucy
'Submission Dauphin! 'Tis a mere French word;
We English warriors wot not what it means
I come to know what prisoners thou has ta'en
And to survey the bodies of the dead.'

It is not hard to imagine the mighty roar that Englishmen, jostling among the groundlings would give that.

He was very conscious of how language could engage, but also how it could put up barriers, with what he dubbed 'taffeta phrases'. As he writes in 'Love's Labour's Lost', as Berowne seeks to woo Rosalind:

'Taffeta phrases, silken terms precise,
Three pil'd hyperboles, spruce affectation
Figures pedantical – these summer-flies
Have blown me full of maggot ostentation.
I do foreswear them; and I here protest,

*By this white glove – how white the hand, God knows! –
Henceforth my wooing mind shall be express'd
In russet yeas and honest kersey noes
And to begin wench – so God help me, law! –
My love to thee is sound, sans crack or flaw.'*

Shakespeare paints pictures with words, to enrich great stories, and to make vivid human emotion. This is why of all writers who have ever existed he is the most read, the most performed, the most translated and rightly the most revered. The great Shakespearian scholar A.L. Rowse puts it powerfully, quoting initially from 'Othello':

> *'Speak of me as I am. Nothing extenuate, nor set down aught in malice... The use of such a word as 'extenuate' reminds us of Shakespeare's lordliness about language. He needed such a range of words to express his ranging imagination; but from the first he had loved grand, echoing, eloquent words.'*

We all have our favourite pieces of Shakespeare. Mine comes from 'Romeo and Juliet'. It was one of Shakespeare's earliest and would have likely been performed at The Theatre. It would have shown off the skills of the company to the full – Burbage as Romeo, Kempe as the Nurse's manservant Peter, and most importantly the young boys playing the female leads. It was initially published in Quarto format in 1597, and was promoted there as 'An excellent conceited tragedie of Romeo and Juliet. As it hath been often (with great applause) plaid publiquely.' I have no doubt it was a crowd-pleaser. It went on to be the inspiration for the greatest and most remarkable musical of modern times, 'West Side Story', which I have always enjoyed producing. Of particular resonance for me was the film in 1968 that Franco Zeffirelli directed, brilliantly then and much more controversially now. My father helped finance it; I remember it happening and often go back to the breathtakingly beautiful town of Pienza in the Tuscan hills, where much of it was filmed. The words still echo around the unchanged streets. Or in the bedroom, as they must surely part.

Juliet
*'Wilt thou be gone? It is not yet near day:
It was the nightingale, and not the lark,
That pierc'd the fearful hollow of thine ear;
Nightly she sings on yond pomegranate tree.
Believe me, love, it was the nightingale.'*

Amorous or Loving?

17. Miniature of Geoffrey Chaucer clutching and pointing at the text of Thomas Hocleve's poem 'De Regimine Principum'. See Chapter Eleven. *Source : British Library.*

18. Manuscript copy of the 'Wycliffe Bible' created 1375-1425. This page is from 'Proverbs to Maccabees'. See Chapter Twelve. *Source : British Library.*

19. The Great Bible published in 1540, with a prologue by Thomas Cranmer, Archbishop of Canterbury. See Chapter Twelve. *Source : British Library.*

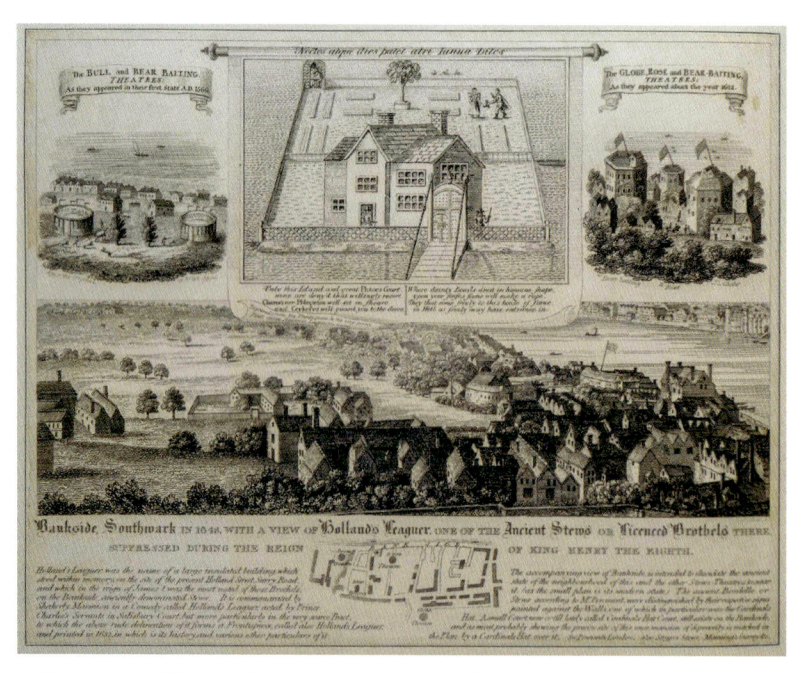

20. A View of 'Bankside Southwark in 1648' showing the 'The Bull and Bear Baiting Theatres as they appeared in 1560', and 'The Globe, Rose and Bear Baiting Theatres as they appeared in the years 1612'. See Chapter Fourteen.
Source : British Library.

Amorous or Loving?

21. The memorial celebrating the publication of Shakespeare's First Folio, edited by Henry Condell and John Heminges. The memorial stands in the gardens of the now ruined church of St Mary Aldermanbury, where Condell and Heminges worshipped all their lives. See Chapter Fourteen. *Source : Shutterstock.*

22. The Great Hall at Hampton Court Palace, constructed in the reign of Henry VIII. A pivotal location for many events in our story. See Chapter Fifteen. *Source : Historic Royal Palaces.*

Amorous or Loving?

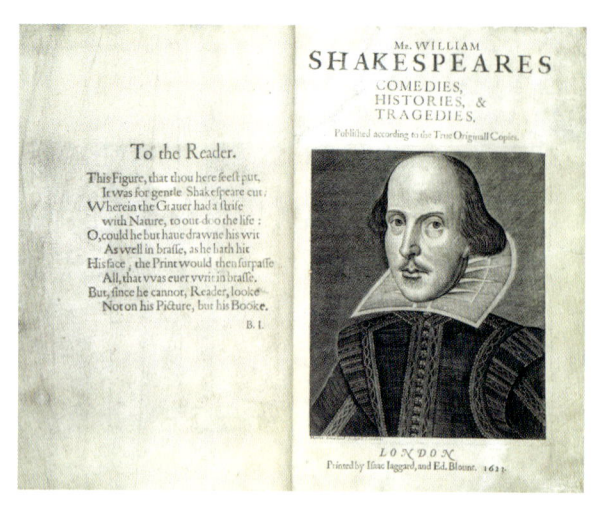

23. William Shakespeare's First Folio, edited by Henry Condell and John Heminges. Published in 1623. With a foreword entitled 'To the Reader' by fellow playwright and rival, Ben Jonson. See Chapter Fourteen.
Source : British Library.

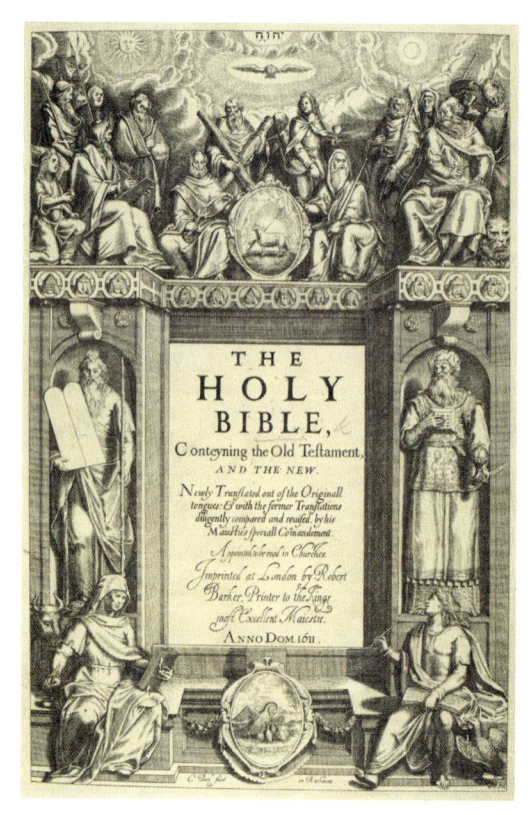

24. Frontispiece of the King James Bible published in 1611. See Chapter Fifteen. *Source : British Library.*

Amorous or Loving?

25. Portrait of Nell Gwyn (1651-1687). After Sir Peter Lely. See Chapter Eighteen. *Source : National Trust Images.*

26. The stage set of 'The Empress of Morocco', a 1673 tragedy by Elkanah Settle, originally staged by the Duke's Company at the Dorset Garden Theatre. See Chapter Eighteen. *Source : Alamy.*

Amorous or Loving?

27. The death portrait of John Donne, which appeared as the frontispiece to 'Death's Duel', the last of Donne's sermons, preached at Whitehall in 1631. See Chapter Nineteen. *Source : British Library.*

28. John Wesley on horseback in a painting by Richard Gilmore Douglas. See Chapter Nineteen. *Source : Epworth Old Rectory.*

Amorous or Loving?

29. Gillray cartoon in 1783, on the loss of the American colonies. Britain regrets while France gloats, Spain blames the French for the failure to take back Gibraltar and Holland looks on impassively. See Chapter Twenty.
Source : British Museum.

30. French allegorical illustration of the Treaty of Paris, signed 3 September 1783, by representatives of George III, and representatives of the United States of America. See Chapter Twenty. *Source : Alamy.*

31. William Petty, Lord Shelburne, Prime Minister 1782-1783, painting by Jean-Laurent Mosnier. See Chapter Twenty. *Source : Sotheby's.*

32. Dickens's Dream by R.W. Buss, 1875. See Chapter Twenty-One. *Source : Charles Dickens Museum.*

Romeo
'It was the lark, the herald of the morn,
No nightingale. Look, love, what envious streaks
Do lace the severing clouds in yonder east;
Night's candles are burnt out, and jocund day
Stands tiptoe on the misty mountain tops.
I must be gone and live, or stay and die.'

Juliet
'Yond light is not daylight; I know it, I:
It is some meteor that the sun exhales
To be to thee this night a torch-bearer,
And light thee on thy way to Mantua;
Therefore stay yet; thou need'st not to be gone.'

Romeo
'Let me be ta'en, let me be put to death;
I am content, so thou wilt have it so.'

Those who still doubt the true authorship of all the plays, ignore the regard that Shakespeare was held in by his own contemporaries. Heminges and Condell laboured hard to preserve his work. They had spent a good part of their lives working alongside him both professionally and as friends; they had no recorded cause to doubt his authorship. Were other hands involved? Definitely. It was a collaborative age. But that is as far as I would venture. I would rely on the words of Ben Jonson, who knew Shakespeare well, and sufficient a rival to give him no unearned credit. He wrote in the First Folio an introduction, positioned opposite the engraving of Shakespeare himself:

'This Figure, that thou here seest put,
It was for gentle Shakespeare cut;
Wherein the Graver had a strife
with Naure, to out-doo the life.
O, could he but have drawne his wit
As well in brasse, as he hath hit
His face; the Print would then surpasse
All, that was ever writ in brasse.
But, since he cannot, Reader, looke
Not on his Picture, but his Booke.'

B(en) J(onson)

o o o

It is estimated that 83 per cent of the New Testament in the King James Bible was Tyndale's and 76 per cent of the Old Testament. This was not just because the translators were entranced by Tyndale's version, it directly reflected the brief given them, and the way that they worked. Their task, defined by the Hampton Court Conference, was to take the Bishops' Bible Version, work back through the previous versions, remove the offending marginalia (a primary feature of the Geneva Bible), and correct errors and infelicities. As the final preface said, their purpose was 'to make a good one better, or out of many good ones, one principal good one'. Thus they worked on the Bishops' Bible as their text to correct, which in turn was based on the Matthew version, based on the Coverdale version, based in turn on Tyndale's. It was no surprise that Tyndale's writings came shining through the final draft. The preservation of the archaic forms, such as Ye, Thou, and -est, was determined by a wish to keep everything they could; their brief was to correct, not to modernise previous translations.

Almost all of the translators, working on the King James version, came from southern England. The Bible, like Chaucer's work, like Shakespeare's, like the Book of Common Prayer all reinforced one particular dialectic of English – that of London, Oxford, Cambridge and the southern counties. As George Puttenham wrote in 'The Art of English Poesie' in 1589, a highly influential work among writers of the day: an author must not use 'the terms of Northern men…nor in effect any speech used beyond the river of Trent… ye shall therefore take the usual speech of the court, and that of London, and the shires lying about London'. An early statement of the principles upon which Received Pronunciation (or 'RP') are based today.

We are the lucky beneficiaries. William Rosenau, the Hebrew expert, wrote: 'The King James Bible has been – it can be said without any fear of being charged with exaggeration – the most powerful factor in the history of the English literature'. Robert Lowth, the 18th century Professor of Poetry at Oxford, called it 'the noblest monument of English prose'.

The King James version was beautifully written. It was every bit as powerful as Shakespeare's plays, but its use of English was different. Its purpose was different. Although the same length as Shakespeare's complete works, its selection of words was narrower. Pointedly. The Bible text was to be spoken, it was to be memorised, and it was to be understood line by line by everyone. Its success was the power and the simplicity of the language. It was not afraid to repeat itself, because through repetition came impression. Its global success as it travelled the world was as much in the words it left out, as in the words it included. It was the master of the simple evocative phrase. Who can forget the shortest verse in the whole Bible: 'Jesus wept'.

Although the King James Bible appeared in print after most of Shakespeare's plays had been written, the language of the Bible reflected an earlier form of English. It provides good witness to how much the language had evolved in a relatively short period. David Crystal in 'The Stories of English' does a detailed word by word analysis, looking at where the Bible and Shakespeare used the old form of a word or a new form of a word. So for example, 'gat' and 'gotten' were the old forms of the newer form 'got'. The Bible used 'gat'/'gotten' 45 times while using 'got' only 7. Whereas Shakespeare used the former only 5 times, but the latter 115. The Bible used the older 'spake' 585 times but the newer 'spoke' not at all, while Shakespeare used 'spake' 48 times to 'spoke' 142. The Bible used 'goeth' 135 times but never used 'goes', while Shakespeare never used 'goeth' but used 'goes' 166 times. And so on. Consistently Shakespeare's language was more modern. The Bible translators had their brief and stuck to it. To the first readers of the Bible, it must have seemed already archaic. Possibly that was part of its timeless magic.

Little was initially made of Tyndale's contribution in the early centuries of the Bible's global success. Now too little attention is paid to the body of scholars who worked a full seven years on the edition that was printed. They went meticulously passage by passage comparing back to the original Greek and the original Hebrew. They were using exactly the same sources as Tyndale, and obviously knew his work well. They ended up mainly basing their final version on his. Much of the seven years was spent in gaining consensus across the various factions, but also in gently improving Tyndale's version. They put focus on the declamatory value and the poetic rhythms of the translations. They were deeply aware that most congregations would hear the words rather than read them. Lancelot Andrewes was too accomplished a preacher not to have a sharp ear for what would resonate when spoken. Time was spent by the teams endlessly reading their texts aloud to each other to spot aural infelicities, ensuring the final version was as euphonious as possible.

Shakespeare was most likely influenced by Tyndale's writing as a young man. On a weekly basis he would have heard Tyndale's words read out in Church. Equally I think Shakespeare and his peers will have influenced the editors of the King James Bible, as they sought to harness the power of spoken verse to the rhythm of their translations.

In terms of Shakespeare leaning on Tyndale, there are lots of examples. In 'Hamlet', Shakespeare writes: *'…There's a special providence in the fall of a sparrow. If it be now, 'tis not to come: if it be not to come, it will be now; if it be not now, yet it will come – the readiness is all.'* He borrows from

Tyndale in Matthew, Chapter 10: *'Are not two sparrows sold for a farthing? And none of them shall fall on the ground without your Father.'* And the King James Bible writes this line almost identically.

The traffic also went the other way, in terms of the influence of poetic patterns. For one of the most beautiful passages of the same Gospel, Tyndale did a superb piece of composition as follows:

> *'Beholde the lylies off the felde, how they growe. They labour not nether spyne. And yet for all that I saie unto you that even Solomon in all his royalte was not arayed lyke unto one of these.'*

But the King James Bible translators added a rhythm to the lines.

> *'Consider the lillies of the field, how they grow: they toil not, neither do they spin. And yet, I say unto you, That even Solomon in all his glory was not arrayed like one of these.'*

So similar, but you can detect how the editors must have been challenging each other to get the most perfect sounding phraseology. I am sure that they were mindful that any reference to Solomon would have the King's full attention. Finally to the comparison of the opening lines of Genesis.

Tyndale wrote:

> *'In the beginning God created heaven and earth. The earth was void and empty; and darkness was upon the deep and the spirit of God moved upon the water.'*

The King James Bible presented the same opening as:

> *'In the beginning God created the heaven and the earth. And the earth was without form, and void; and darkness was upon the face of the deep. And the Spirit of God moved upon the face of the waters.'*

The editors managed to adapt a work of exceptional prose into a text that had a subtle rhythm and metre to it, sounding perceptibly better when read. I like to think that the pattern of Shakespearian verse was in the editors' mouths, and steered their hands. It is in this form that the King James Bible swept the world, transported by missionaries, and preachers across many continents. While the spread of Christianity through these centuries was not free of considerable blemish, the actual word of the scriptures and the beautifully written message of kindness, love, forgiveness and charity, is something that has brought inspiration, solace and good guidance to every walk of life. For that we have to thank Tyndale and the editors of the King James Bible.

And when put alongside the complete set of plays of William Shakespeare, you then have the two greatest advertisements for the English language globally. While today, we can reflect on their worldwide impact and its massive uptake as a language, at the time of their writing, it must be remembered how marginal English a language was. Richard Mulcaster, in his 'Elementarie of 1582', opined at the time:

> *'Our English tung...is of small reatch, it stretcheth no further than this Iland of ours, naie not there ouer all.'*

Finally to emphasise the highly spoken nature of English, it is worth dwelling for a moment on a small curio. Shakespeare's name almost certainly was not Shakespeare. There are six remaining records of his signature, and his own spelling of his name varied, but at no point did he write 'Shakespeare'. The most likely name he had was 'Shakspear' or something sounding like it. It is posited that typographers found it hard to combine the florid curls of the 'k' alongside the elaborate 's' used in those days. For layout purposes, they may have decided to insert an 'e' between the 'k' and the 's', as the most benign vowel to use but changing forever the way we remember the name of our greatest dramatist.

To add further supporting evidence to this contention, his brother Edmund and his brother's son, William's nephew (also called Edmund), both died in the same year, 1607. The brother's burial record at St Mary Overie church records his name as 'Shakspeare', and the death register at Saint Giles Cripplegate records his nephew's name as 'Shackspeere', both reiterating the absent first 'e'.

It is yet one more enduring mystery about the man whose work we know so well, but whose life leaves us so often puzzled.

CHAPTER SEVENTEEN

AND THE LIGHTS WENT OUT

'I cannot but please myself to think how greedily we shall put down profaneness.'

– One of Cromwell's major generals

On 2 September 1642, eleven days after Charles I raised his standard in Nottingham, it was decreed that public sports and playgoing should be for the moment suspended. The wording implied there was scope for the decision to be revisited, but that was not to be. Not in Cromwell's days. The theatres remained as good as closed for eighteen years until 1660, long after the military emergency had passed.

The parliamentary cause was supported at the outset by the City leaders. The City support served as a reminder of how any successful political movement, usually required London to be in favour. In this case, it was underpinned by an effective military machine. Cromwell and Fairfax established a capable fighting force, in the New Model Army which they led with vision. Charles I was in effect replaced by Oliver Cromwell, who was repeatedly offered the Crown by his supporters, but chose the title of Lord Protector instead. This may have been an act of humility, or an expression of Republican fervour, but given his penchant for taking over so many of the trappings of royalty, it may have been more due to his aversion to the constitutional constraints on the monarchy, that did not apply to the new and undefined role of Lord Protector.

Cromwell readily embraced kingship. He was peculiarly fond of Hampton Court Palace, which he used as his out-of-town residence. When it came to his acclamation as Lord Protector, he chose the epitome of Stuart monarchy, the Banqueting House, as the place of general celebration. Other trappings were dispensed with more easily, such as the royal art collection (funds could be raised from that). What went most swiftly were the Crown Jewels. Apart from their secondary market value when broken up, they always held spiritual symbolic value of the monarch's divine right to rule. In the heated arguments about the role of the Church and the power of the monarch, the Crown and the regalia symbolised the direct connection to God, which they provided the King. That connection could not be interrupted by Church or politician.

Even to this day, this thinking subtly prevails. Filming of the Crown Jewels and especially the Coronation Crown, has to be carefully arranged, for fear of draining, in some mysterious way, their spiritual potency. Especially any filming that necessitates an overhead shot; this is usually not permitted. As in Stuart days, nothing can come between the monarch's Crown and the God above – not even a film camera.

Commonwealth parliaments came and went, and Cromwell was soon every bit as much at odds with them as Charles had been. The City aligned easily at first with the parliamentary cause, finding common ground in shared Puritanical principles, and tempted by the prospect of a more balanced mercantile environment than a capricious King would allow. The army was the power base for Cromwell's rule. Nineteen major generals were appointed to run various sections of England outside London. They commanded the local militia, were responsible for raising the decimation tax from known Royalists, and most significantly for supervising the moral regeneration of the country – punishing all manner of vice – as noted in the opening quote to this chapter.

The playhouses were closed and Christmas was so curtailed as to be almost cancelled.

The rule of the Major Generals ensured that swearing, inebriation and sexual behaviour were punished severely. Many pubs were closed. Animals used for baiting were killed – just to confirm that there was little concern for the animals being baited, solely for the morals of those watching. It was proposed that prostitutes be packed off to Jamaica. Adultery became a capital offence. One pregnant adulteress, Susan Bounty, was convicted, allowed to give birth to her baby, and was then hanged. Churches were banned from using Cranmer's Book of Common Prayer and forced to use the Directory of Public Worship. One Puritan writer described the Book of Common Prayer as an 'imperfect book, culled and picked out of the popish dunghill, the... Mass book full of abominations.' The Directory in contrast was devised by a parliamentary sub-committee; it provided a detailed manual of how pastoral practice should be conducted. The major part of all services was devoted to sequential readings of the scriptures, interspersed with prayer.

The closure of the theatres and the persecution of the acting profession should be seen in the context of the repression of anything morally loose. Nobody should have been particularly surprised. The puritan anti-theatre view was well known; a pursuit so blatantly representative of the devil's work had long been high on the target list.

Theatre in England in the 16th and 17th centuries had flourished by being a sublimation of the country's historic Catholic instincts – it was the antidote.

Therefore to the Puritan mind, theatre should be eliminated as vigorously, as the Catholic Church itself should be eradicated.

The advancement of the English language had to withstand poisonous attacks. Its flexibility made it the perfect vehicle. Its richness leant itself well to its new purpose. English has always been the perfect language to swear in. The Puritans developed its ability to deliver coruscating and full-throttled critique, with masterful dexterity.

None of the Puritan writers were more notorious than William Prynne, the lawyer and polemicist. He wrote over 200 books and pamphlets. The most famous of which was his coruscating diatribe against theatre, entitled 'Histriomastix – The Player's Scourge'. It was published in November 1632. He pulled no punches; he ripped into every aspect of the theatre industry, including any attempt by women to appear onstage. 'Our Christmas lords of misrule, together with dancing, masks, mummeries, state players, and such other Christmas disorders, now in use with Christmas, were derived from these Roman Saturnalia and Bacchanalian festivals which would cause all pious Christians eternally to abominate them,' he raged. Female actors, he dismissed as 'notorious whores'. On and on he went for 1,000 pages, leaving no aspect of the dramatic world spared from his vituperative pen.

Theatre was not only closed, but dismantled. In 1644, the Globe Theatre was pulled down to make way for low-cost housing. The interiors of the Cockpit, Fortune and Salisbury Court Theatres were all removed. There were attempts to continue play performances at the indoor Blackfriars Theatre. Within days, complaints were registered in the Commons that 'stage players were playing at public houses in the City'. The Lord Mayor and City justices were empowered 'to enter into all houses, and other places...where stage plays, interludes, or other common plays are' and to call any actors discovered there before the Courts 'to be punished as Rogues'. The Blackfriars Theatre was demolished in 1655, to make way, once again, for low-cost housing.

Only one stage in London remained consistently active – the Red Bull Playhouse. Performances were intermittent, but court records do indicate actors had occasionally been bound over for unlawful playmaking. The cases allege that actors had collaborated with the parishioners of Clerkenwell; they had offered twenty shillings a day for the hire of the playhouse, and in addition, they had paid money towards the relief of the poor, and the repair of the highways. Proving that a solution to potholes trumps religious beliefs in any century.

○ ○ ○

The return of theatre started a little before the end of the Commonwealth. Ultimately all administrations learn the propaganda power of the performed word. As the Puritan administration started to falter, they reached for the solution that they had so vehemently argued against. William Davenant provided the catalyst. A poet and playwright, often considered in his day an heir to Shakespeare, was staunchly Royalist. He was named unofficially Poet Laureate, arrested several times by the parliamentary regime, before escaping to France.

The start of the Commonwealth's death knell came with Cromwell's humiliation in the only major military defeat of his career. The seaborne expedition to seize Hispaniola from the Spanish failed miserably. The island that Drake had previously 'captured' with but a handful of men, Cromwell failed to secure with a full fleet and a small army. The subsequent ejection of the Spanish from Jamaica, by the English expeditionary force, was seen as no consolation, despite becoming subsequently a more substantial prize than Hispaniola. Cromwell implicitly believed that victory on the battlefield was synonymous with God's approval, and defeat was God's punishment. He had never had to suffer military failure before, and was left in fundamental turmoil. The expedition was known as 'The Western Design'. It had been envisioned as the perfect way to deploy the almighty parliamentary forces to disrupt the Spanish gold shipments and to secure the additional funds required to meet the massive cost of the army. The dismal failure of the mission, compounded by Cromwell's continuing unwillingness to settle the question of succession, caused the irreversible erosion of his power.

Davenant saw his opportunity. Returning to London, he had been busy in the second half of the 1650s secretly mounting theatre productions, mainly in private homes. His production of 'The Siege of Rhodes', presented covertly at Rutland House is believed to be the first performance of opera in English. He daringly proposed to the authorities that two plays should be performed that would encourage appropriate jingoistic fervour to distract from the failures of the Western Design. The aim was to gloss over the defeat, but also to stoke fiery resentment of the Spanish. The appeal of foreigner-bashing as a diversion of the public mood, proved too tempting to resist. So he wrote and produced two plays. One was entitled 'The History of Sir Francis Drake' (the jingoistic piece), performed in 1658, and the other, 'The Cruelty of the Spaniards in Peru' (the foreigner-bashing piece), the following year. The path to bringing theatre back was begun. Even the die-hard Puritans could get over their objections to its immorality and ungodly nature, if it served their political purpose.

Neither play managed to save the Commonwealth. Richard, Cromwell's son, and successor, proved a pale imitation. For a while he kept the support of the army, but foolishly upset them in the middle of 1659. Upon his resignation, Parliament was still hopelessly divided, and no decisions could be made. Samuel Pepys waspishly noted that 'boys do now cry 'Kiss my parliament' rather than 'Kiss my arse'.' The army too was fragmented between the potentially most powerful successor to Cromwell, the Commander of the Army in the North, Lambert, and the Commander of the Army in Scotland, Monck. The latter proved to be the better prepared. He had purged his force of radical officers and counted wholeheartedly on the support of the remainder. Come early 1660, Monck gambled. He decamped his soldiers from Coldstream, in the Border country, and crossed the River Tweed into England. This was his own personal Rubicon. While Lambert dithered, Monck marched 400 miles to London. On the evening of 8 February, he and his senior officers dined in Grocers' Hall, at the invitation of the Lord Mayor, a Grocer, Thomas Alleyn. The deal was soon sealed between the City and the army, now led by General Monck, to seek to bring back Charles I's son from Holland.

This feast took place in exactly the same Hall where Cromwell and Fairfax had dined on 7 June 1649, to celebrate the overthrow of the Levellers. That night both Cromwell and Fairfax were showered with precious gifts including a gold basin and ewer, and expensive pieces of silverware; all of which they were very content to keep, despite their puritanical principles. Cromwell obviously enjoyed himself as he returned as Lord Protector to Grocers' Hall in 1654, where according to the minutes he dined, ironically, 'in regal splendour'. The City had been strong supporters of the Commonwealth. Cromwell had built an effective army, and had invested heavily in naval power. But the City was to become discouraged by the failure of Cromwell's Western Design, and the indecision following his death. The prospect of muscular kingship, ready to take on their main mercantile foes, the Dutch, was, in my opinion, too tempting. Monck's bold moves convinced them that the Royalist cause would win, and bring benefits for the City. Throughout history, the City has never seen shame in switching sides, when a better mercantile outcome was in the offing.

On 8 May, the 'Convention Parliament' abandoned their Republican experiment, and unanimously declared Charles II to be their future King. Charles II set sail, landing in England on 25 May. He progressed to London, and paused on Blackheath. He entered the City triumphantly on his birthday, on 29 May. At the gates, he was greeted by the Lord Mayor, who acknowledged him as King, and was promptly knighted on the spot as recompense for his trouble.

The Restoration had happened, and without much bloodshed apart from those of the signatories to the King's father's death warrant, or at least those who had not had the good sense to die beforehand, or escape into exile. You can still see on Runaway Bay in north Jamaica, the house built, in 1655, by the one of the few regicides, Daniel Blagrave, who managed to make a lucky escape. Daniel himself died in Aachen and his son inherited the house – which these days is a hotel.

CHAPTER EIGHTEEN

RESTORATION – LIFE RENEWED

'His gentleness was such
And Love, he lov'd. For he lov'd
Fucking much
Nor was his desire above his Strength
His Scepter and his Prick were of a length...
This to evince wou'd be to long to tell yee
The painfull Tricks of the laborious Nelly
Imploying Hands, Armes, Fingers, Mouth and Thighs
To raise the Limb which shee each Night enjoyes.'

– Earl of Rochester's poem on the King's relationship with Nell Gwyn

Changes came quickly from the restricted days of the Puritans, as is evident from the poem above which the Court wit, the Earl of Rochester, felt able to publish on the sexual prowess, or lack of it, of the monarch. Rochester died aged thirty-three of venereal disease.

The Act of Free and General Pardon, Indemnity and Oblivion was passed in August 1660. An Act of Uniformity was passed in 1662 mandating the Book of Common Prayer as the basis of church service. In 1664 the Conventicle Act banned private nonconformity from all forms of worship. In 1673, the Test Act required all public employees to take an oath of allegiance and observe the Anglican faith. A significant number of church ministers, and teachers were ejected for refusing to accept the Anglican orthodoxy. The King James Bible became the definitive Bible for the Anglican Church and the English-speaking world as a whole. The popularity of the King James version continued to grow from this point onward. Theatres reopened, returning with even greater vigour, and London, as expected, led the way. In short order, England had thrown off Puritan strictures and returned to the Anglican middle ground of Elizabethan times. Charles II cemented in place the building blocks that made English a global phenomenon – the King James Bible, the Book of Common Prayer, and English theatre.

The new King delivered on several of his promises internationally. His brother, James, Duke of York, grabbed New Amsterdam from the Dutch and renamed it New York. The basis for further English expansion in North America was laid, and formed a major part of the country's global mercantile growth for the next hundred years.

Certain disasters of course were to follow: the plague, the Great Fire, and the humiliation of the Dutch navy trouncing the English in their own waters of the Medway. However, the direction was set and English temperament was satisfied in general by this version of the Protestant way of life.

Thomas Rugg, a London barber, happened to record in his diary, as early as autumn 1660: 'Playes much in request and great resort to them.' The impact of the Great Fire saw the West End emerge as the centre of polite society and also of playmaking. With much of the City devastated and laid to waste, the nobility and 'well to do' moved quickly to establish themselves outside the walls. Given the need to stay in close touch with the main transport artery, the river, the options were to move either to the East or to the West. The prevailing wind determined the outcome. By going to the West, the upper classes of London reduced the impact of the terrible stench of the City that would have pursued them to the East.

Two companies were royally authorised and dominated the London theatre scene in the new West End. The first was formed unsurprisingly by Davenant, and was called the Duke of York's Men, occupying the theatre at Lisle's Tennis Court, before moving into the purpose-built Dorset Garden Theatre near the Strand. The other was managed by his great rival, Thomas Killigrew; his company was called the King's Men and after a period in another old tennis court building, went on to establish the Theatre Royal Drury Lane. Both companies moved away from the City/Southwark confines, they abandoned the open staged structure of Elizabethan theatre, and built more upon the tradition of the Stuart masque and European theatre, with all its visual splendour. Both adopted an indoor proscenium stage and arch configuration. This maximised the sense of spectacle. They packed in as much stage machinery as their buildings would allow. This approach forms the basis of most of our theatres today.

A group of talented playwrights emerged: Vanbrugh ('The Provoked Wife'), Congreve ('The Way of the World'), Farquhar ('The Recruiting Officer'), Dryden ('Marriage à la Mode'). The style was frothy, witty and satirical. The audiences were back in growing number, and most importantly royal patronage was even more pronounced than before. The style of the plays fitted the style of the monarchy. While tragedy, and Shakespeare were indeed played, of the Jacobean authors the witty scripts of Jonson and those of Beaumont and Fletcher were more often preferred. The bare board approach of Jacobean theatre was out, and fussy multiple sets aiming to conjure 3D representations of real life were in. Or satires of them at least. Shakespeare did not fit easily into this template. The performance records show that comedies significantly outweighed tragedies, and even these could end up being adapted for the age. Davenant famously mounted a version of Macbeth with the witches appearing on trapezes to satisfy contemporary tastes. The theatre manager, Colley Cibber, developed the version of 'Richard III' that became the standard text for many decades, despite it cutting the original severely, shifting the famous 'Summer of our discontent' opening, and adding several 'hit' speeches from other Shakespeare plays. The poet, Nahum Tate, adapted 'Lear' in 1681, to give it several happy endings – much more in keeping with the audience sentiments of the day.

The other great innovation of the day was the introduction of women, primarily attractive women, to play the female parts. The permission to allow women on the stage was included in the Royal Patents issued in August 1660. They were quick to implement this stipulation. The first female actress to appear on the stage in a theatre (rather than a masque) was on 8 December 1660, when Killigrew mounted a production of 'Othello' with a woman playing Desdemona. The stated reason for the new policy was to discourage the promotion of homoerotic tendencies that men playing women would inevitably create. This helped appease the residual Puritan concern about the reopenings. The private reasons were different, and not unconnected with the interests of the box office, in these uncertain times.

The King himself was personally involved in the ruling, and declared its potential positive impact on homosexual deviancy. To prove as much, he acquired a close interest in the actresses.

The actress Moll Davis initially took his fancy. She performed in the Duke's company, and lived with Davenant himself. Moll kept Charles's affections for about a year, sufficient for her to be showered with enough gifts to buy a house in St James's Square. Pepys, who was a close observer of theatre life, described her as 'the most impertinent slut in the world'. She was adroitly replaced, by the newest actress to catch Charles's fancy, Nell Gwyn. The acting star of the King's company, Charles Hart, had spotted her, coached her in the dramatic arts, put her onstage, and placed her in his bed. Her vivacious light touch and sensual looks proved a winner with the Drury Lane audiences. Samuel Pepys had a wholly different opinion of her talents to those of Moll; upon observing her first performance in April 1665, he described her as 'witty, pretty Nell'.

This entry in Pepys's diary allows us to speculate on the first moment that King Charles probably set eyes on her. With the onset of plague in London we know that the King and his court left for Hampton Court Palace on 29 June of that year. We know he sent for the King's company to provide entertainment for him. Since Nell was now an established performing member of the company, and one of only a few female actresses, it is inconceivable that she did not come to Hampton Court with the company. If correct, then this means that Charles first caught sight of her in action there over the summer, presumably performing in exactly the same Great Hall that Shakespeare had performed for Charles's grandfather. Another interlocking coincidence in our story.

She was first cast in a leading role in 1666, playing the part of Lady Wealthy in the 'English Monsieur' by James Howard. Nell moved on from her dalliance with Charles Hart, to take up with the aristocrat Charles Sackville. But by January 1668, Pepys records that she had dropped Sackville (who was appropriately royally compensated) and begun her affair with the King. Nell would refer to the King, even to his face, as her Charles the Third.

It is to be credited to her skills, charms and wit that she lasted both as his mistress, but also in his affections for a full sixteen years. A completely different tenure to the 'impertinent' Moll. What is more, she survived heavy-weight competition from well-born, and expert mistresses, such as Barbara Palmer, Duchess of Cleveland, and Louise de Kérouaille, Duchess of Portsmouth. She successfully manipulated the complexities of court life. Famously she was proud to proclaim when once mistaken by a jeering crowd to be Louise, and thus 'the Catholic Whore' that she was in fact 'the Protestant Whore'. Such was her earthy wit. She was granted a Crown property on Pall Mall, a country residence on Windsor Home Park, and a summer house on what is now King's Cross Road. Even on his deathbed, the King remembered her, allegedly instructing his brother and successor, 'Let not poor Nelly starve'.

Further insight into the background of Nell came from research I did into the identity of the Master of the Grocers' Company in 1620 – Roger Gwyn. He was one of the leading Apothecaries of the day. The genealogical records in Oxford, where his family came from, indicate that Nell might have been the daughter of the illegitimate son of Roger's brother, who was Canon of Christchurch. If so, then the actor Charles Hart would have been in the same Royalist cavalry regiment as her father. This may have explained Charles Hart's readiness to employ her (in addition to his purely amorous intentions). Perhaps her background was a great deal more complex than the popular portrait of her as a gutter wench, and this may help explain her natural skill at navigating aristocratic circles. What Nell certainly managed to do was to keep up royal and society interest in the dramatic arts. Albeit of the frothier type.

The performance of Shakespeare did not return to the pre-eminence that we consider natural today, until the middle of the 18th century. The first modern edition of Shakespeare appeared in 1709, and a publishing war in the 1730s meant his play scripts became much more affordable. His popularity was in due course assured in 1769, when the actor/manager, David Garrick mounted at Stratford a Shakespeare Jubilee celebration, to commemorate the 200th anniversary of the Bard's birth (albeit five years late). Like Burbage before him, and Olivier after him, Garrick knew instinctively that Shakespeare provides the platform for the greatest actors. Garrick's renditions of 'Richard III', 'King Lear' and 'Hamlet' were all famous in their time. His more naturalistic style of acting was revolutionary and lent itself to these roles. The fashion of the day for bombastic and mannered delivery was not for him. Equally, Garrick rejected the gimmickry that was habitually deployed to popularise classic texts, especially the penchant for onstage rope dancers and acrobats. He is said to have commented: 'I cannot agree to such a prostitution on any account, and nothing but downright starving would induce me to bring such defilement and abomination to the house of William Shakespeare'. From Garrick's moments of rediscovery and ever since, Shakespeare has been the pinnacle of the English dramatic repertoire. Garrick's style of interpretation and purity of staging has become a benchmark for Shakespearian performance. We have not looked back.

o o o

From this time onwards, the English passion for drama sailed on, as if uninterrupted. There have been better periods, there have been worse periods, but its centrality in English (and now British) cultural life has never wavered. Today, drama and performance play a continuous role in every child's education – quite unlike any other educational system in the world. The output of students of drama from universities and drama schools exceeds proportionately any other country. We have unique structures for proving new talent in the multiplicity of regional theatres, provincial arts centres, and most importantly festivals like the Edinburgh Fringe Festival. Edinburgh is the biggest arts festival in the world. Founded in 1947, it now hosts in its four-week duration around 3,700 different productions, and in over 250 different venues. Underneath this growth lies an essential anarchy. Nobody invites you to go to the Fringe Festival. Nobody scrutinises or sanctions what you do. If you have a show to present, and you wish to present it, then you can go. All you need is a space to perform in, and the few hundred pounds to have yourself inserted in the main Fringe programme. It is a magnet for theatrical enthusiasts. It is an accepted proving ground for the young and talented, and even for the young and untalented, of all ages. It is an essential part of the theatrical and comedic ecology in the world, that no other country has the equivalence.

The same spirit guides our language. Unlike other more disciplined tongues, there are no rules as to who can and who cannot create words or figures of speech. It is a creative free for all. Good additions survive and become part of the everyday discourse. Bad additions disappear.

As to our theatre industry, which is a prime user of the language, we have, in a haphazard manner come to create a web of theatres and producing companies, both commercial and subsidised, that exceeds anything anywhere in any other country, and also works remarkably well together. Like many things in this tale, you could not have invented it, if you had been planning for it entirely logically. At time of writing there are seventy-seven 'West End houses' as determined by the number of auditoria who are specified as eligible for work to be considered for the West End Olivier awards. By comparison there are forty-one Broadway theatres for the equivalent Tony awards. In 2022/23, there were 19,224 West End performances with a combined audience of 16.4 million versus Broadway's 11,506 performances and 12.3 million total audience. Broadway is London's closest competitor.

Then in the UK as a whole, there are 1,100 active theatre buildings. We have preserved, since Elizabethan London days, our appetite for theatre going. In 2018, some 34 million attended major scale professional theatres in the whole country including the West End. This is more than the combined attendance at all football league matches in the same year. If football is our national sport, then theatre must be our national art form.

Apart from all the direct economic benefits, it is also a driver of tourism. It brings international prestige. The strength of our theatre culture has directly fuelled our pre-eminence in television and strength in film making, where in global market share, we are second only to the US. Theatre nurtures many of our great screen performers, screen writers, and screen designers. Above all, the reason for dwelling so much on the history of theatre, is that it has provided a creative engine for the English language to become THE global language. Shakespeare is our obvious standard-bearer. But to him you have to add Wilde, Pinter, Jonson, Stoppard, Shaw, Priestley, Coward, Osborne, Congreve, Butterworth, and on and on and on.

This country flirted with Republicanism. It flirted with an ascetic purity. It flirted with strict authoritarianism. You could speculate that if Cromwell had been as good at anointing successors, as he had been at marshalling armies on the battlefield, then this flirtation might have developed into a longer-term romance. If his elder son Henry, and not Richard, had been chosen to succeed him, and if Hispaniola had not been an unmitigated disaster, then Puritan rule might have prevailed for longer. Our theatres would have remained closed, our prowess would not exist, and our language would have been poorer. Our lives would certainly have been markedly more colourless. The bounce-back from eighteen years of bleak existence gives hope today that the recovery from the enforced closure of the pandemic will likewise continue to be strong. If at times the audience feels that they are being offered a surfeit of comedy and lighthearted musicals, that is because producers have learnt the lessons of 1660.

CHAPTER NINETEEN

WHEN ALL IS SAID AND DONNE

'I design plain Truth for plain people... I labour to avoid all words which are not easy to be understood, all which are not used in common life.'
– John Wesley, preacher and founder of The Methodist Church

To chart the growth of English and the English, we have focused on literature, on drama, on poetry, on legal documents, and on Bibles. These are the things that are constant presences in our lives today; we inevitably understand them better. Yet for many centuries, these were not the most ever-present uses of our language. We often ignore the impact of the preachers and the creators of hymns. Today, these seem less influential. Few of us sit through hour-long sermons, nor do we know the words to a thousand hymns, as our forebears did. What was central then, has become marginalised now. Yet at their time, sermons and hymns, linked to readings from the Bibles and the Book of Common Prayer, were the most powerful influences on the way the language developed. They provided the constant exposure to a vocabulary and structure of expression outside the normally conversational. As the mass media of the day, they were the source of linguistic usage for all but the most highly educated.

The first impact of preaching outside the constraints of the Church structure came with Wycliffe's Bible-men. These groups of laymen were armed with sections of the vernacular translations that Wycliffe and his followers had originated; they travelled the country reading from the text and preaching wherever they could.

After Wycliffe's death, a range of powerful preachers kept the message going, inspiring the movement known as Lollardy. There were three particular concentrations of Lollardy: around Leicester, in the West of England and in London. Leicester's concentration owed much to Wycliffe's long-standing base in the county, right up to his death. The West and London were more dependent on where Wycliffe's preachers travelled. They were distinguished by their long russet-coloured gowns with their deep pockets. They would preach using references to the text of the scriptures, enriched with argument and exhortation. Teaching or preaching from the Bible in English was soon declared to be a heresy, and heresy was made a capital offence. The relentless pursuit of the Lollards by the authorities, their banishment from the established Church, and the threat of execution kept Lollardy suppressed. But its spirit never disappeared, and the template for the travelling preacher, operating outside the constraints of the traditional church had been born.

∘ ∘ ∘

The next significant phase for preaching came after the Reformation. The Protestant movement removed visual symbolism and the more ornate ceremonies of religion, replacing these with a steely focus on the word of God. The sermon would play a pivotal role in communicating the meaning of the scriptures. Normally the sermon would take as its start point a particular passage of the Bible, and using this as a basis, extemporise on the meaning and consequence of the passage in question. In London, at the turn of the 16th century a third of the population may have been going to the theatre every month, but this was eclipsed by church attendance. Almost every person in the country was hearing a sermon (many lasting for an hour or even longer) every week. The printed sermons of the greatest preachers were much in demand, not solely from lay readers, but also from members of the clergy lacking the skill to write their own, who leant on the work of the star preachers of the day.

During the Elizabethan and Stuart periods, the business of sermonising became an industry. It is not possible to do justice to all the powerful religious communicators of this time, but two stand out as exceptional and meriting further examination. They provided very different but complementary templates of how a sermon should be composed and delivered: Lancelot Andrewes and John Donne.

∘ ∘ ∘

Lancelot Andrewes was born in 1555 in London, the offspring of an old Suffolk family, and son of the Master of Trinity House. Andrewes was no outsider. He was educated at Merchant Taylors' School, Pembroke College, Cambridge, and became an MA at Oxford. He was clearly a bright scholar, mastering all the major languages of Europe, almost as a sideline. He was ordained in 1581, went on to become Bishop of Chichester, subsequently Bishop of Winchester, and was generally regarded as one of the foremost religious scholars and writers of the age. We have noted his role in leading the translators of the King James Bible; this in itself represents a major contribution to the development of our language. But in his day, he was better known and recognised as the court preacher, appointed Royal Almoner in 1605, and author of some of the most beautiful and stirring sermons written. For a total of nineteen years he preached at court at almost every Christmas, Easter, Whitsun and anniversary of the Gunpowder plot. These were the big formal annual occasions, but they would have been interspersed with many other sermons on lesser days. During James's reign, the King, a great enthusiast for the complex and scholarly sermon, would have heard many times more words composed and uttered by Andrewes, than he would have heard by Shakespeare. Despite the King's huge enthusiasm for the theatre, the stage was no rival to the pulpit.

The task was daunting. The Stuart monarchs insisted that their chosen preachers did not read their sermons. They were required to extemporise from a collection of notes, and pointers. In keeping with our national characteristic, they were meant to be performed rather than declaimed. We have a form of record of what they said. Andrewes and Donne would usually write up their notes into full texts at a later moment, for distribution to other members of the clergy. The written sermon would inevitably vary from the spoken version. Notwithstanding the challenges, Andrewes was dubbed the 'stella praedicantium' – the star of preachers. The editors of his sermons, Laud and Buckeridge, strongly hint at this in their dedication of the sermons to the King: 'Though they could not live with all the elegancy which they had upon his tongue, yet you were graciously pleased to think a paper-life better than none'. Underneath all the scholarship, the devotion and the scriptural analysis, this was a performance art.

Although his preaching was serious, his success derived from the popularity of his approach. His aim was not to get his congregation thinking analytically about the divinity, but to give them the experience of God through language. He would become remarkably colloquial for his time. I use some examples from Raymond Chapman's work on Andrewes. In his Christmas sermon of 1622, he admonishes his listeners on their lack of purpose or urgency. He postulates that they would not hurry to the newborn Christ as the Wise Men did, but instead would speculate: 'Christ is no wild-cat. What talk ye of twelve days? And if it be forty days hence, ye shall be sure to find his Mother and Him; she cannot be churched till then. What needs such haste?'

He would play with words, in an almost pun-like fashion. 'If without Him in this (world), without Him in the next, and if without Him there – if it be not *Immanu-el*, it will be *Immanu-hell*.' (Nativity sermon 9). He would speak in almost rhythmic structures. 'A gardener He is then. The first, the fairest garden that ever was, Paradise. He was the gardener; it was of His plantings. So a gardener.' (Easter 1620).

o o o

The two men were different in background. Unlike Andrewes, Donne was an outsider. His family were staunchly Catholic in the face of the brutal exertion of Protestant dogma. His uncle was the Superior of the English Jesuit mission, and was banished. His brother Henry was arrested for harbouring a Catholic priest and died in Newgate prison. His father died when Donne was only four, and he was brought up by his mother who remarried a wealthy widower called, Syminges. This enabled Donne to go to Oxford, followed possibly by Cambridge, but he never received a degree, refusing to take the Oath of Supremacy. After university he trained as a lawyer, and worked as a clerk. His rebellious, passionate spirit clearly never left him. While in the employ of the Lord Keeper of the Great Seal, Sir Thomas Egerton, as his secretary, in York House on the Strand (at the point of the overflowing river referred to earlier), he fell unstoppably in love with his employer's niece, Anne. Against the strongly expressed wishes of both Anne's uncle and father, they married secretly in 1601. This act got Donne fired, thrown into Fleet prison, and his career ruined, prompting his possibly apocryphal, brief outburst: 'John Donne, Anne Donne, Un-done.' The marriage survived the opprobrium; they retreated to the country, where Anne bore twelve children, and Donne, not unlike many others subsequently, started to rebuild his career, by being elected an MP, firstly for Brackley, and then for Taunton. It was polemics, surprisingly anti-Catholic, that brought him to the King's attention.

From 1615, an entirely different phase of his career began; with the King's encouragement, he accepted the position of Royal Chaplain. Six years later, he was promoted to be Dean of St Paul's, achieving one of the most visible and influential roles in the Anglican Church. He was to remain in this position until his death. It is a remarkable personal journey for an ardent Roman Catholic and an outsider, who had always managed to display an intemperate and often indulgent approach to life. This is part of the fascination of the mercurial genius of John Donne.

What we remember today most is his brilliance as poet. But only a few of these poetic works were ever published in print in his lifetime. They circulated among a close group of friends solely in manuscript form.

Among his contemporaries, he was recognised most as an exceptional preacher, and communicator on divinity and the scriptures. The true rival of Andrewes, but exceeding him in terms of mass popularity. We have today 160 extant sermons of his. Many of these were printed in his own lifetime. They were undoubtedly only a fraction of all the sermons he composed. He was at times writing a new sermon a week, and he was Chaplain and Dean for sixteen years. He saw preaching as his primary calling: 'It hath been my desire (and God may be pleased to grant it!) that I might die in the pulpit…' He came close to achieving his wish.

However Donne as poet and as preacher in my opinion cannot be divided. He applied the same passion and beauty of language to both. His poetry had various aspects. Firstly, there was his passion for the purely erotic. A contemporary described him when a bachelor, as 'a great visitor of ladies', which provided ample source material. Never meant for publication, but for private circulation, they demonstrate his ability to deploy language to the expression of powerful emotions.

In 'To His Mistress Going to Bed' he writes:

> 'Licence my roving hands and let them go
> Behind, before, above, between, below
> Oh my America, my new found land!'

And…

> 'Your gown going off, such beautous state reveals,
> As when from flowery meads th' hill's shadow steals.
> Off with that wiry coronet and show
> The hairy diadem which on you doth grow.'

His second passion was for love and for life itself, both sources of constant inspiration:

> 'For God's sake hold your tongue and let me love…'

> 'Busy old fool, unruly sun,
> Why dost thou thus,
> Through windows, and through curtains call on us?'

And after the tragic death of Anne:

> 'Sweetest love, I do not go
> For weariness of thee…'

And to his sponsor, muse and close friend, Magdalen Herbert, Lady Danvers:

> 'No spring, nor summer beauty hath such grace
> As I have seen in one autumnal face.'

And probably his most famous text:

> 'No man is an island, entire of itself, every man is a piece of the continent a part of the main...
>
> any man's death diminishes me, because I am involved in mankind, and therefore never send to know for whom the bell tolls; it tolls for thee.'

In addition, his writing spoke of his religious devotion ('Batter my heart, three-personed God'), and this intensity of devotion led him to his role as pre-eminent preacher. His impact was in part due to his regular appearance at court services, but also to the prominence of the role as Dean of St Paul's. He had access to one of the best attended Cathedral pulpits, but also the right to deliver sermons from Paul's Cross. This was an outdoor pulpit to the north-east of the Cathedral, in one of the largest open areas in the increasingly congested City. The right preacher would draw massive crowds from all strata of London life to hear them. Women as well as men, apprentices as well as masters, the low born as well as the high born. John Donne's sermons were definitely star attractions. This pulpit gave him a breadth of reach that church confines alone could not provide. He knew how to pull crowds. When he preached at Lincoln's Inn on one occasion, Constantine Huygens from the Dutch embassy who was listening, noted that due to the vast gathering of noblemen and gentlemen, 'whereof two or three were endangered and taken up dead for the time, with the extreme press and thronging.' More akin to a Beatles concert, and less to a Sunday sermon today.

His format followed that of the age, namely expanding at length on a specific portion of scriptural text. He deployed rhetoric, metaphor and powerful visionary phraseology to capture his audience's imagination. What is remarkable to us today, is how learned, textual and detailed much of his sermons are; the audiences seemed willing to accept the complexity, because at heart there were strong emotional messages. His subject matters were repeatedly Sin, Death and God. The powerful big three of the preaching worlds. He himself specified that a sermon is not a lecture. '...a sermon intends *Exhortation* principally, and *Edification*, and a holy stirring of religious affections.' Or Donne again: every word from the lips of the preacher is 'a drop of the *dew of heaven*, a dram of the *balme of Gilead*, a portion of the bloud of thy Saviour...'

He consciously pitched his texts into what would now be termed the middle brow, which was the source of much of his popularity. 'Preaching is the thunder, that clears the air, disperses all clouds of ignorance; and then the *Sacrament* is the lightning, the glorious light and the presence of Christ Jesus himself.'

All of which led Quiller-Couch to conclude subsequently that Donne's sermons were 'the most magnificent prose ever uttered from an English pulpit, if not the most magnificent prose ever spoken in our tongue.' Huge audiences were inspired by Donne's vivid use of language.

At the heart of this was of course the need to perform. This was an essential part of the successful preacher's art. Donne would come to his pulpit, and carefully place his upturned hourglass in front of him, before starting. He would speak from a series of notes that would outline the source text and the principal themes to be covered. His natural fluency would then take over, albeit under the close watch of the emptying hourglass.

His friend and contemporary, Izaak Walton, described his unique style as:

> '...a preacher in earnest; weeping sometimes for his auditory, sometimes with them; always preaching to himself, like an angel from a cloud, but in none: carrying some, as St Paul was, to heaven in holy raptures, and enticing others by a sacred art and courtship to amend their lives; here picturing a vice so as it to make it ugly to those that practised it; and a virtue so as to make it beloved, even by those that loved it not.'

He kept this innate theatricality up until the very end. His final sermon was entitled 'Death's Duel'; he delivered it in Whitehall in 1631 in front of the King. He appeared in the pulpit in almost cadaverous condition, and despite his frailty managed to deliver a booming sermon, that painted a horrific vision of hell, the eternal presence of Death and the doom to which Sin would lead. 'We have a winding sheet in our Mother's womb which grows with us from our conception...the whole world is but a universal churchyard...that which we call life is but a week of deaths, seven days, seven periods of our life, spent dying...'

Five weeks after this apocalyptic vision of death, he himself passed away, but not before arranging a detailed portrait of himself standing almost skeletally in his death robes. A brutal, unflinching vision of him that he has bequeathed us.

His contribution to the language through all his writing and preaching was considerable. There are over 300 words first attributed to him, such as 'emancipate', 'enripen', 'apprehensible', etc. Most relevant to today's vernacular he made extensive use of the 'super-' prefix, coining terms such as 'superinfuse' and 'super-infinite', which Katherine Rundell used as the title to her recent, insightful book on Donne. For those who now think that 'super-' is a thoroughly contemporary idiom ('super cool', 'super special', etc.) Donne was there doing this, 400 years ago.

He was buried in St Paul's Cathedral. Lancelot Andrewes's tomb resides in Southwark Cathedral. These were the two greatest preachers of the age; they brought the vivacity and imagery of the English language to the mass of the English population, fuelled not just by a love of God, but of language itself.

o o o

The third star preacher in our sequence came almost a hundred years later. His reach and impact were even greater than Donne and Andrewes.

John Wesley was born in 1703 in Lincolnshire, the fifteenth child of Samuel and Susanna Wesley, and grandson of the famous non-conformist preacher, Samuel Annesley, who refused to accept the 1662 Act of Uniformity. As with Donne, albeit from the other end of the religious spectrum, we have a family that intrinsically rejected the constraints of official doctrine. Wesley would live true to that principle throughout his adult life. His upbringing however was more traditional and middle class. He was sent to school at Charterhouse, and from there to Christ Church, Oxford. He was ordained as a priest in 1728, shortly after receiving his MA. His formative experience was being sent to serve a ministry in Savannah in Georgia. The ministry itself was not successful, but brought him into contact with a religious society led by Moravian Christians. Upon his return to London, he had his Damascene moment at a Moravian meeting house in Aldersgate Street in 1738. He heard there a reading of Martin Luther's preface to the Epistle to the Romans, in which the principles of 'universal redemption of all through Christ', irrespective of their sin, and of deep-rooted faith in piety, were espoused. These formed the central planks of Moravian Christian belief.

He developed his sermons and preachings to advocate the concept of personal salvation through faith and the accessibility of God's grace to be 'free in all, and free for all'. He believed that he was reinventing the Anglican Church to embrace a much more hopeful, more welcoming and more personally spiritual set of beliefs. This proved at odds with official Anglican thinking. In short order, he found himself banned from preaching in parish churches. It was his friend and fellow evangelist, George Whitefield, who introduced him, somewhat reluctantly to field preaching as the alternative.

This practice made his message accessible to a much wider audience, with very little limitation of attendance numbers. Wesley himself described his friend's activities as follows: '...our dear brother, Whitefield expounded...on Sunday morning to six or seven thousand at the Bowling Green; at noon to much the same number at Hanham Mount, and at five to I believe thirty thousand from a little mount on Rose Green. At one today he left Bristol.' Wesley quickly followed in Whitefield's steps, and discovered how field preaching could take his message to ever larger audiences.

His appearances had a snowball effect. People who heard Wesley preach initially in either London or Bristol, travelled back to their homes, brimming with enthusiasm for what they had heard. Methodist Societies were springing into existence in places that Wesley had never been to, and urgent invitations were sent begging him to come. For example a man called John Nelson heard Wesley preach at Moorfields in London, before returning to his native Yorkshire. There Nelson began preaching himself with great success, and in due course Wesley accepted an invitation to travel north. He describes what he found:

> *'(Nelson's) labour had not been in vain. Many of the great profligates in all the country were now changed. Their blasphemies were turned to praise. Many of the most abandoned drunkards were now sober; many sabbath-breakers remembered the Sabbath to keep it holy. The whole town wore a new face. Such a change did God work by the artless testimony of one plain man! And from thence his word sounded forth to Leeds, Wakefield, Halifax and all the West Riding of Yorkshire.'*

His preferred method of travelling was on horseback. It is estimated that in his life he rode some 250,000 miles, delivering 40,000 sermons. There are inevitably no estimates of how many people heard him, but in my opinion, it must be counted in millions.

A supporting structure and organisation were quickly established to assist the promulgation of the message. A cadre of preachers, both lay and ordained, were introduced to travel the country more broadly than a single man could achieve. Local presences were formed in individual societies, with their chapels and their meeting houses. A whole new language was formed for their activities, and a parallel organisational hierarchy, all of it pointedly different from Anglican principles. This formed the basis of the Methodist Church which considers Wesley to be their founder. They still celebrate 24 May, as Aldersgate Day, honouring the moment when Wesley embraced his new doctrine.

Wesley was a polymath, much as Donne was. Not only was he a churchman and a preacher, but he was also a writer and a grammarian with a fascination in language. He wrote books of Latin grammar, Hebrew grammar, as well as English grammar. He published his own dictionary. In all he wrote or edited some 400 publications. Of his letters, 2,800 have been preserved. He had wide interests in history, geography, science and languages. He was obsessed with the degraded conditions of the common man. He was a vehement advocate for Abolition at any early stage. In 1772, he wrote that slavery is 'that execrable sum of all villainies.' He was a pioneer in introducing female preachers. He was a vegetarian and teetotal, long before these ever became fashionable. It is perhaps not surprising that his only attempt at marriage, at the age of forty-eight, was not a success. He was just too busy for something so formal.

His love of, and mastery of language permeated both his writings and his preaching. He prided himself on being a direct speaker. He considered grammar to be simply the art of speaking and writing properly. He wrote in his journal 'I dare no more write in a *fine style* than wear a fine coat'. He professed a dislike of those sermons and prayers which he dubbed 'luscious'. He dismissed sentimentality; Rousseau for example he described as 'sure a more consummate coxcomb never saw the sun'. His definition of simplicity in religion was a model of his own sense of humanity: '…to refine religion is to spoil it. It is the simplest thing that can be conceived; it is only humble, gentle, patient, love.'

His directness of speech was a cornerstone of his writing, but while direct, it was not sparse. He spoke evangelically of 'execrable wretches', of 'worms of the earth', 'backsliders', 'mourners', 'penitents', 'blockheads', 'drones', and 'vulgar herd' – often calling his own congregations in such terms. Hence in 1759, he addressed the Society in Norwich, in plain terms, that they were 'the most ignorant, self-conceited, self-willed, fickle, intractable, disorderly, disjointed society that I knew in the three kingdoms.' It has been commented that 'few Englishmen succeeded so well as he did in clothing the Divine Word with flesh and blood', and there are many examples to bear that out.

He developed a unique vocabulary for Methodism as a whole, and very specifically for the roles and officers of the Church, to distinguish them from what came before. He named concepts such as the 'Watchnight', and the 'Love-feast'. The Oxford English Dictionary records that Wesley was the first writer to use a good number of words, either absolutely, or in a particular sense. Words such as 'bluff', 'caved in', 'irrecollection', 'aggrandising' and the term, 'accountable for'. He was also an inveterate coiner of expressions and idioms. In the OED of English Proverbs, some 584 are taken from Wesley's writings. Such as: 'Catch on fire and others will love to come watch you burn', and 'We should be rigorous in judging ourselves, and gracious in judging others.'

He was acutely aware of the theatrical demands of his job. To engage the sizeable numbers that attended his sermons, and to overcome the open-air conditions, required performance ability. He himself distrusted theatre, traditional theatre; he referred to it as the 'sink of all profaneness'. That opinion however never stopped him deploying the best theatrical tricks of the trade. Being Wesley, he recorded all of these in a pamphlet entitled 'Directions concerning Pronunciation and Gesture'. Reading this tells you he was as much a theatre man as any of our finest performers. In his pamphlet, the first section is: 'How we may speak so as to be heard without Difficulty and with Pleasure'. He warns against speaking too loudly, or too low, or in a 'thick, cluttering manner'. He urges strong articulation and clear pronunciation of every word. He counsels against speaking in a fashion that is 'womanish', 'singing', 'squeaking' or 'solemn'. Speech should 'flow like a gliding stream, and not as a rapid torrent'. He prepared meticulously like an experienced stage manager. On one occasion he paced the ground to establish that he could be heard clearly up to 140 yards away. At St Ives, he successfully contended with a raging sea, whipped up by a northerly wind. At Chapel-le-Frith, he overcame a disapproving nearby miller noisily letting out the water from his pond.

In his pamphlet, he also advises on gesture and posture, giving minutely detailed instructions. The head needed to be kept 'modestly and decently upright'. He puts great emphasis on the face. The eyes must meet those of the listeners directly, each in turn. The mouth should not be angled; lips should not be bitten or licked; the expression should match the emotions being spoken of. As to posture, he strongly advises against shrugging, leaning on the elbow, or any form of incessant movement. There should be no hand-clapping or thumping of the pulpit. The right hand should be used more frequently than the left. The arms should not be stretched out more than six inches from the body. 'Beware of clownishness, either in speech or dress'. And so on.

His intricate instructions on how to perform to open-air congregations is understandable, given the conditions. But in the end, they all boiled down to very simple precepts: communicate the words clearly and directly with as little distraction as possible. This is no different to how our theatre directors often instruct their actors: 'Deliver the text, pure and simple. Be true to what the author has given us.'

Wesley kept preaching until almost the very end. Aged eighty-six and only eighteen months before his death, he wrote that 'my strength is much lessened, so that I cannot easily preach above twice a day'. But this still challenging schedule was kept going with enthusiasm. Six months later he commented that 'it does me no harm, but rather good, to preach once or twice a day'. He attributed his longevity to 'constant preaching at five in the morning for above fifty years.'

He died in March 1791; his dying statement expressed his lifelong faith in redemption being available for everyone. 'The best of all is, God is with us!' At his death, there were 135,000 members of the Church he founded, and over 500 itinerant preachers. Today, Methodism has 80 million followers globally, making true Wesley's aspiration, as Whitefield had expressed it: 'I look on all the world as my parish.' This was achieved by a clear mind, a very human sense of faith, a deployment of the English language, and an innate sense of how to hold a crowd.

○ ○ ○

From the art of preaching, we turn to hymns, and the importance of congregational singing. Music has always been a part of worship – but not in the congregational and popular form that we are now used to. Psalm singing by priests was a well-established part of Hebrew temple life. Gregorian chanting in Latin by monks was similarly a customary feature of monastic life. With the Reformation, services reverted to psalm singing by choirs, albeit now using the English translation. Any attempt to introduce freshly written hymns, to be sung by a congregation, was controversial. The marriage of participatory singing, with the power of the English language and the strength of devotional feeling, was of course irresistible, however much the Church authorities may have disapproved. It should be noted that the Church of England did not officially accept hymn singing until 1820. But by that date, thousands of very popular hymns had been written and were being sung regularly.

One of the earliest recorded surviving English hymns was published in 1562. It was written by John Marckant, Vicar of Great Clacton. It is a model of beautifully written simplicity, with the power and rhythm that any modern lyricist would be proud of. I quote the beginning and the end.

> 'O lord turn not away thy face,
> From him that lieth prostrate
> Lamenting sore his sinfull life,
> Before thy mercy gate.

*Which gate thou openest wide to those
That doo lament their sinne,
Shut not that gate against me lord,
But let me enter in.*

*And call me not to mine accompts,
How I have lived here,
For then I know right well (O Lorde)
How vile I shall appere...*

*...So come I to thy mercy gate,
Where mercy doth abound
Requiring mercy for my sinne.'*

The first hymn book for general use was published in 1691, by Benjamin Keach, who pioneered their introduction into regular worship. His book 'Spiritual Melody' included a total of 300 hymns.

The breakthrough came with the hymn writing genius of Isaac Watts. Once more, he was a typical outsider. Born in 1674, his father was a deacon of the Independent Church and was regularly imprisoned, or on the run from the authorities. His highly talented son, Isaac, was offered a place at either Oxford or Cambridge. His refusal to subscribe to the Church of England eliminated him from consideration. He went to Stoke Newington Academy instead and devoted the rest of his life to the writing of the first great body of hymns. He is credited with some 750. Such was their power of authorship, the strength of melody and the natural urge of every congregation to participate, his work became familiar to every practising Christian. Many still sing his work today. 'O God, Our Help in Ages Past' is a perennial favourite. As is 'When I Survey the Wondrous Cross', and 'Joy to the World'. And phrases he coined are part of our normal vernacular like:

*'For Satan finds some mischief still
For idle hands to do.'*

From Watts onward, the printing of hymn collections surged exponentially. The master of the art form came a generation after Watts, with Charles Wesley. While his brother concentrated on sermons, Charles was the prodigious exponent of the hymn. During his life he authored around 7,000. It would be impossible to consider the impact of the Methodist Church without the contribution of his hymns and congregational singing. These acted as the centrepiece of their services. His constant emphasis was on the universality of God's love, the presence of the Holy Spirit within us, and our personal accountability to God. All powerful and highly accessible themes.

Any hymn book today is full of Wesley's work, from 'Love Divine, All Loves Excelling,' to 'Soldiers of Christ, Arise'. He also wrote the original 'Hark! How all the welkin rings/Glory to the King of Kings', before his Methodist colleague George Whitefield usefully tweaked it to what we know today as 'Hark! The Herald Angels Sing/Glory to the Newborn King.'

With Watts and Wesley, hymn writing and singing became unstoppable. It swept all of England, throughout America and all the English-speaking world. Hymns followed the King James Bible and the Book of Common Prayer globally, as manifestations of the power and richness of the English language. Towards the end of the 19th century this trend experienced a further uplift with the development of gospel hymns, which used a strong lead vocal, supported by a choir of exciting harmonies. Gospel has swept the modern church, especially in America, and influenced the direction of contemporary music.

At the heart of all these hymns is the marriage of music, the human voice and the English language. There are many cultural fields at which the English have been especially capable over the centuries – and some of which they are probably pre-eminent. But the creation of musical work is not especially high on that list. England has of course produced some wonderful individual composers, like Purcell, over the centuries, and the 20th century in particular saw a renaissance in English composition with Elgar, Holst and Vaughan Williams, followed by Britten and Walton and latterly Ades, Benjamin and Wallen. But they do not rival the depth of centuries of genius that Germany or Italy or Austria or Russia has boasted over the past 400 years. There are times however when English prowess in music-based creation has come to the fore. Two moments especially strike me. The first is the height of hymn writing in the 18th and 19th centuries. The second is in contemporary song, both in record release and staged musical theatre, that has occurred since 1964. I pick that year because it marked the Beatles' first number-one hit in the USA. The work in both periods has had proper global reach, and tellingly these explosions of musical creation both have the lyric as an essential and critical component. A hymn, a number-one hit, or a musical classic, all have the fluency and power of the English language as part of the package. It is that which distinguishes it. It is our strongest card.

CHAPTER TWENTY

THE GREAT AMERICAN EXPERIMENT

'The inherent and permanent fact that North America speaks English.'

– Bismarck's reputed reply in 1898 when asked what he thought the most important factor was in modern history

The Stuart era ended with the death of Queen Anne in 1714. Her achievements included the formation of the Union, of Great Britain and of the United Kingdom. She made a reality of the Pretanic Isles, and thus the Land of the Tattooed People. The House of Stuart was followed by the House of Hanover, and the next phase of the constitutional monarchy. By the pointed selection of a minor, but staunchly Protestant set of descendants of King James, who helpfully spoke no English, a new political partnership was formed between monarch, his ministers and Parliament. It was a further step in the progression of the Anglo-Saxon principle of rule made legitimate by the consent of the elders and the people. The arrangement was not without its teething problems, nor without its hisses and fits, but it left the nation to get on with trade, progress, commercial growth, industrial innovation and global expansion. London was at the very centre of everything, and quickly to become capital of the world.

Military prowess, maritime power, mercantile strength and industrial development all went hand in hand to make Britain the pre-eminent global power. The Bank of England was formed, and the country kept its credit record, unlike some of its major competitors. London, its independence and its financial capabilities, were prime assets to the country. The ability to borrow affordably lay at the heart of the ability to wage war and to expand globally. A highly effective system of trade came into play, fuelled by this availability of funding. Colonial expansion brought sources of raw materials. These were shipped home to be turned into finished products using the latest capabilities of the industrial revolution; these were then sold to the domestic market, or transported back to sale in the colonial territories in the very ships that would be refilled with more materials. With an active and protective navy, this massive web of trading flourished. The trade in the enslaved was one horrific component of this mercantile merry-go-round, which was not abolished until 1807.

The turning point for Britain's influence on the world came with the Seven Years' War, which started in 1756. Considered the first world war, it was fought nominally over the issue of Austrian succession, but turned into an outbreak of monumental global muscle flexing between the European nations. The outright success of Britain in this war put paid to France's claim for European supremacy (an outcome that was then reiterated in the American colonial wars, and the Napoleonic Wars, for additional good measure). Britain emerged from the war's concluding treaty in 1763, with a dominant position versus the French in North America, several territories in the West Indies, Senegal in Africa, and an unassailable position in the Indian subcontinent. It gave Britain control of all North America east of the Mississippi apart from the very south. On the flip side, this triumph created an unwarranted level of hubris in George III, and his leading politicians. This would have consequences.

o o o

The American colonies were the stars of this fast-expanding Empire: full of resources, well organised, industrious, and loyal to the home country. Given the strength of devotion among the founding fathers, the Geneva Bible had been their preferred scripture. But the English throttled the supply of this Bible, and consequently, the King James version became the default option. It was on the back of the King James Bible that English spread across the thirteen colonies. They embraced it even more assiduously than the English ever did.

Its popularity undoubtedly helped. There are certain examples of American English preserving more of the language of the 16th century, when England itself has moved on. There are lots of good examples. The phrase 'I guess', the noun 'platter', the verb 'gotten', 'pitcher' for 'jug', the season 'fall', all show Americans continuing to use an early English. And 'herb' being pronounced without sounding the 'h', continues the Middle English 'erbe'. The dropping of 'u's in 'color' and in 'tremor', and the rotation of 'e's and 'r's in 'theater' and 'center', are however all later inventions.

There are then differences between the English of north-east America, and that of the southern States. These hark back to the separate development of the two areas of early settlement – around Boston in the North and around Jamestown in the South. The inhabitants of the latter were more likely to have come from south-west England. They have preserved some facets of that dialect, such as the long vowels, the buzzing 's', the 'y'all' greeting, and the preservation of the verb form 'I be...you be...we be'. The latter is an Old English verbal structure that clung on longest in old Wessex.

The finished copies of the King James Bible were printed in Britain and shipped over for sale. The first locally produced Bible was in fact a German language translation. The number of German-speaking settlers in the American colonies was second only to English speaking. A locally printed version of the King James Bible in English was only allowed to appear in 1782. A Scots-born American, Robert Aitken, engineered congressional authority for his edition, and presented it to the market, proclaiming on its frontispiece to be the 'official' American version. The date is significant. 1782 was the penultimate year of the War of Independence and separation must have seemed tantalisingly possible.

Just as the American colonies were becoming the most valuable part of the British Empire, the English allowed an argument to break out that probably should have never been allowed to get out of control. A row over who had the duty to defend the colonies, and who had the obligation to pay for that defence, spiralled into an all-comprehensive argument about self-determination, about taxation, and about representation – familiar Anglo-Saxon principles. The colonies never wanted to sever ties with the home country, they wanted a better deal. The English never saw it like that. They reacted to it as impudence, as a wish for something for nothing, and a lack of humility towards their imperial masters. The challenge of communicating across the distance of the Atlantic, and the lack of politicians in London with any first-hand experience of America, led to misunderstandings that a supposedly common language was incapable of resolving.

In 'The March of Folly', Barbara Tuchman presents a compendium of moments in history when stupid decisions were taken which the perpetrators knew (and had often been warned of) were stupid. Alongside such prime examples as the Trojans taking the wooden horse into their city, and the Americans believing that the ruinous bombing operation 'Rolling Thunder' would end the Vietnam War, Tuchman lists the English decision to wage war against its own American colonies. The English were driven by a sense of invincible superiority over their American subjects, by an unrealistic belief in their own military might, and by a conviction that compromise would be a dangerous precedent. Yet they were repeatedly warned that they would fail. George III had a dread of being remembered as the monarch that had allowed the Empire to unravel. He would only have to see his portrayal in the musical 'Hamilton', to see his worst fear was more than justified.

To compound the folly even further, the early rebel successes prompted Britain's enemies, France and Spain, to move from fence-sitting to joining in wholeheartedly. The European powers found the perfect opportunity to embarrass England, and to reverse the territorial losses they had suffered from the Seven Years' War. France saw the chance of reasserting French as the true global language. And Spain saw the opportunity of grabbing not just chunks of North America but also Gibraltar – lost at the Treaty of Utrecht back in 1713.

My interest in the American War of Independence is less the ins and outs of folly in England's prosecution of the war, nor its much more capable performance against its traditional foes especially at sea, but the bigger and longer-term picture. For many various reasons the English lost the war against the Americans, but remarkably and quite uniquely, albeit not without subsequent argy-bargy and the odd conflict, they went on to manage to win the peace. They bamboozled their traditional European foes and gained something nearly as valuable as the continued retention of the American colonies.

○ ○ ○

The architect of the peace was Lord Shelburne, Prime Minister from 1782 until 1783. Shelburne was an Irish born, Oxford-educated soldier who had fought with distinction in the Seven Years' War. As a politician, he was an ally of Pitt, and a vocal opponent of North and of his confrontational stance towards the Americans. When North's approach was clearly failing, Rockingham became Prime Minister with Shelburne as a Secretary of State. Rockingham died of flu three months later and Shelburne stepped into his shoes, aged forty-five, with a clear vision of how to resolve the intractable problem of the American colonies. An excellent account of these is included in Richard B. Morris's 'The Peacemakers', which has served as an invaluable reference.

The negotiations were conducted in Paris; they were meant to be closely scrutinised by the Americans' allies, the French. The process had dragged on for months into years. On the American side the negotiating team included Benjamin Franklin, John Jay, Henry Laurens and John Adams. On the British side, the negotiations were done almost entirely by the Scottish lawyer Richard Oswald, before being succeeded in the final phase by David Hartley. It was the months of discussion between Jay and Oswald that enabled the intractable differences between the two sides to move towards resolution. Neither negotiating team kept their constitutional bodies properly aware of the concessions, trade-offs and red lines that were forming the heart of the deal. On the British side, Shelburne kept closely in touch with Oswald, but informed few others in Parliament, and certainly not the King. On the American side, the Atlantic posed a significant barrier; Franklin had to act as a senior overseer to the process, but Congress was only sporadically updated. By the time any message reached them, the arguments had moved on. In contravention of Congress's specific instructions, the French were kept totally in the dark.

The French had already put forward their solution. They proposed that America be declared independent, that the American colonies have no rights to land west of the Appalachians, that Britain be allowed to maintain all territory north of the Ohio River, that the southern section of America including Florida come under Spanish control, that Spain get Gibraltar and Menorca, that France be given various Caribbean islands from Britain, and able to advance its interests in India.

The French wanted to grab as much for themselves first, Spain second, that Britain be penalised, but America gets as little as possible. As a colonial power, France had no motive to reward outbreaks of independent spirit.

The value of France's proposal was it annoyed everyone. The Spanish were not pleased, the English hated it, and the Americans felt insulted.

Austria and then Russia made attempts to negotiate peace deals as 'honest brokers', but these were quickly exposed as nakedly self-interested.

Oswald, with Shelburne's support, approached the American team, and persuaded them that both sides should deal with each other direct and in secret. He convinced them that an amicable agreement, more generous to the Americans, and more to the taste of the English, could be achieved between the two of them directly. The French and Spanish could be dealt with later. For the Americans to accept this approach, they needed an unequivocal assurance from the English of their commitment to independence, as an up-front *sine qua non*. Shelburne knew that both King and Parliament were emphatically opposed. He himself had initially wanted some form of Dominion status for the colonies. But he soon realised that his secret negotiation would only work if full Independence was put on the table at the outset, and the Americans felt they were negotiating as equals. It was a very brave decision. He knew the consequences for him personally, but also knew it was fundamental for success. He agreed to the demand.

This enabled the detailed further negotiations to proceed in private, until what was termed the Preliminary Draft was delivered. This was the agreed template for the final agreement. It was to be signed by both parties, and although not binding, it was expected that any further variations would be minor.

In the Preliminary Draft, the American colonies were offered rights to expand up to the Mississippi in the West, and up to the Canadian border in the North – significantly more than the French deal had offered them. The Spanish were constrained to a small and ambiguous section in the South, that stopped short of the mouth of the Mississippi. The Americans were granted navigation access to that great river. Americans were offered important fishing rights off the Newfoundland coastline (showing how often fish have been a pivotal point for major international treaties). England committed to remove the balance of its troops, including their garrison in New York.

In return for the British generosity, the Americans dropped their demands for the secession of Canada, they supported the principle of restitution of British property, they agreed to the mutual settlement of claims, they agreed to share with England navigation access to the Mississippi, with the exclusion of all other nations. Above all, the Americans offered through this more beneficial deal the basis of a close future relationship with specific benefits in continuing trade. The extraordinary vision of Shelburne and of Oswald was to appreciate that continued pettiness and rancour would achieve little, but that generosity would in the long term concede not much more, but achieve the biggest prizes of all: a strong economic and cultural bond with these former colonies, and remove them from the clutches of France and Spain.

When the Preliminary Draft was signed in November 1782, the response was clear and emphatic. The French and Spanish denounced it. They had been left in the dark; they saw the terms as unnecessarily generous and an assault on all colonial rights. The American Congress hated it too. Not because of any specific term, but because of the covert manner of its preparation, without their specific approval and behind the backs of their French allies. Hamilton himself was quick to denounce it on the floor of the House.

The British Parliament was appalled by the terms, in particular the unequivocal recognition of America's Independence. The King was coruscating and reduced to noisy hand-wringing. He wrote in November 1782 about the 'dismemberment of America from this Empire', in the knowledge 'that knavery seems to be so much the striking feature of its inhabitants that it may not in the end be an evil that they become aliens to this kingdom'. When it came to the moment to commend it to Parliament, he did holding his nose with both hands. He offered his 'humble and earnest prayer to Almighty God' that Great Britain would not 'feel the evils which might result from so great a dismemberment of the Empire; and that America may be free from those calamities, which have formerly proved, in the mother country, how essential monarchy is to the enjoyment of constitutional liberty.' You can hear him already writing his own part in 'Hamilton'. In the parliamentary debate itself, Shelburne's arch critic, Viscount Stormont, took cruel pleasure in reminding Shelburne how he had previously declared to Parliament that the sun of Great Britain would set when America was granted independence. Stormont declared, 'That sun is set, there is not a ray of light left, all is darkness.'

In Congress matters fared no better. While not disagreeing with the specifics of the deal, the American secretary of Foreign Affairs, Robert Livingston, declared 'no little pain at the distrust' in which it was concluded. Not just Hamilton, but other senior members of Congress lined up to denigrate the negotiators openly in the House.

In Britain, the storm against Shelburne grew and grew. The *coup de grâce* came in February, when two Cabinet Ministers, Keppel and Richmond, resigned. Shelburne could not continue and so resigned as well. The King was left with few options. Shelburne's critic, Fox, allied as he was with North, was the only politician who commanded parliamentary support. The King detested Fox. He had previously gone to exceptional lengths to avoid a Fox-North administration. Earlier he had actually drafted an abdication speech and had his yacht wait in readiness to take him to Hanover, a dominion that he had never been to, and in fact never would. As Shelburne resigned, the King once again threatened to go to Hanover rather than accept Fox. The only solution was for an amenable, forty-five year-old aristocrat and associate of Rockingham, called the Duke of Portland, to be invited to be prime minister. Fox was to serve as Foreign Secretary; this arrangement avoided the King having to deal with Fox, he need only speak to the more acceptable Portland.

Fox's public position was that the Preliminary Draft made him 'sicken at its very name'. It was 'more calamitous, more dreadful, more ruinous than war could possibly be.' Fox changed the leadership of the negotiating team replacing Oswald with Hartley. However Fox's real priority was not to unpick the Preliminary Draft, whatever he said in public, his focus was to conclude deals with France, with Spain and Holland, on the best terms for England – now that the trump card of potentially mutinous American colonies was no longer available. He derived too much sport from running rings around them, to worry about the core American deal. In the end, Spain got Menorca, and some ambiguous bits of Florida but no access to the Mississippi delta. They failed to get Gibraltar. France got Tobago and Senegal. But France and Spain handed back the Bahamas, Grenada and Montserrat. Most importantly, England cemented the carve-up of North America between themselves and the Americans.

The Definitive Treaty of Paris was signed on 3 September 1783. Its final form was similar in almost every detail to the Preliminary Draft. What Shelburne had predicted was to come about. The British were the primary trading partners of the Americans; huge wealth and prosperity was created for both sides. There is often discussion of the 'Special Relationship', what it is and how it arose. In my view, it was formed in 1782, by the generosity in the negotiation of Shelburne and Oswald. Every sensible person would have predicted not a 'Special Relationship' but a lastingly antagonistic one. It was sufficiently special to survive the English burning down of The White House in 1814, albeit in retaliation for an American armed incursion into Canada.

While the immediate benefits were economic, it had big consequence in language. Various attempts had been made within the American colonies to consider alternatives to English as their national language. These came to nothing. Despite the considerable presence of German/Dutch speakers, and the siren calls of their allies, the French, the choice of English prevailed.

In the build-up to the war, various influential figures doubted that English would be the resulting language of America. In 1776, Franklin predicted that unless Britain and the colonies found a proper reconciliation, English and American would become as different as Spanish and Portuguese. John Pickering, author of an American dictionary forecast that '*Americans* shall no longer be able to understand the works of Milton, Pope, Swift, Addison and other English authors…without the aid of *a translation*'. Webster himself held the view that American English would be 'as different from the future language of England, as modern Dutch, Danish, and Swedish are from German or one another.'

But a telling exchange took place after the signing of the Preliminary Draft. Richard Morris in 'The Peacemakers' recounts:

> *The signing over, the participants rode out to Passy (where Franklin resided) together to celebrate the event. There they were joined by some French guests, one of whom took the occasion to rub salt into the wound. Turning to the British, he harped on the theme of 'the growing greatness of America', and predicted that the '13 United States would form the greatest empire in the world'. 'Yes, sir' Caleb Whiteford (an old English friend of Franklin's) replied, 'and they will all speak English, every one of them'.*

The same point was made by John Adams, subsequently the second US President. He wrote in a letter:

'English is destined to be in the next and succeeding centuries more generally the language of the world than Latin was in the last or French is in the present age. The reason for this is obvious, because the increasing population in America, and their universal connection and correspondence with all nations will, aided by the influence of England in the world, whether great or small, force their language into general use, in spite of all the obstacles that may be thrown in their way, if any such there should be.'

All three men (one French, one English and one American) proved accurate in their predictions. In their cups and their celebrations, something remarkable had been achieved. With America firmly and lastingly in the English-speaking fold, the decision of language for the world had been taken – and they could see it even at the time. Fuelled by a remarkably rich and versatile construction, supercharged by some of the most powerful works that deployed this language to its full potential, and with the supporting base of the next great Empire and the Empire to follow, the task had been completed.

English had the advantage of both the embedded position of the King James Bible in much of American daily worship, and the invasive power of Shakespeare. He was a point of constant reference to the revolutionary leaders. Shakespeare's tales of power, rebellion, insurrection and overthrow, provided words and characters to their feelings. Kevin J. Hayes quotes some good examples in his book on this topic. John Adams and his wife Abigail would pepper their correspondence to each other with Shakespearian quotes and references. Franklin considered 'Othello' his favourite play; indeed he even owned a slave called Othello. Jefferson opined that 'To learn filial piety, don't read moral philosophy, read King Lear'. John Jay, the American negotiator, used 'Henry V' to defend the draft of the constitution: 'We few, we happy few, we band of brothers', and finished off by quoting from 'Henry VIII'. When the national delegates gathered in 1787 in Philadelphia for their Constitutional Convention, they paused their proceedings to go to a performance of 'The Tempest'. Shakespeare was a constant ghost at the table. If the heads of the American leaders had good, sound separatist-minded reasons for taking a break in language, their hearts were won over by Shakespeare, and their heads by the negotiating position of Shelburne and Oswald. Bismarck's assessment a hundred years later, quoted at the head of this chapter, was that the choice of the language in North America had determined the course of modern history. This was prescient, coming long before the two subsequent world wars.

This creates an end point to a narrative arc of the development of our language. It is one that began with the Battle of Edington and the Treaty of Wedmore. It finishes with the siege of Yorktown, the surrender of the English army to the rebels, and the Treaty of Paris. The journey of English from its near obliterated minority status to the achievement of its destiny as the first true global language was set. This is not to pretend that language stood still thereafter. Quite the reverse. If anything, changes have accelerated. But its future pre-eminence was largely determined by this point.

CHAPTER TWENTY-ONE

GREAT EXPECTATIONS

'Sparkler of Albion'
— Charles Dickens's description of himself

The progress of the English language was relentless from the moment of its defining acceptance in America, in a form very similar to its mother tongue. Expectations for its future from that point had been great, and they did not disappoint. It expanded and evolved continuously, matching pace with globalisation.

At no point in its history has English suffered regulation or control, and its global expansion into every part of the world has failed to trigger a system of governance. The English language is similar to the English Constitution; it is governed by practice and by precedent. If a word works, if it gains traction, then it enters our language. The compilers of dictionaries acknowledge its presence, but there is no process of approval or authorisation. It is an especially English approach to rule-making.

By contrast, in France, Richelieu established the Académie Française. It had, and still has, a primary purpose of policing their language. In 1635, one of its main aims was 'to render (French) pure, eloquent, and capable of treating the Arts and Sciences'. In Italy, in 1582, the Accademia della Crusca was founded with a similar aim for Italian.

There were various attempts made in England to do the same. The most vigorously prosecuted was by Johnathan Swift, in the early 18th century. Swift was vocal on many subjects and this was one. He lamented the parlous state of the language. He formulated 'A Proposal for Correcting, Improving and Ascertaining the English Language'. In 1712, he wrote to the leader of the government, Robert Harley as follows:

> 'My LORD, I do here, in the Name of all the Learned and Polite Persons of the Nation, complain to your LORDSHIP, as First Minister, that our Language is extremely imperfect, that its daily Improvements are by no means in proportion to its daily Corruptions that the Pretenders to polish and refine it, have

chiefly multiplied Abuses and Absurdities and, that, in many Instances, it offends against every Part of Grammar.'

His solution was an academy to oversee the language. He urged Harley to become a member. He never did and the academy soon petered out.

Swift was not the first, nor the last to propose such a solution. In 1664, the writer and thinker, John Evelyn backed the formation of a similar academy to opine on all matters relating to grammar, and dictionaries. But the meetings soon dissipated and the academy disappeared. This method of control of something so culturally central to our way of life, is not the English way.

Not only did the English initiatives fail, but also the American various attempts. One in 1774. One again in 1788, with the ardent lexicographer, Noah Webster, at the helm. Another in 1820. Despite John Adams arguing strongly in the favour of such a body, none worked or survived for long.

Webster was not a man to give up easily. He was driven by a revolutionary zeal, inspired not just by a wish for freedom, but by a disgust at the corrupt indolence of their former English masters. He wrote that America will be '(raised) to a pitch of greatness and lustre, before which the glory of ancient Greece and Rome shall dwindle to a point, and the splendour of modern Empires shall fade into obscurity'. He set about defining the role that language could make to the attainment of 'greatness and lustre'. He made his intent plain. '*Now* is the time and *this* is the country, in which we may expect success in attempting changes favourable to language, science and government… Let us, then, seize the present moment, and establish a *national language*, as well as a national government.' He set about his work with vigour. He wished to achieve 'the omission of all superfluous or silent letters' and 'a substitution of a character that has a certain definite sound for one that is vaguer and more indeterminate.' His grand vision was a process of simplification. He published his recommendations in his dictionary in 1806. Some of these were implemented and survive in American today. He advocated the removal of the 'u' in '-our' words where the 'u' is not being pronounced as in 'harbour' or 'humour', etc. He argued for changing '-re' to '-er', as in 'theater', 'center' and 'meter'. The suffix '-ise' in English became '-ize' in American, as in 'organize' or 'recognize'. He replaced complex double vowels in words like 'diarrhoea'. He managed to get silent vowels dropped like the 'e's in 'axe' and 'storey'. He implemented simplifications like 'tire' for 'tyre'. But a good number of his proposals were rejected, for example the dropping of the final 'e' in 'nightmare', 'give', 'determine' and 'medicine', or simplifying 'tongue' to 'tong'. Or 'cloak' to 'cloke'. Or 'soup' to 'soop'. Or 'although' to 'altho'. All the English originals are still there today. At the end of the procrastination, America achieved a very slightly modified version of English, which they could just about call their own. Tellingly, Webster's assistant, Joseph Worcester, produced his own more anglicised dictionary, which considerably outsold Webster's.

While today we recognise the difference between American 'English' and English 'English' and make fun, as George Bernard Shaw said of 'two countries separated by a common language', we need to acknowledge the importance of the failure to make the two versions of the same language more separate. The close similarity grammatically and lexicographically of the two tongues has been an important contributor to the emergence of English as the global means of communication.

o o o

The language also has resisted various earlier attempts to halt its process of endless assimilation. The 'Inkhorn Controversy' had raged through the 16th and 17th centuries, and had denounced the 'corruption' of the English language by Classical and French influences, well before any American and other foreign infusions from around the world had wrought their damage to the pure Anglo-Saxon tongue. The Inkhorn adherents (so called because of the inkwells they used) attempted to rewrite core texts such as the Bible, in an English that was free of such corruptions, often to ludicrous effect.

But the Inkhorn case gained no real traction. The language was at liberty to do what it naturally did best: to nurture and absorb new words from new cultures. What had begun as a facility of the language to ingest conquerors' linguistic structures and vocabularies, reversed direction and managed to appropriate words, idioms and terms from countries all over the world, especially the British Empire.

A whole book in itself could be written recording and examining all the riches that English absorbed from its colonies and global trading routes. David Crystal does a good compendium of these in 'The Stories of English'.

From American Indian came 'racoon', 'skunk' and 'moose'. From Hindi, we have acquired great words such as 'bungalow', 'chintz', 'cot', 'juggernaut'. From Marathi, 'dungaree'. From Sanskrit, 'pundit'. From Tamil, we have acquired 'catamaran', 'curry', 'pariah', and by way of French, 'cheroot'. From Far Eastern tongues we have acquired 'kethcup', 'kimono'. From Maldivian, 'atoll'. From our Caribbean pirate days came 'pieces of eight' and 'dubloons'. From the Arawak came 'hurricane', 'maize' and 'hammocks'. From the Aztecs and Mexicans came 'chocolate', 'avocado', 'cocoa', 'guacamole', 'tomato'. From the Peruvians came 'condor', 'llama', 'puma' and 'cocaine'. From the Brazilians came 'cashew', 'toucan' and 'tapioca'. From Australia came 'kangaroo' (an indigenous word for a large, dark-coloured animal, and not for 'I don't know' in response to the question, 'What is that?'), 'koala', 'boomerang' and 'wombat'. From Arabic came 'alchemy', 'alcohol', 'algebra', 'amber', 'candy', 'coffee', 'lemon' and 'sugar'.

Our word 'tattoo' is not ancient English. The word only entered the English language in the 18th century. Captain Cook observed in Tahiti how the islanders painted their bodies. The local word for these was 'tatau', which we adopted and evolved into 'tattoo'.

Whole versions of English were developed such as 'West African Pidgin English'. This simplified version of the language is believed to have been developed by groups of the enslaved, so they could communicate on the ships and in the plantations, with each other and with their owners.

As the global expansion of the British took place during the 18th and 19th centuries, the language showed a remarkable ability to be a sponge to exciting new words, phrases, and even whole grammatical forms, that kept it endlessly rich, and versatile to the needs of peoples of all backgrounds around the world. This has been as much a part of its success, as its earlier formative centuries.

○ ○ ○

The symphonic progress of this narrative, as we traverse the 19th century, then comes to the crescendo that is Charles Dickens – or the 'Sparkler of Albion', as he occasionally called himself.

In many ways, Dickens is the embodiment of all the principles that we have been espousing. Dickens is in my view our greatest writer of secular prose; what Chaucer did in verse, what Tyndale did in religious prose, what Shakespeare did in sonnet and dramatic verse, so Dickens did in his everyday storytelling. He is the creative genius that the progress of English was begging to exist. He commanded the language and the grammar to his service in a way that few writers have done since. Above all, he did it with immense theatricality, resonating quickly with his mass readership, and continuously fuelling film, television and stage versions over the last century.

Dickens was the consummate outsider. Born in Portsmouth, the second of eight children, the son of a navy clerk. He moved to London young, then to Sheerness, then Chatham and eventually Camden. His education was sporadic, and at times almost non-existent. When his father was thrown into debtors' prison, and the family needed every penny that could be earned, he was sent out to work in a blacking factory near Charing Cross.

Somehow through all this disadvantage and adversity, Dickens acquired an ability at storytelling, and an unmatched facility for the language. He always had a devotional respect for Shakespeare: 'the great master who knew everything'. From an early age he could quote lengthy passages, and in later life, he had an ability to recite sections of the plays spontaneously. In his novels, he quotes from 'Macbeth' more than any other play. Like Shakespeare, as a young man, he had wanted to be an actor, but he missed his first professional audition. Despite considerable preparation, he fell ill and could not perform. Before he got the chance for a further audition, he was writing short stories, which magazines proved willing to publish. His career as a writer had begun. The short stories then built up into sequential episodes. His first full length novel, 'Pickwick Papers', was published in instalments. After a slow start, the appearance of the cockney character Sam Weller in the fourth episode, caught the public's imagination and their subsequent popularity was assured. By the final instalment, the magazine was selling 40,000 copies a time. It was 1836 and Dickens was only 24.

This process of publishing novels by instalment was a hallmark of Dickens and how he built an audience. By the time he was done, he had completed twenty novels and novellas. About four and a half million words written in all. It was a prodigious output, almost three times the length of the Complete Works of Shakespeare, and of the King James Bible combined. He was the most read man of his generation. He was read by Queen Victoria and Prince Albert, but also by millions of members of the working classes. His novels were one of the greatest spurs for literacy in England in the 19th century. He was an ardent campaigner against poverty, worker abuse and the exploitation of the disadvantaged. His work did more than anything else to change the landscape for social justice in the mid-19th century.

While he received great public affirmation, critics and writerly circles disliked his style and his talent was distrusted. The author Anthony Trollope satirised him as 'Mr Popular Sentiment', and observed acidly, 'the artist who paints for the million must use glaring colours.' But his popularity inured Dickens to such carping.

That popularity lay in his innate ability to portray vividly all strata of society. His flair was his capability, not just to tell a great story, not just to bring to life a captivating array of characters, but to give them dialogue that conveyed the richness and comedy of all walks of like – from the aristocrat to the thieving pickpocket, from the plutocrat to the humble clerk. His ear for dialect was exceptional, and he poured all of that into his writing. He had Chaucer's knack of weaving the lives of the rich, the poor, the pompous, the downtrodden, the high-faluting, the pretentious, the sincere, into coherent and compelling tapestries. And like Chaucer, he used their vernacular to convincing effect.

Like all great writers before him, he bequeathed a contribution of excellent new words. Often it is difficult to know if he invented these words or merely popularised them. From the Dickens quotations in the OED, some 265 new words or compounds can be identified, and almost 1,600 words used in a new sense. He evolved 'messy' to 'messiness', and 'creepy' to 'the creeps'. In 'David Copperfield', he writes, 'She was constantly complaining of the cold, and of its occasioning a visitation in her back which she called 'the creeps'.' He developed the word 'rampage'. In 'Great Expectations', he writes, 'When I got home at night and delivered this message for Joe, my sister 'went on the Rampage'...'

He is credited with inventing or coining or popularising a fine selection of fabulous words including 'boredom', 'flummox', 'butterfingers', 'tousled', 'confusingly', 'kibosh', 'footlights', 'dustbin' and 'fairy story'. He conjured up 'Gunpowderous', 'platformally pausing' and 'slangular'.

As a proportion of his total words written, the number created was small, compared to Shakespeare. Over 250 new words out of 4.5 million written, versus Shakespeare's 2,000 new words out of circa 800,000. This suggests that the heavy lifting had been done, in previous centuries, of vocabulary expansion. Dickens was presented with a canvas of words that was already broad and commodious.

The descriptive style, he utilised to a point of obsession, and quite uniquely for the time, was the technique of 'as if- ness' (John Mullan's work identifies this convincingly). This stylistic quirk enabled him repeatedly to bring metaphor-like passages to his service. In 'Great Expectations' alone he used 'as if' no fewer than 266 times. In the first chapter, after Pip's encounter in the deserted cemetery with an escaped convict, Pip watches the man's return across the marshes, navigating his way between the graves: 'He looked in my young eyes as if he were eluding the hands of the dead people, stretching up cautiously out of their graves, to get a twist upon his ankle and pull him in.' On and on, Dickens would 'as if' away.

He also stylistically became highly experimental in his use of tenses. Once again, he saw the rules of language as being there to be broken. Thirty-four of the sixty-seven chapters of 'Bleak House' were written in the present; thirty-three were written in the past tense. Every batch of instalments included past chapters as well as present chapters. Towards the end of his career, he then developed a habit of leaping ahead of himself in the narrative, and telling the reader what is to come. He deployed every twist and turn to engage and excite his readers. The acidic Trollope continued to decry him: 'Of Dickens's style it is impossible to speak in praise. It is jerky, ungrammatical, and created by him in defiance of the rules... To readers who have taught themselves to regard language, it must therefore be unpleasant', and 'No young novelist should ever dare to imitate the style of Dickens.'

Where his inventiveness is most visible lexicographically is in the naming of his characters. In book after book, his protagonists are brought zinging to life by the most eye-catching names. It is a Dickens hallmark. 'Scrooge', 'Micawber', 'Jacob Marley', 'Bob Cratchit', 'Uriah Heep', 'Pecksniff', 'Gradgrind', 'Miss Havisham', 'Fezziwig', 'Sweedlepipe', 'Affery Flintwinch', etc. – all are rhythmic, descriptive, or onomatopoeic, and sometimes all three. I remember as a boy at school, calling my umbrella for short, not a 'brolly', but a 'gamp'. We all did. It is a pithy, monosyllabic word, derived from the name of the nurse in Martin Chuzzlewit who always carried one, Mrs Sarah Gamp. An early critic wrote, bizarrely puzzled by Dickens's name: 'Mr Dickens, as if in revenge for his own queer name, does bestow still queerer ones upon his fictitious creations.'

To this skill at fanciful naming has to be added, as is appropriate for any great writer in English, a ready sense of wit and humour. In a 'Christmas Carol', Scrooge, convinced that the apparition of Marley's ghost is a by-product of indigestion, comments:

> 'There's more of gravy than of grave about you, whatever you are!'

and then Dickens goes into a comic riff about door nails, that most comedians would be proud of:

> 'Old Marley was as dead as a door nail... Mind! I don't mean to say that I know, of my own knowledge, what there is particularly dead about a doornail. I might have been inclined myself, to regard a coffin-nail as the deadliest piece of ironmongery in the trade. But the wisdom of our ancestors is in the simile; and my unhallowed hands shall not disturb it, or the Country's done for. You will therefore permit me to repeat emphatically, that Marley was as dead as a doornail.'

While he was the creator of so many characters, his greatest of all was London – his home for much of his life. He seemed to know every aspect of London, from its seediness to its grandness, from its extreme poverty to its bourgeois aspiration. Through all his work you can detect an everlasting fascination with the City. Dickens projected to the world the majesty, the chaos and the grimness of Victorian London, by then the capital of the world. People in far flung corners knew London solely through the writings of Dickens.

He was inherently transatlantic. While it was a complex love-hate relationship, he was appreciated as a writer, as much in the USA as in the UK. His first American tour came in 1842, only five years after his first novel had been completed. The Americans were as much devotees of his theatrical reading style as the English, and his US tours often every bit as long as his English ones. He was not uncritical of American life as he found it. He was disappointed not to be greeted there by his utopian dream of social equality and free speech. He wrote about America: 'They've such a passion for Liberty, that they can't help taking liberties with her.' Describing an outbreak of violence that followed a political election, he wrote in one of his novels, that 'the friends of the disappointed candidate had found it necessary to assert the principles of Purity of Election and Freedom of Opinion by breaking a few legs and arms, and furthermore pursuing one obnoxious gentleman through the streets with the design of slitting his nose.' These candid commentaries on American life created him enemies. Though at times they may not have loved the man, they always loved his writing – whether written or performed.

o o o

Appropriately for our narrative, Dickens was a consummate man of the theatre. It was an important, possibly even the most important, secret of his success.

His literary debut as a young boy was penning a play: 'Misnar, Sultan of India – a tragedy,' which he acted out in his family kitchen in Chatham. He never succeeded in becoming a full-time professional actor, but he adored performance. There were times in his life, especially as a young man, when he said he went to the theatre every night of the week. As he was to write later: 'I have always had a misgiving, in my inmost heart that I was born to be the Manager of a Theatre.'

Theatre infused his writing. His first most famous character, Sam Weller of 'The Pickwick Papers' was modelled on a character in the play 'Beasleys Boarding House'. In his other early novel 'Nicholas Nickleby', dedicated to his friend and the greatest actor of his day, Macready, the protagonist finds himself recruited into a company of moth-eaten thespians under the leadership of Victor Crummles. In his other early hit, 'The Old Curiosity Shop', he counterbalanced the emotional pathos of Little Nell, with the appearance of a group of ragged performers, with waxworks and dancing dogs.

It was not just that he used the theatre and performance as part of his regular subject matter, but the way that he wrote his characters bore all the hallmarks of theatrical performance. The writer's voice was invariably present as narrator conjuring these marvellous figures into three dimensions in front of the readers' eyes. His public responded to the vivid characters of his imagination because he used the theatrical idiom that they were so used to.

In between an utterly hectic schedule of book writing, magazine contributing, and editing, including a complex family and romantic life, he endlessly found time to mount theatre productions. This reflected his innate instinct as impresario. In 1845, Dickens produced, directed and performed in a run of 'Every Man in his Humour', by Ben Jonson. It first appeared in a small theatre on Dean Street, Soho. It was revived countless times over the next three years, including once for Prince Albert, and once for Queen Victoria. *The Morning Post* wrote in its review: 'Should it be this gentleman's fate to witness the ebbtide of his popularity as a novelist, it is evident that there is another road to public favour open to him, in which he is likely to be not less successful than literature.' Another reviewer wrote: 'Mr Dickens assumed the swagger of the 'Paul's Man', with an ease that belonged more to a stage veteran rather than to an amateur.'

'Every Man in his Humour' was not a one-off for him. He went on, in 1848, to mount a new production of Shakespeare's 'The Merry Wives of Windsor' in which he played the role of Justice Shallow. In 1855, he produced 'The Lighthouse', a new play by Wilkie Collins. In 1857, he produced and even stage-managed a play he co-wrote with Collins, called 'The Frozen Deep'. Dickens's performance as Richard Wardour so moved Queen Victoria, that she granted him an audience at Buckingham Palace.

How he found time for all this as well as his prose work is hard to imagine, but he was driven by his love of theatre and performance. Where this came to an apotheosis, representing the ultimate marriage of the two art forms, was in the public readings of his books. The first such reading, he conducted in Birmingham at Christmas 1853; appropriately he read from his ever popular 'A Christmas Carol'. 1,700 people attended despite a heavy snowstorm.

What began as a standard promotional exercise for an author's work, turned, by dint of his actorly expertise, into heavily demanded, and lucrative events. He delivered his stories, in a way that nobody had done previously and probably will never do again. His reading tours became legendary. His 1858/9 tour of the United Kingdom consisted of 129 appearances in

49 different towns. Year after year, he would feed the demand for these personal appearances. His dramatic ability to deliver the text was quite unique. He designed his own bespoke lectern that emphasised the drama. On the lectern, he placed his text, a carafe of water, and a paperknife, which he used as a prop for gesticulation. Above the lectern, he had built a gas-filled frame of metal piping that lit up during the reading. This illuminated both the text and him, casting a giant shadow on the wall behind that enlarged his every gesture.

His rendition onstage of the sequence from 'Oliver Twist' of the killing of Nancy by Bill Sikes, was so physically delivered, that it would reduce him to near exhaustion, and his audience to tearful helplessness. His handwritten stage directions alongside the text indicate the verve with which he tackled the reading. 'Beckon down…Point…Shudder…Look round in terror…Murder coming…Mystery…Terror through to the end.'

On and on, he drove himself, writing and performing, performing and writing. In 1869, while in the middle of conducting a one hundred date tour, he suffered a stroke, and had to cancel the last twenty-five performances. By January 1870, he had recovered sufficiently to deliver a further twelve in St James's Hall in London. He held a special matinee to allow people to be able to hear 'Sikes' once more. Dickens wrote afterwards that it had been 'madness ever to do it continuously. My ordinary pulse is 72, and it runs up under this effort to 112. Besides which, it takes me ten or twelve minutes to get my wind back at all; I being in the meantime like the man who lost the fight.'

In the last of the readings held at St James's Hall in London, on 15 March, he delivered selections from what was to be his most enduringly popular novel, 'A Christmas Carol'. At the end, the audience called him back repeatedly to the stage, until he finally had to quell their clamour and bid them a moving and tearful farewell: 'Ladies and Gentlemen, it would be worse than idle, for it would be hypocritical and unfeeling, if I were to disguise that I close this episode in my life with feelings of very considerable pain.' So he began, and by the end of his final address, it was said that there was literally not a dry eye in the house. Carlyle wrote to his sister:

> *'Dickens does it capitally, such as it is, acts better than any Macready in the world; a whole tragic, comic, heroic theatre visible, performing under one hat and keeping us laughing…the whole night.'*

He suffered a further stroke shortly afterwards. He died that June, at the end of a full day's work on his last novel, 'Edwin Drood'. Unbelievably in his final weeks, he was not only writing 'Edwin Drood' but also producing and directing for stage three comedies: 'The Prima Donna', 'A Happy Air' and 'Le Myosotosis'. His rapidly failing health prevented him from appearing in any of them, but did not diminish his urge to produce and direct. He was working in both literature and drama, up until the very final moment. He died a thousand years after the Battle of Edington, and was one of the most shining examples of the value of the victory on that day.

Dickens was a man of emotion. He was a man of the theatre (no other English prose writer has had his work subsequently converted to stage, to television and to film as frequently and as successfully as he). He was a writer, but also a performer. He was a colossus that straddled the Atlantic. He was the consummate outsider, looking in, and forever championing the cause of the downtrodden and disadvantaged. He spoke to Everyman. He sparked a love of reading, a love of character, a love of stories in millions of people from all backgrounds. He had as his tool, the brilliance of the English language, at its peak of development. Despite his lack of a great education, he found a way to use that tool to brilliant effect. He had his critics. Some found him too sentimental; some felt him to be too populist. But I do not hesitate in advancing him for consideration as the greatest secular prose writer in the English language, and creatively an apotheosis of our highly peculiar tale.

CHAPTER TWENTY-TWO

WHERE WE ARE TODAY

> *'Of all modern languages, not one has acquired such great strength and vigour as the English...none of all the living languages can be compared with it as to richness, rationality and close construction.'*

This was the opinion of Jacob Grimm, co-author of the 'Grimm's Fairy Tales'. Although a writer, Grimm spent the greater part of his life as an expert linguist and renowned philologist. As a German, he brings a degree of objectivity to the merits of English.

We thus finish by delighting in a language that allows us to be amorous one night, and loving another. To commence, to begin, or to start. To ask, to question, to inquire or to interrogate. To respond, to reply or to answer...to be mad or berserk...to be hungry or famished. With all the diversities that those comparable words can deliver.

We can celebrate in a culture that emanates from this language, with its history and its mongrel origins. A culture that is expressive, creative, willing to tackle monumental challenges and ultimately allows us to transcend our natural reserve.

The English tongue has gone from being a dialect spoken by an estimated 200,000 people, in a precarious situation at the end of the 9th century, to a language that circuits the world and is spoken today by around 1,600 million.

It has gone from a vocabulary of about 50,000 words at the end of the Old English period to over half a million now.

Our narratives are seen on television screens in every country across the world. Millions of visitors flock to London to experience the unique wonder of our stages, and experience where our history was forged.

But it is not just cultural. Today, English is the global language used for many sectors of commerce. The whole of the air travel industry and air traffic control depend on English. Shipping too. Financial trading. Ironically, in the last-minute finalisation of the Brexit trade deal in 2020, the only version of the draft deal that could be circulated to all the individual EU administrations for final scrutiny was in English – the mother tongue of the departing nation.

Where We Are Today

This language has a clear and dominant root to it. What you might call a linguistic backbone. If you take the hundred words that we use most frequently, as defined recently by the Oxford English Corpus, you find that the overwhelming majority, ninety-one, can be identified by their Old English roots. Three are from Norse, two from mixed Norse/Germanic/Old English roots and four are derived from French/Latin. A word's history can often be complex and influenced by many sources but the message seems to emerge quite clearly. I quote below the hundred most used, ranked in order of usage. I put beside each word the source it is most strongly derived from, if not directly Anglo-Saxon English.

1. the
2. be
3. to
4. of
5. and
6. a
7. in
8. that
9. have
10. I
11. it
12. for
13. not
14. on
15. with
16. he
17. as
18. you
19. do
20. at
21. this
22. but
23. his
24. by
25. from
26. they (Norse-derived)
27. we
28. say
29. her
30. she
31. or
32. an
33. will
34. my
35. one
36. all
37. would
38. there
39. their (Norse-derived)
40. what
41. so
42. up
43. out
44. if
45. about
46. who
47. get (Old English/Germanic/Norse-derived)
48. which
49. go
50. me
51. when
52. make
53. can
54. like
55. time
56. no

57. just (French/Latin-derived)	79. think
58. him	80. also
59. know	81. back
60. take	82. after
61. people (French/Latin-derived)	83. use (French/Latin-derived)
62. into	84. two
63. year	85. how
64. your	86. our
65. good	87. work
66. some	88. first
67. could	89. well
68. them (Norse-derived)	90. way
69. see	91. even
70. other	92. new
71. than	93. want (Old English/Germanic/Norse-derived)
72. then	94. because (French/Latin-derived)
73. now	95. any
74. look	96. these
75. only	97. give
76. come	98. day
77. its	99. most
78. over	100. us

The three Norse words (they/them/their) are telling. As mentioned earlier, when English was simplified by the interaction with Norse, suffixes disappeared. This worked well so long as the nouns and pronouns, carrying the meaning, were clear and distinct. In common-place Old English, these three were not. The difference between he and they, his and their, him and them was small, and potentially confusing. Expediently the Norse/Scandinavian variants were kept for the plurals.

For all the multifarious subsequent infusions, our language at its core, and at its most used, is Anglo-Saxon. That core has benefitted from borrowings from Celtic and the wonderful enrichment of Norman, French, Latin, Norse and all the other languages we have absorbed and cherry picked from. But the core is Anglo-Saxon Old English. The same too, I believe for our culture. Its core is the wonderful creativity, and storytelling of our Anglo-Saxon heritage, enhanced by Norman pragmatism and organisational skill, with an underpinning of the lyrical beauty of Celtic.

o o o

To help validate this overall thesis, some double-checking is helpful. I make a few, international comparisons as reference points. I start with the data about dictionaries. Then the global metrics for theatre. A brief comparison in the world of swearing and obscenities. Before cross referencing the thesis to the field of music. To test if it holds water.

The word 'dictionary' was coined originally by John of Garland in 1220. The first substantive English dictionary, however, appeared in 1721. It was produced by Bailey, with 40,000 words, but with little illustration or guidance on the use of the words. It was Samuel Johnson's Dictionary of the English Language in 1755, that first provided an alphabetical ordering of words, with full context and explanation. He employed only six assistants, five of whom were Scottish. His first edition also included 40,000 words, but achieved such popularity that it became the standard for dictionaries for 150 years. He was probably the closest the English had to a recognised arbiter on words.

Johnson tackled his gargantuan task with humility and humour, producing a thoroughly English piece of work. He defined his own profession, that of being a 'lexicographer' as 'A writer of dictionaries, a harmless drudge...' Self-heckling that Chaucer would have been proud of. To tease his assistants, he defined 'oats' as 'a grain, which in England is generally given to horses, but in Scotland supports the people'.

He demonstrated a fundamental understanding of the unruliness of the language. In his preface, he wrote:

> 'When we see men grow old and die at a certain time one after another, from century to century, we laugh at the elixir that promises to prolong life to a thousand years; and with equal justice may the lexicographer be derided, who being able to produce no example of a ion that has preserved their words and phrases from mutability, shall imagine that his dictionary can embalm his language, and secure it from corruption and decay.'

The documenting of words in English dictionaries has expanded endlessly since Johnson's masterpiece. The most epic endeavour was the development of the Oxford English Dictionary. Begun initially in 1857, it took on the scale of a Victorian engineering project, collecting submissions of words and phrases from the whole of the English-speaking world; these were meticulously annotated and distilled by its longest serving editor, James Murray. By 1884, the work was still not complete, and the publishers started issuing it in instalments beginning with the letter 'A'. The final complete work was not available until 1928. It quickly became the gold standard of the language. Today, the Oxford English Dictionary contains 500,000 words. By comparison Webster's Dictionary (named after Noah Webster, the evangelist for American English) lists 470,000 words. The English Wiktionary online edition claims 711,000 words.

The first French dictionary, the Catholicon, appeared in 1499. The Académie Française subsequently took responsibility for the official French dictionary. Its first edition appeared in 1687. It took fifty-five years to compile, and a further eighteen to revise. Johnson achieved his dictionary almost single handedly in seven years. The eighth edition of the Académie Française dictionary was published in 1935, it contained only 35,000 words. The ninth edition was begun in 1986 and was finally published in 2024, some 38 years later. It has managed to add only 21,000, finally recognising words like 'vegan', 'photocopy' and unbelievably 'le wokisme'. This is the gold standard for proper French; it has staunchly tried to resist the invasion of Anglo derivations. Other French dictionaries include more words, but even the Dictionnaire Le Grand Robert published in 2019 includes only 100,000, and Trésor de la Langue Française 135,000. The French Wiktionary achieves 408,000.

The fundamental difference between the fundamental nature of French and English vocabularies is also comically endorsed by a recent work by Professor Bernard Cerquiglini, entitled 'La langue anglaise n'existe pas – c'est du français mal prononcé' ('English as language does not exist, it is simply French mispronounced'). His thesis is that 80,000 current English words can be identified as being derived (and linguistically distorted) from French. The mistake, he makes, is assuming that 80,000 constitutes a whole language (or in his terms, the important bits of the language), as it does in official French. This is his basis for ascertaining that English does not exist as a language. In fact the expansive, absorptive and evolutionary nature of English means that these French derivations take a proud place in our tongue, but constitute no more than 15 per cent of the English we use today.

Wikipedia itself provides a useful schedule of comparison not only for French but also for other languages. In German, the Deutsche Worterbuch contains 330,000 words of which only 200,000 are said to be in contemporary use. In Russian, the Explanatory Dictionary of the Living Great Russian Language contains 220,000 words. In Spanish the Diccionario de la lengua española de la Real Academia Española includes 93,000 words.

Robert McCrum in his 'The Story of English' endorses this analysis. He writes:

> '*The statistics are astonishing. Of all the world's languages, which now number some 2700, (English) is arguably the richest in vocabulary. The compendious Oxford English Dictionary lists about 500,000 words; and a further half a million technical and scientific terms remain uncatalogued. According to traditional estimates, neighbouring Germany has a vocabulary of about 185,000 words and French fewer than 100,000, including such Franglais vocabulary as 'le snaque-barre' and 'le hit parade.'*

o o o

I move next to theatre.

In Britain, just prior to the pandemic, the annual total audience was 34 million in the professional theatre sector (West End, major off-West End, major regional and touring venues) across 63,000 performances a year. This excludes countless small scale and amateur. By contrast, according to a substantial 2022 EU report assessing the theatre sector, Germany has 18.5 million attendances per year. Germany is one of the more theatre-loving countries in the world, but does not come close to our frequency of attendance, in spite of 20 per cent more population. Spain had only 11.5 million attendances a year, with Italy at 11.8 million. The French did not, or were not able to submit data to this EU survey, which tends to confirm both a proportionately low number and a lack of importance given to theatre (by comparison to its well-supported film industry).

America is obviously the other great theatre powerhouse, reflecting our shared cultural roots. London and New York are the two theatre capitals of the world. But in 2022/23, Broadway's annual audience was 12 million versus London's West End at 16 million. Professional major regional theatre attendance in the US was reported to be about 18 million – comparable to UK regional theatre. Given the relative scale of the two countries, this means that the British are at least five times more frequent theatre goers than their American counterparts.

No nation in the world puts so much emphasis on-stage performance. Every school in the country involves its children in dramatic playmaking almost continuously. To a degree that surprised even my American East Coast theatre-loving wife, when it came to the education of our children in England.

Every university brims with drama groups; every town, and even village, has their amateur performance clubs. The visit to the theatre especially at

Christmas time is an embedded cultural tradition. This does not happen globally to any equivalent extent.

Not surprisingly, America and Britain are disproportionately significant in the TV and film industry. Both benefit from the talents and skills developed in the theatre world. Acting, writing, producing, designing, set-making, prop-making, costume-making and so on. The launch of a new film into cinemas is still referred to as its 'theatrical release'. The term reflects the shared legacy.

o o o

I consider swearing and obscenities next. Verse, prose and high drama have not been the only beneficiaries of a rich, flexible and highly phonetic tongue, but also cussing, oaths and profanities.

Richard Marriott wrote in *The Times* recently:

> *'If our language's highest pleasure is Shakespeare, its second highest pleasure is its swear words. English with its abundance of plosive and fricative sounds and its versatile syntax, might have been designed for profanity. German is too sinister. The European romance languages too beautiful (the Spanish 'puta madre' sounds like a kind of rose; the French 'putain' sounds like a cake you might buy in a patisserie), English swear words are comic, heartfelt and charged with ancient malice.'*

I concur with this overview but in order to make the comparative analysis a touch more scientific, I asked the comedian, writer and radio broadcaster, Arthur Smith, to consider the relative merits of English and French as languages to swear in. He is fluent in both, and regularly performs stand-up comedy in both Paris and London. He is expert in the options for oaths, put-downs and heckles in both languages. He writes:

> *'I have a degree in French, spent a year teaching English in Paris, and was the first English stand-up comic to perform a show in French. I feel qualified to contend that swearing in English is miles better than swearing in French. Yes, 'vas te faire enculer' is nearly as rude as 'fuck off' but it lacks those sharp, satisfying Anglo-Saxon spiteful expulsions. The French choose prostitutes and buggery as their favoured arenas for insults while we prefer genitalia and self-pleasure. The French have no 'bollocks' and for them, being a 'wanker' or a 'tosser' ('bronleur') carries no negative connotations. 'Merde' is equal to 'shit' but*

cannot act as a verb, and no single word in French is as offensive as 'cunt'. ('La chatte'? That is just a sweet cat).

We may imagine the French, with their continental ways and slouched shoulders, are liable to be more sweary than us but the reality is that the English are much more fluent both at swearing and heckling than the French. From personal experience, I have found that the line 'I have shat better comics than you', is a punchier put down when delivered by the Geordie battle-axe in the front row, than 'vous êtes une pomme de terre avec le visage d'un cochon d'inde'. Personally, I am happy to be a 'potato with the face of a guinea pig'.

The battle-axe in the front row was clearly honouring Chaucer and his self-heckle, noted earlier: 'Thy drasty rymyng is nat worth a toord'.

I cannot think of a culture that would name the streets habituated by brothels and streetwalkers, so directly, bluntly and descriptively as 'Gropecunt Lane'. But in medieval England this was commonplace. London had several of this name. These were not just in Southwark, home to the stews and lewderies of the day, but in the very heart of the City. A 'Gropecunt Lane' was cited for example alongside 'PuppekirtyLane', and 'Bordhawelane', in the red light district opposite Mercers' Hall on Cheapside. The English language revelled in highly evocative compound terms, even in their rudest forms.

I finish by quoting the anecdote from Niall Ferguson's book 'Empire – How Britain made the Modern World'. The Governor of Aden, Sir Richard Turnbull, just prior to its independence, mused to Dennis Healey, then defence minister, 'When the British Empire finally sank beneath the waves of history, it would leave behind it only two monuments: one was the game of Association Football, the other was the expression 'Fuck off''.

o o o

My final cross-reference is to music. The role of music in English culture warrants a book in its own right. I can at best be cursory.

Music has always been central to our artistic life, from the sung delivery of 'Beowulf' onward. However taking the whole of the last two millennia, you would not consider England consistently pre-eminent globally in music making or composition. There are odd exceptions like the renaissance in the early 20th century with Elgar, Holst and Vaughan Williams, but looking at the bigger picture, the European nations that appear constantly in the forefront are Germany, Austria, Italy, France, Russia. Each boasts a list of topflight, truly first-rank composers over a sustained number of centuries. Africa, the Caribbean and Black America have comparably been the source of blues, of jazz, of reggae, of rock and R&B for the world. The German writer, Oscar Schmitz put his finger on it famously in 1904 in his work 'Das Land Ohne Musik'. 'I have found something which distinguishes English people from all cultures to quite an astonishing degree,' he writes, 'a lack which everybody acknowledges, therefore nothing new, but has not been emphasised enough. The English are the only cultured nation without its own music.'

But despite what Schmitz concludes, and as mentioned as a conclusion to Chapter Nineteen, there are two periods of history when English musical prowess has achieved global recognition sustainably. The first is Hymns. In the 17th, 18th and 19th centuries, hymns written by English writers circled the world. They represent a total body of work that few other nations could rival.

The second period has been from 1964 onwards. In 1964 the Beatles achieved their first number-one single in the USA. Almost from nowhere, the Sixties saw an explosion in English music making that took the world by storm. In the matter of a few months we moved from the parochial talents of domestic chart toppers like Frank Ifield, Russ Conway and Lonnie Donegan, to the global phenomena of the Beatles, the Rolling Stones, the Kinks, Pink Floyd, Led Zeppelin, Cream, Bowie, Elton John, etc. This has been an era of extraordinary English pre-eminence. This explosion is equivalent to the paradigm shift in English drama in the 16th century.

In parallel to the contemporary music revolution came the wave of English stage musical writing. What had been an exclusively American area of expertise, suddenly had English contenders taking the crown. We moved from the delightful but very insular 'Salad Days' of the 1950s, by way of Lionel Bart's 'Oliver' in 1960, to the full force of 'Jesus Christ Superstar' by 1970, 'The Rocky Horror Show' in 1973, 'Evita' in 1978. English musical stage craft has not looked back since. It is extraordinary to see today an English musical about the six wives of Henry VIII, not just winning awards, but playing to full houses on both Broadway and the West End.

I think that there is an obvious reason why these two phases of music became quintessentially English. Hymns, rock and pop, musical numbers are all uniquely lyric-based. Suddenly the popular format of the day moved in the direction of language. They are all music where the words count as much as the composition itself. Suddenly English creators had the unique advantage of the language, and our innate skill with words rhythmic, poetic and emotionally expressive.

There are too many great lyric examples to quote from music since the Sixties. You can marvel at the brilliance of the Beatles' 'A Day in the Life', or Ray Davies' 'Waterloo Sunset', through to more recent great lyrics, such as Florence and the Machine's 'Ship to Wreck' or 'The End of Love', or Arlo Parks' 'Black Dog', Sam Fender's 'Spit of You', or Self Esteem's 'I Do This All the Time'. These are just personal favourites but the list is ever long.

In musicals, English traditional weakness is no more with the lyrical work of Tim Rice, Don Black, Charles Hart, Richard O'Brien and even T.S. Eliot, the lyricist for 'Cats'. Consider the great lyrical show numbers like 'Memories', 'I Don't Know How to Love Him' or 'Sweet Transvestite'.

Backing up this language-based creativity has been an organisational capability that nowadays, in the music and musicals industry is pivotal. From the scale and diversity of festivals to the sophistication of music production, recording techniques, and the daunting complexity of staging musicals, this is an art form that needs the discipline and organisational skills, central to the English temperament. The statistics reflect this sea change. By the 1990s it was estimated that of global contemporary music sales, around 25 per cent was attributable to British writers, versus UK's 2 per cent of global GDP and 1 per cent of global population. That over-indexing has diminished but still continues. According to the industry, UK's total export revenue of the music industry hit 4.6 billion pounds in 2023. And UK artists generated 10 per cent of global music revenue, second only to the US.

CHAPTER TWENTY-THREE

DRAWING TO CONCLUSIONS

I began with a series of questions. Why is English such a uniquely successful language? Why are its people such a mix of the creative and of the organised – often in a single individual? Why are they notoriously so reserved and emotionally constipated in normal life, yet capable of expressing feeling with such power when required? I summarise my suggested conclusions.

A maritime climate and a rich agrarian economy
England's climate and soil have been critical. These have created a productive and munificent agrarian economy. This has made us tempting to invaders, and four major waves of such invasions came in the first eleven hundred years AD. These brought the melting pot of influences from which our mongrel tongue emerged enriched, simplified, versatile and powerful. It also created sufficient wealth that a class of scholars, thinkers and priests could be supported, instigating the first great creative and philosophical wave of the Anglo-Saxon period. It also generated the wealth for churches and monasteries, which in turn made possible the plunder of that wealth by Henry VIII, and the economic redistribution that its broad disposal prompted. Norman strength, brutality and organisation meant the island became unconquerable. The tables could then be turned; the underlying agrarian wealth supplemented by the ingenuity, fuelled the industrial revolution, and created the wherewithal for exploring the world.

The English have preserved an inherent fear of invasion – a comprehensible psychological scarring from our past experiences. Hitler, Napoleon and the Spanish Armada sailors are all familiar invasion-minded bogey men. In 1871, for example, during the Franco-German conflict, a novel entitled 'The Battle of Dorking' was published. Written by a serving army colonel it told the fictional tale, in intricate detail, of England's invasion and occupation by a powerful enemy German army. It became an overnight best seller, and the Prime Minister, Gladstone, had to make urgent public statements, proclaiming that an invasion was not underway, and that 'The Battle of Dorking' was nothing more than a work of fiction.

An island, and sea-faring power
Much of this tale has been influenced by our island status. We are the largest island in Europe. England emerged as an enduring major nation state earlier than any other in Europe. It created a distinct identity, ready to leave or to join Europe, on various occasions in our history. It has shaped our national personality, and given us the basis of a strong unified language. It has also meant that we have put disproportionate focus on being a maritime power. As opportunities started to grow faster outside Europe, England moved from being at the edge of things, to being at the centre. That gave us advantage when it came to the building of an Empire. We have seen throughout this book, the way that English survived, and indeed was, in many ways, improved by conquest. This improved version was then taken to the four corners of the world, was improved again, and benefitted from further infusion from so many different tongues. This has been an active organic process, which would have been impossible for a land-locked nation, with no maritime aspirations.

A capital city like no other
The Romans came to the 'place at the overflowing river', and decided to build a bridge. Partly because they could. Upon this small, seemingly inconsequential event, so much followed. The 'place at the overflowing river' turned into the engine for the whole nation, London. What the Romans started, Alfred endorsed and William's Charter enshrined for the future. Without this congruence of the economic, cultural, political, legal, monarchical and religious, all in a single place, English would not be in the position that it is today. That statement is counter to current regional-minded orthodoxy. However, for this narrative, London's centrality has been crucial; its independence, via its structures of Companies, has enabled it to trade and finance largely according to its own parameters. This has produced funding at reasonable cost for so many elements of this adventure. London, and its dominance, determined which specific dialect would be our national tongue. It then projected it powerfully around the world. Today it has a population of 9 million, and contributes a quarter of the UK's total GDP. It is a financial and cultural centre of the world. The story of the English language cannot be separated from the story of London. If anything will keep London in its global position, it is probably the language.

The impact of religion and the passion for theatre
Just as London and language go hand in hand, so does religion and theatre. We have reflected our instinct for independence in our religious choices. Equally, we have followed a path of the middle ground. On King James's

succession, there were calls to revert to Catholicism, there was pressure to move to full scale Puritan worship, but as with many aspects of our history, a central course was chosen. So much of our language has happened on the back of our religious direction.

Initially we chose in Christianity a religion that was based on scholarship, text and knowledge. We then chose a branch of Christianity that was designed to underline our independence from the ways of Rome. That is in our nature as an island. It chimed with our natural instinct to question, and reject unswerving adherence to Vatican dogma, transubstantiation and the sale of indulgences.

It also re-emphasised the importance of the Word.

From our affection for the old ways but an embrace of a new religious doctrine, came our need for and love of theatre – a crucial medium for our language. The performance, the 'magic' and the storytelling sublimated from the nave to the stage. And what is more, despite arousing endless suspicion from many authorities, managed to survive every attempt to stamp it out.

Our independent nature, and our quest for legitimacy

It has not just been our language which has flourished from essentially Anglo-Saxon roots, but also our approach to power and the constant questioning of legitimacy. Innate within our psychology is a distrust of princes. I attribute that largely to the Anglo-Saxon need for legitimacy of authority. Succession was never preordained, but dependent on a degree of consensus. Whenever the exercise of authority moved from that principle, the consequences were predictable. The stool always required several legs of support to remain upright. King John could not rule without the Barons and the City forcing him to sign the Magna Carta. Charles I was executed when he moved out of the accepted parameters of royal power. Similarly, the Cromwells could not sustain the Protectorate when it became dependent overly on the army.

The same spirit has been applied to our language. Any attempt to control it has been resisted. It expands, contracts and develops on the basis of the consensus of writers and speakers. There is no Constitution of Language in the same way that there is no Constitution of Political Authority. It would be antithetical to our pedigree.

The role of genius

Inevitably none of this can be achieved but for the geniuses who have trodden over these pages. The giants of our narrative have included Alfred, Athelstan, Chaucer, Wycliffe, Tyndale, Shakespeare. To these are added Bede, Ine,

Drawing to Conclusions

William I, Julian of Norwich, Margery Kempe, Langland, Cranmer, James I, Donne, Jonson, Andrewes, and Watts. And more recently are added the Wesleys, Shelburne, Oswald, Dickens, T.S. Eliot and all our contemporary songsmiths.

Direction in history is obviously often determined by the individual genius who transcends the thinking of the time, inspires a generation and sets a fresh course. That will be true of any country at any time. What I find interesting about our selection is how many are either 'outsiders' or what I would call 'unchosen ones'.

This echoes the way in which our narrative has pivoted on key events in our history, that are invariably little known to a modern audience: Edington, Bouvines, the Treaty of Paris, for example. These are not stand-out topics of our history curriculum, and yet they have shaped our destiny. They have certainly shaped the course of our language.

Equally, while many of our protagonists are well known, many are relatively less well known to us today: Athelstan, Shelburne, Tyndale, Watts and Wycliffe, for example. What unites them is the genius they brought but also their relationship with the people of their time, and especially the established order.

Some of course were born into the purple. Shelburne was a second Earl, and eldest son of the first Earl. But that is an exception.

The clear outsiders are apparent: Wycliffe, Langland, Cranmer, Shakespeare and Dickens all came from humble origins and found a way to make their genius tell. Then there are the non-conformists: men like Donne, the two Wesleys and Watts. Chaucer, Andrewes and Oswald were from middle-class families, but entered into circles way beyond their natural experience.

And then there is the category of what I call 'unchosen ones'.

Alfred, Athelstan. William and James, all became Kings of England against natural probability. Alfred was the youngest son of his father. Athelstan, although the eldest son, had been passed over in favour of his younger half-brother. William was of course 'the Bastard', and despite what he protested, had very arguable rights to the English throne. James succeeded the Queen that put his very Catholic and Francophile mother to death. All therefore fall into my category of the 'unchosen ones'; all have been highly influential to the narrative. My opinion is that because none were specifically groomed for the role they assumed, they acquired skills, aptitudes, perspective and aspirations that natural successors often lack. There is nothing like believing that you have the God-given right to a position, to limit your ambition.

Although English society is often considered to be closed and hard to penetrate, consistently over the centuries it has actually been open to the talented outsider. While our attitude to arriving foreigners, or to those that break the class ceiling, has ebbed and flowed, there have been sustained periods of acceptance based on talent, irrespective of origin. Much of our success has been down to very skilled and talented people coming from abroad and settling in this country. Men like the first Governor of the Bank of England, Sir John Houblon, who came from strong French Huguenot stock. Same too for those who have consistently been considered minorities. We have had strong female monarchs for five hundred years. We have had doughty female prime ministers for over forty years. We had a prime minister of overt Jewish heritage some 150 years ago, and recently a prime minister of Hindi descent. By comparison, as at time of writing, neither America nor France has had a female president, and neither have had one of direct Jewish, Muslim or Hindi descent – with the recent exception of Sarkozy in France, who is a quarter Greek/Jewish. Germany finally had a female chancellor in Angela Merkel, but she is their first, and they have never had a Jewish or ethnically diverse chancellor.

This relative acceptance of the outside and unchosen genius has been an important contribution to our narrative. It helps explain why figures of such genius from all backgrounds have regularly stepped forward and made astonishing contributions. Shakespeare's prodigious output, his extraordinary playmaking ability, his breadth of knowledge given his modest background, prompts the question: 'Was it he who wrote all these plays?' It should prompt a different question: 'What is the system that has enabled someone of his background to flourish and to fulfil their genius?' Personally I think the answer lies in our underlying Anglo-Saxon attributes, our Celtic roots, our love of independence, our island separateness, our passion for storytelling on epic scale, and our skill at organising. Dreams are not only encouraged, but also can be realised.

The all-important Norman contribution to this heady mix
For me, '1066 and All That' should be renamed '878 and All That'. This would mark the watershed of King Alfred's victory at Edington, over William's at Hastings.

However the Vikings, the Romans and the original Britons cannot be, and are not, excluded from our story, nor can the Normans be. There are enduring contributions that are fundamental to how we are now.

The Norman's ability to defend the shores from further invasion ranks high. As does their investment in infrastructure. Where the Romans brought us roads and bridges, the Normans brought us castles and cathedrals, around which towns grew stronger and larger. They strengthened our capital markets with the Jewish community. Without the Normans we would not have had the infusion of French that came with them. We might have been solely 'loving', and never 'amorous', and our lives would be greyer as a consequence. Of most interest to me is what they have contributed to our national psychology. The Normans brought a brutal efficiency and organisational focus that is still an enduring aspect of our national make-up.

My belief is that our unusual combination of creative talent and organisational ability is the merging in the national genes of these great influences: the Anglo-Saxon and the Norman, with Roman and Celtic underpinning. No other culture has had the benefit of that combination. As I stand atop the Norman-built White Tower with its forceful presence, its impressive highly geometric design, its advanced latrine system ejecting its waste relentlessly towards London, and stare out over what is still an Anglo-Saxon city with its winding streets, its quirky charms, its churches, its Halls and performance spaces, built within its Roman walls and connected by its Roman bridge, all sited on its Celtic birthplace, the argument feels persuasive.

When you then add to this Anglo-Saxon/Norman mix, our religious history, driven as it was by our island-minded wish to be independent, and apply a brilliantly expressive language, then it is no surprise, you get a people, fundamentally reserved and private, but who have found ways to sublimate their feelings into other art forms and other methods of expression.

And what the world gets in return is a global language, that is rich, diverse, expressive, copious in its options and constantly evolving. And is relatively simple to master. No unnecessary genders. Complex suffixes. No need for intricate variations in tone and sound required to define meaning, as for example in Mandarin and Arabic. It is capable of precision. But it is also capable of conveying sentiment, and emotion. For a buttoned-up body of people, it is a beautiful emotional safety valve. For the rest of the world it is a way of communicating easily from one to another across borders, and to do so with not just words, but with poetry, sentiment and above all in ceremony and performance, in a tongue that allows deviation, change and flexibility.

Of all the world's languages, Mandarin comes second in terms of number of speakers at currently about 1,100 million (aggregating all the various dialects), Hindi 600 million, Spanish 550 million, French 280 million, Arabic 270 million. English at 1,600 million has not only the largest number, but it also has the largest proportion speaking it as a second language – some 75 per cent, versus Mandarin at 20 per cent. This emphasises its accessibility.

There are lots of issues and debates, rightly, about the negative impacts of empires (past and present), globalisation, and cultural appropriation. They are a subject of research and scrutiny beyond the scope of this book. But on the other side of the coin, the benefits derived from having a widely spoken global common language of this beauty and practicality, cannot be ignored.

Iris Murdoch caught the spirit of this when she wrote:

'We live continually in and through words. Memories of words, poetic and sacred, travel with us through life... The great traditional words of the Bible and the Prayer Book are high instances of sacred art, of beauty as sacrament...language and spirit conjoined to produce a high unique religious eloquence. These books have been loved because of their inspired linguistic perfection. Treasured words encourage, console and save.'

I have to hope that the current focus on exorcising words from the language that could possibly offend, and the dizzying shift month by month in determining what language is right and what is wrong, does not reverse the historic process of our vocabulary and its expansion. We have a long tradition of free speech. We have a history of organic growth based on influx and usage, and have always resisted linguistic diktats. We lose that as a core feature of English at its peril.

o o o

That is my thesis. Many will find issue, but at the least I hope it prompts debate. I hope that I have taken you to some places you have not previously been, and introduced you to people you have not previously met.

By way of finale, I wanted to end with the relatively recent past.

Like many of our greatest literary creators, T.S. Eliot was both dramatist and poet. He was another 'outsider'. He was legendarily unknowable. He was born in Missouri with an inguinal hernia that excluded him from sport and physical activities, and made him an oddity among his classmates. He went on to spend his adult life in England, where he was greatly accepted but seemed to remain an outsider, nonetheless. He converted from Unitarianism to the Anglican faith, and found great inspiration from the church of St Magnus the Martyr, in the City. St Magnus was a Norse, Orkney-based warlord, and the church dedicated to him formed the original northern stepping-off point for London Bridge, until the bridge was moved fifty yards westward, where it stands today. The church was probably frequented by Chaucer, and was where Miles Coverdale, the assistant to Tyndale, preached for several years. Many of our narrative strands intertwine in this quiet location.

Eliot studied and appreciated many of the figures from our story: Shakespeare, Andrewes, Julian of Norwich. His supreme mastery of the language meant he wrote some of the greatest English poetry of the 20th century. Much could be quoted, but as my final example, I chose the poem he dedicated to his second wife. In his late sixties, he fell passionately in love with Valerie, some thirty-eight years younger than he. In complete contrast to the tempestuous storms of his first marriage, he remained lovingly devoted to Valerie, until his death.

This dedication appeared first in the preface to his last and most confessional play, 'The Elder Statesman', which included the telling disclosure. '...like the asthmatic struggling for breath, so the lover must struggle for words.' I quote the final revised version, because of the quiet beauty of the writing, because of his characteristic careful use of words, and because he captures in the closing line, in nine words only, the quintessential thesis of Englishness, core to our argument.

> 'A Dedication to my Wife
>
> To whom I owe the leaping delight
> That quickens my senses in our wakingtime
> And the rhythm that governs the repose of our sleepingtime,
> The breathing in unison
>
> Of lovers whose bodies smell of each other
> Who think the same thoughts without need of speech
> And babble the same speech without need of meaning.
>
> No peevish winter wind shall chill
> No sullen tropic sun shall wither
> The roses in the rose-garden which is ours and ours only.
>
> But this dedication is for others to read:
> These are private words addressed to you in public.'

It took an Anglophile born on the banks of the Mississippi, to be able to express the abiding ethos of English expressiveness, probably better than any Englishman could. To me, it is the defining concept of 'private words addressed to you in public'. It is this, that is being played out on our stages, in our theatres every night, at our music arenas, and at every festival time. It is this that which our language was uniquely designed to do. Utterly reserved people able to express feelings of a deeply emotional nature through the medium of public performance, expertly mounted and through words in English. Private words addressed to you in public.

○ ○ ○

T.S. Eliot also wrote about the pervasive feeling of antiquity that permeates England, and spoke of the countless generations lying beneath the soil standing witness to our current lives. These are themes which the play 'Jerusalem' constantly returns to. So as I was writing the initial drafts of this book, it felt appropriate that the decision was made to bring 'Jerusalem' back to the West End, twelve years after its first performance. Following two years of pandemic induced darkness, producers wondered, just as they did in 1660, what would bring the audiences back. One conclusion was the unique performance of 'Jerusalem'. The director, Ian Rickson, and the core of the original performers, Mark Rylance, Mackenzie Crook, Gerard Horan, Alan David, Barry Sloane, all embraced the significance of the opportunity.

Prior to the first performance in April 2022, every ticket had been sold for its full three month run. Once again Mark Rylance had no understudy. This time we did lose a few performances, three to be precise. During the run, Mark's brother was tragically killed riding a bike in Los Angeles. It took the duration of three performances for Mark to fly to California, attend the funeral and fly back straight to the theatre. Three performances were added at the end of the run. The final of these was on Wednesday 10 August 2022. The auditorium was packed as it had been throughout the run. At the end, the audience gave a standing ovation in a way that the English very rarely do. They cheered and stomped for a full fifteen minutes, not wishing the actors to leave or for the moment to pass. They would have done so for much longer, if Mark had not brought proceedings to a reluctant close. The primordial English gods had been woken, stories old and new had been told, authority had been defied, the forest had been brought to vivid life and the magic of our language and our ancient myths had been welded together into an experience that reminded us that feelings can be expressed and words can be found for our deepest emotions.

The final, moving, defiant lines of Rooster Byron boomed out.

> *Surrender! South Wiltshire! You are outnumbered. I have you surrounded. For at my back is every Byron boy that e'er was born an Englishman. And behind them bay the drunken devil's army and we are numberless. Rise up! Rise up. Cormoran.*

Woden. Jack-of-green. Jack-in-irons. Thunderdell. Buri, Blunderbore, Gog and Magog, Galligantus, Vili and Ve, Yggdrasil, Brutus of Albion. Come, you drunken spirits. Come, you battalions. You fields of ghosts who walk these green plains still. Come, you giants!'

The wind roared through the trees, the earth shook, as Rooster called up his guardians by the relentless beat of his ancient drum. Their approaching footsteps told us that once more, against all the odds of aversion, the English dream would survive and a new dawn beckoned.

SOURCES, ATTRIBUTIONS, REFERENCES, AND TRANSLATIONS USED

All quotations from the plays of William Shakespeare are taken from the 'Tudor Shakespeare' edition, edited by Professor Peter Alexander and first published by Collins Classics in 1951.

Word derivations have been sourced predominantly from the current (2023) online version of the Oxford English Dictionary.

All sources are listed alphabetically by chapter.

CHAPTER ONE: 'AMONG THESE DARK SATANIC MILLS'

'Blood Swept Lands and Seas of Red', created by artist Paul Cummins and designer Tom Piper, for Historic Royal Palaces 2014.

Historic Royal Palaces websites.

'Jerusalem' by Jez Butterworth. Nick Hern Books 2009

'Jerusalem' by William Blake. Poetry Foundation : source 'Preface to Milton's Poem', 1810.

Mary Borden's 'Sonnets to a Soldier', Dare-Gale Press 2015.

CHAPTER TWO: THE LAND OF THE TATTOOED PEOPLE

'French Leave' by P.G. Wodehouse. Herbert Jenkins 1956.

Gildas quoted from 'The Ruin of Britain and Other Works', edited and translated by Michael Winterbottom. Philimore 1978.

'In Search of the Dark Ages' by Michael Wood. BBC Books 2005.

'Kings' Letters from the Days of Alfred to the Coming of the Tudors', edited by Robert Steele, Alexander Moring. De la More Press 1900.

Source of Pretannike : Diodorus Siculus in 'The Library of History' Book 5. 21.

'The Emergence of the English' by Susan Oosthuizen. Arc Humanities Press 2019.

'The Earth Transformed. An Untold History' by Peter Frankopan. Bloomsbury 2023.

CHAPTER THREE: WHEN GIANTS WALKED THIS LAND

'Alfred the Great : Asser's Life of King Alfred and Other Contemporary Sources' by John Asser : De Rebus Gestis Aelfredi. English : Simon Keynes 1952 and Michael Lapidge 1983.

'King Ine (688–726) and the Writing of English Law in Latin' by Ingrid Ivarsen, English Historical Review (137).
'Kings' Letters from the Days of Alfred to the Coming of the Tudors', edited by Robert Steele, Alexander Moring. De la More Press 1900.
'Place Names Dictionary of London' by Johannes Hoops. Oxford University Press.
'The Anglo-Saxon Chronicles', from a translation by J.A. Giles published in Monumenta Historica Britannica, G. Bell & Sons 1914. 787 entry from manuscript C, 793 entry from manuscript D.
'The Cult of Alfred the Great' by Simon Keynes. Anglo-Saxons England (28) 1999.
'The Tribal Hidage' by Cyril Hart. Transactions of the Royal Historical Society 21. 1971.
Wedmore Treaty quoted as translated on the British Library website.

CHAPTER FOUR: REX ANGLORUM

'Athelstan : First English King' by Sarah Foot. 2011.
'Athelstan : The Making of England' by Tom Holland. 2016.
'Edward the Elder and the Making of England' by Harriet Harvey Wood. Sharpe Books 2019.
'In Search of the Dark Ages' by Michael Wood. BBC Books 2022.
'Jerusalem' by William Blake. Poetry Foundation : source 'Preface to Milton's Poem', 1810.

CHAPTER FIVE: THE FORGOTTEN TRIBES

'In Search of the Dark Ages' by Michael Wood. BBC Books 2022.
'Our Magnificent Bastard Tongue' by John McWhorter. Gotham Books 2008.
'How English Became English' by Simon Horobin. OUP 2016.

CHAPTER SIX: NORSE CODE

'Havamal' from the Codex Regius, The Poetic Edda. Translated by Henry Adams Bellows. 1936.
'Our Magnificent Bastard Tongue' by John McWhorter. Gotham Books 2008.
'The Story of English' by Philip Gooden. Quercus 2009.

CHAPTER SEVEN: THE UNIQUELY ENGLISH CULTURAL REVOLUTION

'A Medieval Mercantile Community' by Pamela Nightingale. Yale University Press 1995.
'Beowulf' by Anonymous. Opening section quoted from a translation by Richard Hamer. Faber and Faber 2020. Lake section quoted from translation by Burton Raffel 1999. Closing section quoted from translation by Seamus Heaney, W.W. Norton 2000.

'Dream of the Rood' from Complete Old English Poems, edited by Tom Shipping and translated by Craig Williamson. 2017.

'How English Became English' by Simon Horobin. Oxford University Press 2016.

'Humour in Anglo-Saxon Literature', edited by Jonathan Wilcox. D.S. Brewer 2000. In particular 'Humor in Hiding : Laughter Between the Sheets in the Exeter Book of Riddles' by, and with translation by, D.K. Smith quoted.

'Music in Anglo-Saxon England' by Alison Hudson. The British Library.

Tacitus' 'Life of Cnaeus Julius Agricola' Ch 21. Translated by Alfred John Church and William Jackson Brodribb.

'The Alfred Jewel', The British Library website.

'The Battle of Maldon' by Mark Atherton based on David Casley's transcript. Bloomsbury Academic 2021.

'The Buildings of England – Cumberland and Westmoreland' by Nikolaus Pevsner. Penguin 1967.

'The English' by Geoffrrey Elton. Blackwell 1992.

'The Making of England : Anglo-Saxon Art and Culture AD600–900' by Marion Archibald, Janet Backhouse, Leslie Webster. British Museum 1991.

'The Seafarer', from Complete Old English Poems, translated by Craig Williamson.

CHAPTER EIGHT: LIVING WITH THE NEW NORMAN

'A Description of London' by William Fitzstephens, from Corporation of London Records, transcription by Henry Thomas Riley d.1878.

'Carmen de Hastingae Proelio' of Guy Bishop of Amiens, edited by Catherine Morton and Hope Muntz. 1972.

'Facsimiles of English Royal Writs to AD 1100', presented to Vivian Hunter Galbraith.

'History of England under the Norman Kings' by J.M. Lappenberg

'History of the Conquest' by Guil. Pictav.

'London under Danish Rule : Cnut's Politics and Policies as a Demonstration of Power' by Matthew Firth. Eras Journal.

'Norman Conquest' and 'Norman Yoke' entries in Oxford Companion of British History 2009.

'Protection, Power and Persecution : The Tower of London and the Jewish Community until 1290' by Sally Dixon-Smith. Historic Royal Palaces.

Population estimates from Encyclopedia Britannica.

Rhigyfarch's quote taken from 'The Welsh-Latin Poetry' by M. Lapidge. Studia Celtica.

'Richard I' by John Gillingham. Yale University Press 1999.

'Richard Devises, concerning the deeds of Richard I, King of England', translated and edited by J.A. Giles. Jmes Bohm, London 1841.

'The Anglo-Saxon Chronicles', from a translation by J.A. Giles published in Monumenta Historica Britannice, G. Bell & Sons 1914. 1066 entry from manuscript D.

'The Anglo-Saxon Chronicles', 1124 entry taken from a translation of manuscript E published by Malasree Home. Boydell Press 2015.

'The Anglo-Saxon Chronicles', 1153 entry quotation taken from a revised translation of manuscript E, edited by Dorothy Whitelock, Eyre & Spottiswoode 1965.

'The Chronicle of Richard of Devizes of the time of King Richard the First', edited and translated by John T. Appleby. Thomas Nelson & Sons, London 1963.

'The Danish Attacks on London and the South in 1016' by Tony Sharp. Academia edu.

'The Earth Transformed. An Untold History' by Peter Frankopan. Bloomsbury 2023.

'The Social History of Jews in England' by Vivian Lipman. 1954.

'The Stories of English' by David Crystal. Allen Lane 2004.

'The William Charter' from London Metropolitan Archives.

'The William Charter', translation as per City of London archives website. 1999.

'War and Society in Medieval Wales' by S. Davies 2004.

William of Malmesbury quotation from 'The English and Their History' by Robert Tombs.

'William the Conqueror's Lost Writ for London Rediscovered' by Nicholas Karn, Wiley Online Library 2023.

'William the Conqueror's Wait for the City of London' by Nicholas Karn. Historical Research vol. 96, 2013.

CHAPTER NINE: THE PLACE AT THE OVERFLOWING RIVER

'A Medieval Mercantile Community' by Pamela Nightingale. Yale University Press 1995.

'Citadels of the Saxons – London' by Rory Naismith. Bloomsbury Academic 2019.

'Dunbar the Makar' by Priscilla Bawcutt. Clarendon Press 1992.

'Henry VII's London in the Great Chronicle', edited by Julia Boffey 2019.

'In Honour of the City of London', poem originally attributed to William Dunbar : 'The Poems of William Dunbar', edited by W. Mackay Mackenzie. Porpoise Press 1932.

'Kingship and Government' by Ann Williams. Bloomsbury 1999.

'London' by Walter Besant. Chatto & Windus 1892.

'London in the Roman World' by D. Perring. OUP 2022.
'Maintaining the Balance of Power' by R.L. Hopcraft. Sociological Perspective 42. 1999.
'Roman Law in England Before the Time of Bracton' by R.V. Turner in Journal of British Studies 15. 1975.

CHAPTER TEN: LE LANGAGE NOUVEAU EST ARRIVÉE
'1415 Henry V's Year of Glory' by Ian Mortimer. Vintage 2010.
'Froissart Chronicles' quoted in 'The Hundred Years War' vol. 1, by Jonathan Sumption, Faber and Faber 1990.
'Henry V, the English Chancery and Chancery English' by M. Richardson. Speculum 55. 1980.
John of Trevisa quoted from 'Stories of English' by David Crystal. Allen Lane 2004.
'Ladies of Magna Carta' by S.B. Connolly 2020.
'Magna Carta : Lincoln Text', edited and translated by David Carpenter. Penguin Classics 2015.
'Shaping the Nation. England 1360–1461' by G.L.Harriss. 2005.
'The Adventure of English' by Melvyn Bragg. Hodder and Stoughton 2003.
'The Cambridge Encyclopedia of the English Language' by David Crystal. Cambridge University Press 2019.
'Wardens' Accounts and Court Minutes Books of the Goldsmiths' Mistery of London 1334-1446', edited by Lisa Jefferson. The Boydell Press 2003.
'The Owl and the Nightingale', Jesus College edition, translated by Neil Cartlidge. University of Exeter Press 2001.
'The Stories of English' by David Crystal. Allen Lane 2004.

CHAPTER ELEVEN: CHAUCER – 'THE FATHER OF ENGLISH POETRY'
'Chaucer' by Peter Ackroyd. Vintage Books 2005.
'Chaucer : a European Link' by Marion Turner. Princeton University Press 2019.
C.S. Lewis quoting Julian of Norwich in a letter of 1940.
English Language and Usage Stack Exchange.
Eustache Deschamps quoted as source for 'Ovid of your poetry'; Dryden quoted as source for 'Father of English poetry'.
'In the beginning : The Story of the King James Bible' by A.E. McGrath. 2001.
Language Oasis blog.
Polydore Vergil quoted by Alison Weir in 'Lancaster and York', Cape 1995.
'Prologue of The Canterbury Tales' quoted from the original by Geoffrey Chaucer. The Riverside edition.

'Shakespeare's Richard II and Rebellion' by Ellen Castelow. Historic UK (historicuk.com).

'The Canterbury Tales' by Geoffrey Chaucer. Opening lines quoted from a version rendered into modern English by Frank Pitt-Taylor. Chapman and Hall 1884. Section from 'The Miller's Tale' quoted from the translation into modern English by Nevill Coghill. Penguin 1951.

'The Imperfect Life of T.S. Eliot' by Lindall Gordon 1998.

'The Making of Chaucer's English' by C. Cannon. 1998.

'Troilus & Criseyde', quoted from the original by Geoffrey Chaucer. The Riverside edition.

CHAPTER TWELVE: THE WORD IS GOD

'England in the Age of Wycliffe' by G.M. Trevelyan and as quoted by David Fountain in 'John Wycliffe'.

Hampton Court Palace information from Historic Royal Palaces Inside Story edition 39.

'Lollards and Reformers : Images and Literacy in Late Medieval Religion' by M. Aston. 1984

'The Bible in its Ancient and English Versions' by Henry Wheeler Robinson. Oxford University Press 1940.

'The English and their History,' by Robert Tombs. Allen Lane 2014.

'The Tyndale Bible', edited for the Tyndale Society by W.R.Cooper. The British Library 2000.

'The Wycliffe Bible'. Modern spelling version based on the text of the British Library MS. The MS was selected by Forshall and Madden on the basis of the old spelling edition of the Wycliffe Bible 1850. 'The Wycliffe New Testament', 1388, printed by the British Library 2002.

'Writings of John Wycliffe' – The Wycliffe Society.

'John Wycliffe – The Dawn of Reformation,' by John Fountain. Mayflower Christian Books.

CHAPTER THIRTEEN: FINAL BUILDING BLOCKS – REFORMATION AND BREAK WITH EUROPE

'Dissolution of the Monasteries : An Economic Study' by J.C. Solomon. 1982.

Historic Royal Palaces websites.

'Mulcaster's Elementarie', edited by E.T. Campagnac. Clarendon Press 1925.

'The Adventure of English' by Melvyn Bragg. Hodder and Stoughton 2003.

'The Book of Common Prayer' by Thomas Cranmer. The 1662 text used, as edited by Brian Cummings. Oxford University Press 2011. Also the 1844 London edition by William Pickering.

CHAPTER FOURTEEN: THE THUNDER RUN

'Drama and Debate at the Court of James I' by Brett Dolman. 2004.

'John Heminge and Henry Condell : Friends and Fellow-actors of Shakespeare, and What the World Owes Them' by Charles Clement Walker 1896. Kessingers Legacy Reprints.

'Shakespeare and the Year of Lear : 1606' by Robert Shapiro.

'The Adventure of English' by Melvyn Bragg. Hodder and Stoughton 2002.

'The Cambridge History of British Theatre', in particular 'Theatre and Controversy 1603–42' by Janette Dillon, and 'Working Playwrights 1580–1642' by Roslyn Knutson. Cambridge University Press 2004.

The edition of 'The Knight of the Burning Pestle' by Fletcher and Beaumont, taken from 'Six Plays of Contemporaries of Shakespeare', edited by C.B. Wheeler 1935.

'The Essential Erasmus' by John Masters. The New American Edition 1956.

CHAPTER FIFTEEN: AN EXTRAORDINARY CONJUNCTION IN TIME AND SPACE

'1599 : A Year in the Life of William Shakespeare' by James Shapiro. Faber and Faber 2005.

'1606 and the Year of King Lear' by James Shapiro. Faber and Faber 2015.

'Drama and Debate at the Court of James I' by Brett Dolman 2004.

'From Grossers to Grocers Volume 1' by Helen Clifford. The Grocers' Company 2018.

'In Search of Shakespeare' by Michael Wood. BBC Books 2003.

'Shadowplay' by Claire Asquith. Public Affairs 2005.

'Shakespeare : The King's Playwright' by Alvin Kernan. 1995.

'Shakespeare's Religious Background' by Peter Milward. Sidgwick and Jackson 1973.

'Shakespeare the Man' by A.L. Rowse. Macmillan 2011.

'Theatre and Reformation' by Paul Whitefield White. Cambridge University Press 1993.

'The Cambridge History of British Theatre'. Cambridge University Press 2004.

'The Earth Transformed. An Untold Story' by Peter Frankopan. Bloomsbury 2023.

CHAPTER SIXTEEN: 'GRAND, ECHOING, ELOQUENT WORDS'

Shakespeare Birthplace Trust on 'Shakespeare's Words'. Online.

'Shakespeare's Vocabulary : Did it Dwarf All Others?' by Ward E.Y. Elliott and Robert J. Valepa. Claremont McKenna College.

'The Adventure of English' by Melvin Bragg. Hodder and Stoughton 2003.

Sources, Attributions, Refereneces, and Translations Used

'The Art of English Poesie' by George Puttenham. 1589.
'The King James Bible'. Oxford University Press edition.
'The Stories of English' by David Crystal. Allen Lane 2004.
'The Story of the King James Bible : In the Beginning' by Alister McGrath. 2001.
'When God Spoke English' by Adam Nicolson. Collins 2011.

CHAPTER SEVENTEEN: AND THE LIGHTS WENT OUT
'Providence Lost' by Paul Lay. Apollo Books 2020.
The Diary of Samuel Pepys, entry for Tuesday February 7th 1659/60.
The Grocers' Company archives and records accessed and researched by Helen Clifford.
'From Grossers to Grocers Volumes 1 and 2' by Helen Clifford. The Grocers' Company 2018 and 2023.
'The King's City' by Don Jordan. Little, Brown 2017.
'Theatre and Commonwealth' by Janet Clare in the Cambridge History of British Theatre. Cambridge University Press 2004.

CHAPTER EIGHTEEN: RESTORATION – LIFE RENEWED
Earl of Rochester quoted from 'The Poems and Lucina's Rape', edited by Kath Walker and Nicholas Fisher 2010.
'London and the 17th Century' by Margaret Lincoln.
'Nell Gwynne : A passionate Life' by Graham Hopkins. Robson Books 2003.
'The Ancestors of Nell Gwyn' by Paul A. Fox, Genealogical Magazine 2009.
'The Cambridge History of British Theatre', vol. 2 1660–1895. Cambridge University Press 2004. In particular 'Theatre and Repertory' by Robert D. Hume.
Theatre industry data from the Society of London Theatre, UK Theatre and the Theatres Trust.

CHAPTER NINETEEN: WHEN ALL IS SAID AND DONNE
'Before the King's Majesty', edited by Raymond Chapman. 2008.
'John Donne : A Life' by R.C. Bald. 1976.
'John Donne : Devotion upon Emergent Occasions'. Ann Arbor Publications 1959.
'John Donne : Language and Style' by A.C. Partridge. Deutsch 1978.
'John Donne Preacher' by William R. Mueller 1962.
'John Donne : Sermons Selected Passages' by Logan Pearsal Smith.
'John Donne : The Major Works' edited by John Carey 1990.
'John Wesley's English' by George Lawton. 1962.
'John Wesley's Political World' by Glen O'Brien. Abingdon 2023.

'John Wesley – preacher by W.L. Doughty. Wesley Society.
'Lancelot Andrewes Works' edited by J.P. Wilson and James Bliss. Library of Anglo-Catholic Theology 1841.
'Oxford Book of English Prose' by Arthur Quiller Couch. 1923.
'Sermons on Several Occasions' by John Wesley, 10th edition. 1829.
'Super-infinite : The Transformation of John Donne' by Katherine Rundell. Faber & Faber 2022.
'The Cambridge Companion to John Wesley' edited by Randy L. Maddox and Jason E. Vickers. Cambridge 2010.
'The Facts on File : Dictionary of Proverbs'. 2007.
'The Life and Time of John Wesley' by L. Tyerman. New York 1872.
'The Life of John Donne' by Izaak Walton. 1865.
'The Sermons of John Donne', edited by Evelyn M. Simpson and George R. Potter. Berkeley 1957.
'The Wesleys and the English Language' by G.H. Valins 1957.
'The Works of the Rev. John Wesley'. London 1829–31.

CHAPTER TWENTY: THE GREAT AMERICAN EXPERIMENT

'A Vocabulary' by John Pickering. Boston 1816.
'Empire. How Britain Made the Modern World' by Niall Ferguson. Allen Lane 2003.
'English as a Global Language' by David Crystal. Cambridge University Press 1998.
'History of the Formation of the Constitution of the United States of America'. New York 1892.
'How Shakespeare Helped Ratify the US Constitution' by Kevin J. Hayes. The Stage 2020.
'The Adventure of English' by Melvin Bragg. Hodder and Stoughton 2003.
'The English Language : A Very Short Introduction' by Simon Horobin. Oxford University Press 2018.
'The English Language in America' by Harry Morgan Ayres.
'The Life of Thomas Jefferson' by Henry S. Randall. New York 1858.
'The March of Folly' by Barbara Tuchman. 1990.
'The Parliamentary History of England', edited by William Cobbett. London 1814.
'The Peacemakers' by Richard B. Morris. Harper and Row 1965.

CHAPTER TWENTY-ONE: GREAT EXPECTATIONS

'Academic Prize Contests & Intellectual Culture in France 1670–1790' by Jeremy L. Caradonna. Ithaca 2012.
'A Christmas Carol' by Charles Dickens. London 1845

Sources, Attributions, Refereneces, and Translations Used

'A Compendious Dictionary', edited by Noah Webster. New Haven 1806.
'American Men of Letters : Noah Webster', edited by Horace E. Scudder. Boston 1909.
'Charles Dickens and the Great Theatre of the World' by Simon Callow. Harper Press 2011.
'Dickens Letters : Volume Twelve 1868–1876', edited by Graham Storey. Oxford 2002.
'Dickens : The Critical Heritage', edited by Philip Collins. London 1971.
'Great Expectations' by Charles Dickens. London 1868.
'Life, Letters and Speeches of Charles Dickens'. Boston 1894.
'The Actor in Dickens : The Study of the Histrionic and Dramatic Elements in the Novelist's Life and Works' by J.B. Amerongen. New York 1970.
'The Artful Dickens' by John Mullan. Bloomsbury 2020.
'The Idea of Nationalism : a Study in its Origins and Background' by Hans Kohn. Brunswick 2005.
'The Letters of Charles Dickens 1844–1846' by Charles Dickens. Oxford 1977.
'The Life and Adventures of Martin Chuzzlewit' by Charles Dickens. London 1890.
'The Life of Charles Dickens' by Franck T. Marzial. London 1887.
'The Stories of English' by David Crystal. Allen Lane 2004.
'The Warden' by Anthony Trollope. 1865.
'Works : Nicholas Nickleby, Martin Chuzzlewit, American Notes' by Charles Dickens. New York 1868.

CHAPTER TWENTY-TWO: WHERE WE ARE TODAY

'Académie Française' 9th online dictionary edition.
'A Dictionary of the English Language' by Samuel Johnson. 6th edition, London 1785.
'A Comparison of Swearing' by Arthur Smith. London 2021.
'Das Land Ohne Musik' by Oscar A.H. Schmitz, Munchen Bei Georg Muller 1914.
Dictionary word number estimates from 'The Story of English' by Robert McCrum, William Cran, Robert McNeil. Faber & Faber 1987. And also from Wikipedia entry of Dictionaries international comparisons.
'La langue anglaise n'existe pas' by Bernard Cerquiglini. Gallimard 2024.
'Notes and Queries' by Jacob Grimm. 1853.
'The Adventure of English' by Melvyn Bragg. Hodder and Stoughton 2003.
'The Art of Love Poetry' by Eric Irving Gray. Oxford 2018.
'The Stories of English' by David Crystal. Allen Lane 2004.

'The Oxford English Corpus. Facts About the Language'. 2011.
'Thomas Stearns Eliot Poet' by David Moody. Cambridge 1979.
UK Music and BPI industry data for the British Music industry.
'What is a Classic? Postcolonial Rewriting and Invention of the Canon' by Ankhi Mukherjee. Stanford 2014.

CHAPTER TWENTY-THREE: DRAWING TO CONCLUSIONS
'Jerusalem' by Jez Butterworth. Nick Hern Books 2009.
Iris Murdoch quoted from Poetry Nation Review 13 vol. 6 number 5 1980.
'The Elder Statesman' and 'Dedication to My Wife' by T.S. Eliot from 'The Complete Poems and Plays of T.S. Eliot'. Faber and Faber Ltd, London 1969.
'What is a Classic? Postcolonial Rewriting and Invention of the Canon' by Ankhi Mukherjee. Stanford 2014.

BIBLIOGRAPHY

The following works provide a good selection for possible further reading on any particular subject, which the reader might be inspired to make. I categorise them by subject area.

THE ANGLO-SAXONS
'Aelfred's Britain' by Max Adams. Head of Zeus 2017.
'Alfred the Great : Asser's Life of King Alfred' translated by Simon Keynes and Michael Lapidge. Penguin 1983.
'Anglo-Saxon England' by Frank Stenton. Oxford University Press 1943.
'Athelstan. The First English King' by Sarah Foot. Yale University Press 2011.
'Athelstan' by Tom Holland. Allen Lane 2016.
'Citadel of the Saxons' by Rory Naismith. Bloomsbury Academic 2019.
'Conquered : The Last Children of Anglo-Saxon England' by Eleanor Parker. Bloomsbury Academic 2022.
'Edward the Elder and the Making of England' by Harriet Harvey Wood. Sharpe Books 2019.
'In Search of the Dark Ages' by Michael Wood. BBC Books 2022.
'King Arthur' by Norma Goodrich. Franklin Watts 1986.
'Music in Anglo-Saxon England' by Alison Hudson. The British Library.
'The Anglo-Saxons : A History of the Beginnings of England' by Marc Morris. Random House 2021.
'The Anglo-Saxons' by Geoffrey Hindley. Robinson 2006.
'The Emergence of the English' by Susan Oosthuizen. Arc Humanities Press 2019.
'The Making of England : Anglo-Saxon Art and Culture AD600–900' by Marion Archibald, Janet Backhouse, Leslie Webster. British Museum c. 1991.
'The Origins of the Anglo-Saxons' by Jean Manco. Thames & Hudson 2018.

ELIZABETHAN AND STUART HISTORY
'A Gambling Man' by Jenny Uglow. Faber & Faber 2009.
'Nell Gwynne : A Passionate Life' by Graham Hopkins. Robson Books 2003.
'Providence Lost' by Paul Lay. Apollo Books 2020.
'The Blazing World' by Jonathan Healey. Bloomsbury 2023.
'The Diary of Samuel Pepys 1660'. The Echo Library 2006.

'The Dreadful Judgement' by Neil Hanson. Doubleday 2001.
'The Elizabethan Renaissance' by A.L. Rowse. Charles Scribener & Sons 1971.

THE ENGLISH LANGUAGE

'How English became English' by Simon Horobin. Oxford University Press 2016.
'Our Magnificent Bastard Tongue' by John McWhorter. Gotham Books 2008.
'The Adventure of English' by Melvyn Bragg. Hodder & Stoughton 2003.
'The Cambridge Encyclopedia of the English Language' by David Crystal. Cambridge University Press 2019.
'The English Language' by R.G. Latham. Longman, Green, Longman & Roberts 1862.
'The English Language. A Very Short Introduction' by Simon Horobin. Oxford University Press 2018.
'The Prodigal Tongue' by Lynne Morphy. One World 2018.
'The Stories of English' by David Crystal. Allen Lane 2004.
'The Story of English' by Philip Gooden. Quercus 2009.
'The Story of English' by Robert McCrum, William Cran, Robert McNeil. Faber and Faber/BBC Books 1987.
'The Unfolding of Language' by Guy Deutscher. Heinemann 2005.
'When God Spoke English' by Adam Nicolson. Harper Press 2011.

THE HISTORY OF LONDON

'A Medieval Mercantile Community' by Pamela Nightingale. Yale University Press 1995.
'London' by Walter Besant. Chatto and Windus 1892.
'London and the 17th Century' by Margaret Lincoln. Yale University Press 2021.
'London in the Roman World' by Dominic Perring. Oxford University Press 2022.
'London's Triumph' by Stephen Alford. Penguin Random House 2017.
'From Grossers to Grocers' by Helen Clifford. 2018 (vol. 1) and 2023 (vol. 2).
'Protection, Power and Persecution : the Tower of London and the Jewish Community until 1290' by Sally Dixon-Smith. Historic Royal Palaces.
'Restoration London' by Liza Picard. Weidenfeld & Nicolson 1997.
'Some Accounts of the Worshipful Company of Grocers' by Baron Heath. 1869.
'The History of the Grocers' Company through its Collection of Silver and Glass' by Helen Clifford. 2014.
'The History of London' by Walter Besant.
'The Huguenots of London' by Robin Gwynn. Alpha Press 1998.
'The King's City' by Dan Jordan. Little, Brown 2017.

'The London Rich' by Peter Thorold. Viking 1999.
'The Soul of the City of London's Livery Companies' by Robert Blackham. Sampson Low Marston 1932.
'The Worshipful Company of Grocers' by Aubrey Rees. Chapman & Dodd 1923.

MEDIEVAL ENGLAND

'1415 : Henry V's Year of Glory' by Ian Mortimer. Vintage 2010.
'Edward IV' by A.J. Pollard. Allen Lane 2016.
'England in the Age of Wycliffe' by G.M. Trevelyan. Longmans, Green 1920.
'English Social History' by G.M. Trevelyan. Longmans, Green 1942.
'The Domesday Quest' by Michael Wood. BBC Books 1986.
'The Perfect King : The Life of Edward III' by Ian Mortimer. Vintage 2008.
'Medieval English Literature 1100–1500' edited by Larry Scanlon. Cambridge University Press 2009.
'Shaping the Nation. England 1360–1461' by G.L. Harriss. Clarendon Press 2005.
'The High Middle Ages 1200–1550' by Trevor Rowley. Paladin Books 1988.
'The Hundred Years War' by Jonathan Sumption vols. 1–5. Faber and Faber, from 1990–2023.
'The Evolution of Medieval Thought' by David Knowles. Random House 1962.

RELIGION

'Donne : Sermons Selected Passages' by Logan Pearsal Smith. Clarendon Press 1919.
'English Hymns : Their Authors and History' by Samuel W. Duffield. Funk & Wagnalls 1886.
'Hymns in Christian Worship' by H.A.L. Jefferson. London Rockliff 1962.
'John Donne – Preacher' by William Muelle. Princeton University Press 1962.
'John Wesley – Preacher' by W.L. Doughty. Epworth Press 1955.
'John Wycliffe : The Dawn of the Reformation' by David Fountain. Mayflower Christian Books.
'Launcelot Andrewes : Before the King's Majesty' by Raymond Chapman. Canterbury Press 2008.
'Lollards and Reformers' by Margaret Aston. Hambledon Press 1984.
'The Dissolution of the Monasteries – An Economic Study' by J.C. Solomon. 1982.
'The English Hymn' by J.R. Watson. Clarendon Press 1997.
'The Story of the King James Bible : In the Beginning' by Alister McGrath. Doubleday 2001.
'Thomas Cranmer' by Diarmaid MacCulloch. Yale University Press 2016.

'William Tyndale' by Melvyn Bragg. Society for the Promotion of Christian Knowledge 2017.

THE HISTORY OF THE THEATRE

'1599 A Year in the Life of William Shakespeare' by James Shapiro. Faber & Faber 2005.
'1606 Shakespeare and the Year of Lear' by James Shapiro. Faber & Faber 2015.
'Charles Dickens and the Great Theatre of the World' by Simon Callow. Harper Press 2011.
'Drama and Debate at the Court of James I' by Brett Dolman. 2004.
'In Search of Shakespeare' by Michael Wood. BBC Books 2003.
'Shadowplay' by Clare Asquith. Public Affairs 2005.
'Shakespeare and the Making of America' by Kevin J. Hayes. Amberley Publishing 2020.
'Shakespeare's Friends' by Kate Emery Pogue. Praeger Publishers 2006.
'Shakespeare's Religious Background' by Peter Milward. Sidgwick and Jackson 1973.
'Shakespeare : The King's Playwright' by Alvin Kernan. Yale University Press 1995.
'Shakespeare the Man' by A.L. Rowse. Macmillan 2011.
'Shakespeare – the Papist' by Peter Millward. Sapienta Press 2005.
'The Cambridge History of British Theatre' vols. 1 & 2. By various. Cambridge University Press 2004.
'The Making of the First Folio' by Emma Smith. Bodleian Library 2015.
'The Rose Theatre' by Christine Eccles. Nick Hern Books 1990.
'Theatre and Reformation' by Paul Whitefield White. Cambridge University Press 1993.

WRITERS AND WRITINGS

'A Reading of Beowulf' by Edward B. Irving Jnr. New Haven 1968.
'Charles Dickens – A Life' by Claire Tomalin. Viking 2011.
'Chaucer' by Peter Ackroyd. Vintage Books 2005.
'Chaucer, a European Link' by Marion Turner. Princeton University Press 2019.
'John Donne : Language and Style' by A.C. Partridge. Deutsch 1978.
'John Wesley's English' by George Lawton. Allen & Unwin 1962.
'Super-infinite : The Transformation of John Donne' by Katherine Rundell. Faber & Faber 2022.
'The Artful Dickens' by John Mullan. Bloomsbury Publishing 2020.
'The Canterbury Tales of Geoffrey Chaucer. A Modern Rendering' by Percy MacKaye. Grant Richards 1907.

'The Language of Chaucer' by David Burnley. Macmillan 1989.
'The Imperfect Life of T.S. Eliot' by Lyndall Gordon. Vintage 1998.
'The Wesleys and the English Language' by G.H. Valins. Epworth Press 1957.

GENERAL

'Anatomy of a Nation' by Dominic Selwood. Constable 2021.
'Great Tales from English History' by Robert Lacey. Little, Brown 2004.
'The Earth Transformed – An Untold History' by Peter Frankopan. Bloomsbury 2023.
'The English and Their History' by Robert Tombs. Allen Lane 2014.
'The March of Folly : Troy to Vietnam' by Barbara Tuchman. Knopf 1984.
'The Peacemakers' by Richard B. Morris. North Eastern University Press 1983.
'This Sovereign Isle' by Robert Tombs. Allen Lane 2021.

INDEX

A

Académie Française   125, 195, 210
Accademia della Crusca   195
Ackroyd, Peter   97
Adams, John   192, 196
Aelfric   51
Aelfweard   33, 34
Aethelbald   37
Aethelbert   20, 21
Aethelflaed   54, 70
Aethelred   55
Aitken, Robert   187
Albert, Prince   199, 203
Alcuin   48, 53–56
Aldhelm   27, 48, 56
Alexander II   86
Alfred the Great   11, 12, 18–37,
    48–56, 67, 70, 95, 104, 148,
    218–220
Alleyn, Sir Thomas   162
Andrewes, Lancelot   146, 149, 155,
    172–174, 219, 223
'Anglo-Saxon Chronicles'   24, 27, 30,
    32, 49, 51, 57–59, 64, 82
Anne, Queen   185
Anne of Bohemia   96, 109
Anne of Denmark   142
Armin, Robert   143
Ashby, George   100
Asquith, Clare   137
Asser   30
Athelstan   12, 29, 33–37, 49, 56, 90,
    106, 148, 218–219
Augustine, St   20–23, 47, 49

B

Bancroft, Richard   146, 148–149
Bart, Lionel   214
Battle of Agincourt   75, 89, 91
Battle of Bouvines   83–86, 219
Battle of Brunanburh   36
Battle of Edington   12–14, 18, 26, 27,
    194, 205, 219–220
Battle of Maldon   35, 51
Beatles, The   184, 214–215
Beaumont, Francis   111, 166
Beckham, David   15
Bede   20–23, 48, 69, 106, 218
'Beowulf'   1, 47, 49–50, 56, 79, 213
Besant, Walter   73
Bishop of Worcester   13
Bismarck, Otto von   185
Black, Don   215
Blagrave, Daniel   163
Blake, William   3, 33
Boccaccio, Giovanni   98
Boethuis, Anicius   32, 49, 95
Boleyn, Anne   113–114
Borden, Mary   7
Boudicca   68
Bowie, David   214
Boyle, Danny   4
Branagh, Sir Ken   5
Brayne, John   130
Brembre, Sir Nicholas   73
Brewers' Company   89
Burbage, James   130, 135
Burbage, Richard   135, 143, 168
Butchers' Company   72

Index

Butterworth, Jez 1, 169, 224
Byrhnoth 51

C
Cavendish-Bentinck, William, Duke of Portland 191
Caxton, William 103
Cecil, Robert 144
Ceolwulf 11
Cerquiglini, Professor Bernard 210
Chapman, Raymond 173
Charlemagne 35, 48, 53
Charles I 58, 158–159, 218
Charles II 162, 164–168
Charles IV, Holy Roman Emperor 96
Chaucer, Geoffrey 8, 31, 93–104, 125, 154, 200, 209, 213, 218–219
Cnut, King 31, 48, 61
Condell, Henry 131, 140, 143, 151, 153
Conference of Constance 91
Congreve, William 165, 169
Conway, Russ 214
Cottrell-Boyce, Frank 4
Coverdale, Miles 223
Coward, Sir Noel 169
Cranmer, Thomas 114, 118, 123, 124, 125, 159, 219
Cromwell, Oliver 158–162
Cromwell, Richard 162
Cromwell, Thomas 114, 127–128
Crooke, Mackenzie 224
Crystal, David 81, 83, 101, 155, 197

D
Daldry, Stephen 4
Dante Alighieri 22, 94
David, Alan 224
Davies, Sir Ray 215
Davis, Moll 166
Davenant, Sir William 135, 161, 165–166

Dekker, Thomas 133, 151
Deschamps, Eustache 93
Dickens, Charles 195, 198–205, 219
Dolman, Brett 134
'Domesday Book' 59, 64
Donegan, Lonnie 214
Donne, John 172–178, 219
Drapers' Company 70, 74, 90
'Dream of the Rood' 50, 52
Dryden, John 93, 165
Dunbar, William 66

E
Eadburgh, Abbess 55
Ecgbert 11, 34
Edgar 29
Edmund 31, 36
Edward I 75, 76, 86
Edward II 75, 76
Edward III 88, 97
Edward VI 117–118, 127
Edward the Confessor 19, 37
Edward the Elder 33–36, 54
Edinburgh (Fringe) Festival 9, 168
Elgar, Edward 213
Eliot T.S. 102, 215, 219, 222–224
Elizabeth I 95, 118, 124, 127, 137, 142
Elizabeth II 7, 8, 9
Elton, Sir Geoffrey 55
English National Ballet 31
Erasmus, Desiderius 94
Evelyn, John 196

F
Fairfax, Thomas 162
Farquhar, George 165
Fender, Sam 215
Ferguson, Niall 213
Fishmongers' Company 122
Fitzstephen, William 65
Fletcher, John 133, 135, 166

243

Fox, Charles 191
Franklin, Benjamin 188–189
Friedman, Sonia 1
Fury, Tyson 15

G
Garrick, David 168
George III 19, 186–189
Gildas 16, 22
Glastonbury Festival 9
Godley, Simon 1
Goldsmiths' Company 72, 90
Gower, John 95, 97, 100, 125
Grafton, Richard 114–115
Grand Synagogue 63
Gray, Lady Jane 114
'Great Heathen Army' 25, 33
Greene, Robert 133
Gregory the Great 20, 29
Grimm, Jacob 206
Grocers' Company 70, 72–74, 77, 90, 122, 130, 162, 167
Guthrum 12, 30
Guy, Bishop of Amiens 58, 61
Gwyn, Nell 167–168

H
Hamilton, Alexander 190
Hammerton, Stephen 135
Hampton Court Palace 34, 119, 143–146, 158, 167
Harold, King 37, 57
Harriss, G.L. 89
Hart, Charles (actor) 166–167
Hart, Charles (lyricist) 215
Hartley, David 188, 191
Hay Literary Festival 9
Hayes, Kevin J. 193
Heminges, John 131, 132, 140, 143, 151, 153
Henry II 72

Henry III 75
Henry IV 88–89
Henry V 75, 90–91
Henry VI 19, 91
Henry VII 66, 142
Henry VIII 113–114, 117, 119, 127
Hepburn, James, Earl of Bothwell 145
Herbert, Mary, Countess of Pembroke 143
Hilda, St 55
Historic Royal Palaces 4
Hoccleve, Thomas 95
Holst, Gustav 213
Horan, Gerard 224
Houblon, Sir John 74, 220
Hundred Years' War 87, 95, 103
Hus, Jan 91, 96, 107

I
Ifield, Frank 214
Ine 20, 23, 24, 26, 28, 29, 31, 218
'Inkhorn Controversy' 197
Innocent III 126

J
James I 134–135, 142–149, 173, 184, 219
James II 165
Jay, John 188
John, King 83–87, 218
John, Sir Elton 214
John of Gaunt 88, 93, 97
John of Trevisa 83
Johnson, Boris 42
Johnson, Samuel 209
Jonson, Ben 131, 133, 135, 137, 151, 153, 166, 169, 203, 219
Judith of Flanders 55
Julian of Norwich 97, 101–102, 219, 223

Index

K
Karn, Dr Nicholas 63
Kempe, Margery 97, 102, 219
Kérouaille, Louise de 167
Killigrew, Thomas 165–166
King James Bible 148–150, 154–157, 164, 184, 186,–187, 193
King's Men 134–5
Kyd, Thomas 133

L
Lambert, John 162
Langland, William 95, 97, 100–101, 125, 219
Laud, William 173
Laurens, Henry 188
Laxton, Sir William 122
Lindisfarne 21, 24–25, 48
Lollard 106, 109, 171
London Bridge 69, 73
Longchamp, William 86
Lord Chamberlain's Men 130–131, 134, 137
Louis XIV 139
Luther, Martin 96, 109, 111, 112, 117, 178
Lydgate, John 100
Lyons, Sir John 122

M
Madonna 40
'Magna Carta' 34, 75, 85–86, 218
Malory, Sir Thomas 102
Marckant, John 182
Marlowe, Christopher 133
Marriott, Richard 213
Mary I 118, 122, 124, 127, 138
Mary, Queen of Scots 142, 145
Massinger, Philip 135
McCrum, Robert 210
McWhorter, Professor John 39–41

Mercers' Company 70, 77, 90, 122, 213
Merchant Taylors' Company 90, 122
Middleton, Thomas 133–134
Milward, Peter 137
Miller, Ben 1
Molière 139
Monck, General George 162
Montfort, Simon de 75
More, Sir Thomas 94, 113
Morris, Richard 192
Mortimer, Edmund 88
Mulcaster, Richard 122, 157
Mullan, John 200
Murdoch, Iris 222

N
Nicholas of Guildford 82, 93
Nightingale, Pamela 54, 77
North, Frederick 188
Norton, Thomas 129
Notting Hill Carnival 9

O
O'Brien, Richard 215
Odericus Vitalis 81
Offa 37
Olivier, Lord Laurence 168
Orm 83
Osborne, John 169
Osekyn, Isabel 73
Oswald, Richard 188–193, 219
Oundle School 122

P
Palmer, Barbara, Duchess of Cleveland 167
Parks, Arlo 215
Pepys, Samuel 162
Petty, William, Lord Shelburne 188–193, 219
Pevsner, Nikolaus 52

245

Philip III 138
'Pilgrimage of Grace' 120
Pinter, Harold 169
Pippin 53
Polybius 14, 15
Polydore Vergil 103
Priestley, J.B. 169
Prynne, William 160
Ptolemy 15
Puttenham, George 154
Pytheas 14

Q
Quiller-Couch, Arthur 177

R
Racine, Jean-Baptiste 139
Reynolds, John 146–148
Richard II 77, 88–89, 96–97
Richard of Devizes 65
Rice, Sir Tim 215
Rickson, Ian 1, 224
Rizzio, David 147
Rogers, John 114
Rosenau, William 154
Rousseau, Jean-Jacques 180
Rowse, A.L. 152
Rundell, Katherine 178
'Ruthwell Cross' 52
Rhigyfarch 58
Rylance, Sir Mark 1, 2, 5, 224

S
Sackville, Thomas 129
Schmitz, Oscar 214
Self Esteem 215
Seven Years' War 186
Shakespeare, William 5, 35–36, 95–96, 98, 115, 129–157, 161, 165–169, 173, 193, 198–200, 203, 218–220, 223

Shapiro, James 137
Shaw, George Bernard 169, 197
Skinners' Company 122
Sloane, Barry 224
Smith, Arthur 212
Soame, Sir Stephen 74
Solomon, J.C. 119
St Paul's Cathedral 71
Stoppard, Sir Tom 169
Stuart, Henry, Lord Darnley 145
Sweyn 31
Swift, Johnathan 195–196

T
Tacitus, Publius 56
Taylor, Joseph 135
Tombs, Robert 60
Tower of London 4, 6, 7, 60, 63, 71, 72, 97–98, 221
'Treaty of Paris' 86, 192–194, 219
'Treaty of Verdun' 35
'Treaty of Wedmore' 12, 194
Trevelyan, Professor George 108
Trollope, Anthony 199, 201
Tuchman, Barbara 187
Tudor, Margaret 66, 142
Tyndale, William 95, 111–116, 123, 125, 148–150, 154–157, 218–219

U
Udall, Nicholas 128
Ulfcetel 31
Urban V 87

V
Vanbrugh, John 165
Vaughan Williams, Ralph 213
Victoria, Queen 199, 203
Villiers, George, Duke of Buckingham 70

W

Walton, Izaak   177
Walworth, William   89
Watson-Wentworth, Charles, Marquess of Rockingham   188, 191
Watt, Tyler   88
Watts, Isaac   183, 219
Webster, John   129, 133, 151
Webster, Noah   192, 196
Welch, Florence   215
Wesley, Charles   183–184, 219
Wesley, John   171, 178=182, 219
Whitefield, George   178–179, 184
Whittington, Sir Richard   73
Wilde, Oscar   169
'William Charter'   62–63, 75, 86
William I ('the Conqueror')   37, 57–65, 219–220
William of Malmesbury   33, 40, 60
William of Nasington   79, 93
Wilmot, John, Earl of Rochester   164
Wodehouse, P.G.   11
Wolsey, Thomas   113
Wonder, Stevie   38
Wood, Michael   49
Worshipful Company of Woolmen   72
Wulfstan   51
Wycliffe, John   31, 91, 95, 96, 104–112, 115, 117, 123, 125, 171, 218–219
Wynkyn de Worde   103

Z

Zeffirelli, Franco   152

HUNGRY OR FAMISHED? LAUGHABLE OR
GO OR DEPART? THINK OR POND
SMELL OR AROMA? HELP OR AID? GO O
PECULIAR? AWFUL OR TERRIBLE? GOO
AVAIL? GIVE OR OFFER? ODD OR PECULI
TALKATIVE OR GARRULOUS? FUCK
UTIFUL? TRUTHFUL OR HONEST? TALKA
COMMENCE? ASK OR ENQUIRE? FUN O
ER OR RESPOND? BEGIN OR COMMENCE?
R DUKE? LOVING OR AMOROUS? HUNG
UE OR LANGUAGE? EARL OR DUKE? LOVI
LOOKING GLASS OR MIRROR? SMELL OR
GHABLE OR HILARIOUS? LOOKING GLASS
K OR PONDER? WORK OR TRAVAIL? GIV
GO OR DEPART? THINK OR PONDER? WO
RRIBLE? GOOD LOOKING OR BEAUTIFUL
IAR? AWFUL OR TERRIBLE? GOOD LOOK
LOUS? FUCK OR COPULATE? ANSWER O
ATIVE OR GARRULOUS? FUCK OR COPU
UIRE? FUN OR AMUSEMENT? TONGUE O
E? ASK OR ENQUIRE? FUN OR AMUSEME
OUS? HUNGRY OR FAMISHED? LAUGHAB
ING OR AMOROUS? HUNGRY OR FAMISH
SMELL OR AROMA? HELP OR AID? GO O
OR MIRROR? SMELL OR AROMA? HELP
AIL? GIVE OR OFFER? ODD OR PECULIAR
WORK OR TRAVAIL? GIVE OR OFFER? O
TIFUL? TRUTHFUL OR HONEST? TALKAT
LOOKING OR BEAUTIFUL? TRUTHFUL O
OR RESPOND? BEGIN OR COMMENCE?
OR COPULATE? ANSWER OR RESPOND? B
OR LANGUAGE? EARL OR DUKE? LOVIN
AMUSEMENT? TONGUE OR LANGUAGE? E
HABLE OR HILARIOUS? LOOKING GLASS
OR FAMISHED? LAUGHABLE OR HILARIO
O OR DEPART? THINK OR PONDER? WOR
A? HELP OR AID? GO OR DEPART? THIN
AR? AWFUL OR TERRIBLE? GOOD LOOKI
? ODD OR PECULIAR? AWFUL OR TERRI
IVE OR GARRULOUS? FUCK OR COPULA
OR HONEST? TALKATIVE OR GARRULOU
ASK OR ENQUIRE? FUN OR AMUSEMENT
BEGIN OR COMMENCE? ASK OR ENQUI
NG OR AMOROUS? HUNGRY OR FAMISHE
EARL OR DUKE? LOVING OR AMOROU

EARL OR DUKE? LOVING OR AMOROUS?
OR MIRROR? SMELL OR AROMA? HELP
HILARIOUS? LOOKING GLASS OR MIRROR
K OR TRAVAIL? GIVE OR OFFER? ODD
PART? THINK OR PONDER? WORK OR T
KING OR BEAUTIFUL? TRUTHFUL OR HON
UL OR TERRIBLE? GOOD LOOKING OR BE
ULATE? ANSWER OR RESPOND? BEGIN O
GARRULOUS? FUCK OR COPULATE? ANSW
SEMENT? TONGUE OR LANGUAGE? EARL
R ENQUIRE? FUN OR AMUSEMENT? TONG
FAMISHED? LAUGHABLE OR HILARIOUS?
AMOROUS? HUNGRY OR FAMISHED? LAU
MA? HELP OR AID? GO OR DEPART? THI
RROR? SMELL OR AROMA? HELP OR AID?
OFFER? ODD OR PECULIAR? AWFUL OR
TRAVAIL? GIVE OR OFFER? ODD OR PECU
THFUL OR HONEST? TALKATIVE OR GARR
BEAUTIFUL? TRUTHFUL OR HONEST? TAL
OND? BEGIN OR COMMENCE? ASK OR EN
SWER OR RESPOND? BEGIN OR COMMEN
UAGE? EARL OR DUKE? LOVING OR AMO
NGUE OR LANGUAGE? EARL OR DUKE? L
HILARIOUS? LOOKING GLASS OR MIRROR
UGHABLE OR HILARIOUS? LOOKING GLA
ART? THINK OR PONDER? WORK OR TRA
ID? GO OR DEPART? THINK OR PONDER?
L OR TERRIBLE? GOOD LOOKING OR BEA
OR PECULIAR? AWFUL OR TERRIBLE? GOO
RRULOUS? FUCK OR COPULATE? ANSWE
NEST? TALKATIVE OR GARRULOUS? FUCK
ENQUIRE? FUN OR AMUSEMENT? TONGU
COMMENCE? ASK OR ENQUIRE? FUN OR
MOROUS? HUNGRY OR FAMISHED? LAUG
R DUKE? LOVING OR AMOROUS? HUNGR
ROR? SMELL OR AROMA? HELP OR AID?
KING GLASS OR MIRROR? SMELL OR ARO
RAVAIL? GIVE OR OFFER? ODD OR PECUL
NDER? WORK OR TRAVAIL? GIVE OR OFF
AUTIFUL? TRUTHFUL OR HONEST? TALK
OOD LOOKING OR BEAUTIFUL? TRUTHFU
WER OR RESPOND? BEGIN OR COMMENC
CK OR COPULATE? ANSWER OR RESPON
UE OR LANGUAGE? EARL OR DUKE? LOV
N OR AMUSEMENT? TONGUE OR LANGU